Princeton Theological Seminary. Class of 1890

Princeton Theological Seminary Class of 1890

Princeton Theological Seminary. Class of 1890

Princeton Theological Seminary Class of 1890

ISBN/EAN: 9783337172664

Printed in Europe, USA, Canada, Australia, Japan

Cover: Foto ©ninafisch / pixelio.de

More available books at **www.hansebooks.com**

PRINCETON

ОLOGICAL SEMINARY.

CLASS OF 1890.

CRANBURY, N. J.:
G. W. BURROUGHS, BOOK AND JOB PRINTER
1892.

PRINCETON THEOLOGICAL SEMINARY.

At the Class Meeting, May 5th, 1890, the following were elected officers of the Class: C. H. Whitaker, President, and F. B. Everitt, Secretary and Treasurer. It was resolved to have a Reunion of the Class in 1892. Accordingly, on May 3d, 1892, in response to the call of the President, the following members answered the roll-call in Stuart Hall: Carrington, Erskine, Everitt, Oates, Parker, Thompson, Warne, Whitaker and Wylie. It was resolved to meet again in 1895. The report of the Secretary was read and ordered published. He, therefore, issues this pamphlet, asking the indulgence of the Class, and trusting that it will afford them as much pleasure in the reading as it gave him in the writing.

APPENDIX, 1895.

Printed by order of the Class of 1890, at their Reunion, Princeton,
May 6, 1895.

ADAMS. Now without charge. Resigned recently. Writing S. S. lessons for "Presbyterian." Wants a field with hard work. Address, 1510 Chestnut street, Philadelphia. Has done Evangelistic work. Two children.

ALLEN. Now at Pennington, N. J.

ANDERSON. Montgomery, Ala. New church dedicated, April, 1894, finest in the city. Largest per capita contribution of any church in Southern Assembly. Two children living, one dead.

BANNERMAN. Home on furlough. Spent last fall in Switzerland, the winter in Edinburgh, and the summer here. If Board opens new station among the Fang in the mountains, he will take it and return at once. Often preached six times a day in as many towns to souls who had never heard of Jesus.

BASKERVILLE. Now at Goodes Ferry, Va., doing Home Mission work. Voice gave out and had to change. Preaches at five stations.

BULL. Now at Church Hill, Md., supplying Trinity and Worton First churches. Two children living, one dead.

H. M. CAMPBELL. New church dedicated, St. Louis, May 26, 1895, costing $18,000.

R. J. CAMPBELL. Resigned, Felton, Cal., last fall after dedicating a church, free of debt, in the most discouraging field. Went to Ireland. Back, single, and now visiting at Portland, Oregon. May settle there.

CARRINGTON. Married September 26, 1894. Building a church at one out-station and organizing one at another.

CUMMINGS. At Clarence, Iowa.

DOUGHTY. Is at the centre of the war preparations in Hiroshima, Japan. Fully 50,000 soldiers have passed through that city to go to the war. They stay in that city from two weeks to two months, and the missionaries have labored night and day to give these men the Gospel. Doughty has an interesting article in "Church at Home and Abroad" for June, 1895.

DUNLAP. At Wood River, Nebraska. One child. Resigned because of wife's illness, but resignation not accepted, but liberal vacation given.

EDDY. Moved to St. Louis as assistant to Dr. Brookes.

ERSKINE. Married recently, and "therefore could not come."

EVERITT. Soon to follow.

F. L. FRASER. At Crookstown, Minn., strongest church financially in Red River Presbytery. Unmarried. Prefers to "wheel" it alone.

GARDNER. Horseheads, N. Y. At home ——— with English setter.

GIBBONS. Examiner in Hebrew and editor of Lackawanna Presbyterian. "Second in orthodoxy and tone to the Presbyterian and Reformed Review." Two children.

HEANEY. Installed recently over First Church of Shamokin, Pa., new church, costing $40,000. Has a population of 25,000 with but one Presbyterian church.

HEDGES. At Rome, Ga., in the City Mission work. Field encouraging. Married September 12, 1894.

JESSUP. More admissions to church than ever before. Marked increase in gifts. But Board says, "the Beirut Mission must cut expenses $4,222.22." It staggers us. We must give up what we have prayed for and worn ourselves out in doing. I feel that the Church at home had taken away all the good that I have been able to accomplish since I came to Syria nearly five years ago. We have to face now the question, "What! don't your Church stand by you better than that?" (Bro. Jessup's letter was sad, indeed, to your Secretary. From private sources I learn that Jessup will hold his post, even if he has to do it *without any salary*.

JOHNSON. At Pine Ridge Agency, South Dakota, since September, 1892, working among the Indians. Four out-stations. Three native helpers. Preaches in native dialect. Married.

JUNGEBLUT. Wife consumptive and had to leave Milwaukee. Now stationed at Alexandria, Neb., over the Meridian German Presbyterian Church. Two children, one named Calvin.

LEVINGOOD. Installed at Greenwich, N. J.

LYNN. At Bergen, N. Y., near Buffalo. Wife was sick at Pottsville.

McMILLAN. A P. G. at Union Seminary the past winter.

McCUSH. In the college town of Fulton, Mo. Membership, 600; audiences, 700; prayer meetings, 300; 95 on confession in nine months; repairs to church, $1,600. Declined the appointment to Honorary Fellow in Clark University, Worcester, Mass. Unmarried.

McGINNISS. At Troy, and of course has a Helen (child).

McLEOD. Is our coming divine and preacher. At Chester, Pa., new building, costing $15,000. Fifty-four accessions since January 1st. Unmarried.

MASON. After six months rest, has returned to De Soto, Mo., much improved in health. Was on verge of nervous prostration.

E. D. MILLER. Studied in Germany the past winter. Will take another Semester. Now traveling in Italy.

H. MILLER. Stated supply at Ardmore, Penn., near Philadelphia.

MOORE. Has one of the few really self-supporting churches in Japan, at Kochi. Membership, 700. Only ordained man in a province of half a million of the best Japanese. He decries the statement that the missionary's work in Japan is done. Both wife and daughter died in 1893 from congestion of the brain due to malaria. He came home and returned with his boy and sister. Expects to return to America in 1904.

MURCHIE. The first of the Class to pass to the "Father's House." Died May 21st, 1894, after a year's stay in the General Hospital, St. John. Born December 16th, 1860. Very studious when young. Joined church at twenty-two. Graduated at University N. B. in 1886. Taught a year. Entered our class 1887. Licensed 1890. Worked in Scotch settlement N. B. 1890. Took P. G. course in Edinburgh that winter. At Birnscarth, Manitoba, June, 1891 —December, 1892. Left a good field for a harder one at one-half the salary, or $400. Self-sacrificing? Returned home, sick, in December, 1892. Doctored for rheumatism. Proved to be an abscess. Cough increased. Died from consumption mainly. Great sufferer, but very patient and always cheerful. Unmarried.

NELSON. At Ambler, Pa.; recently installed. Institutional church on small scale. Largely increased audiences and Sabbath School.

OATES. Very ill, but now recovered. Still at Delaware City, Del.

PARKER. Change of P. O. to Street P. O., Md. Same charge. New manse. "Three high chairs."

PATTERSON. Prosperous at Mechanicsville, N. Y. One child.

PATON. Prof. of O. T. Criticism and Exegesis at Hartford Seminary. Salary increased. No elementary work in Heb., and only one course in exegesis. So time for study. Had calls to Oberlin, Princeton and Hartford, upon his return from Germany. Responded for Class at Alumni dinner. Unmarried.

PHRANER. Died Jan. 15, 1895. Born May 26, 1860. Reached Siam Dec. 1890. Twice seriously ill. Two years S. S. of Maa Dawk Dang Church. Long rides and hard work. "Personal acquaintance and true pastoral work characterized all his labors." In Dec. '93, was S. S. of four churches to north of Cheung Mai. Did good work in the Dispensary. Expected to open new station at Cheung Hai. Twice ordered home by physicians, but declined. Finally forced to do it, and left Cheung Mai, Dec. 21, '94. Grew worse at once, and died in Singapore Hospital after an operation for hepatic abscess. The operation was successful, but he was too weak to rally. When he entered the hospital he said "I am going either to heaven or to America. I think I am going to heaven." Shortly before his death he said, "I had hoped I was going home, but I am going to heaven." His widow, who is in this country with his two children (one by his former wife), sums up his characteristics as "Consistency, promptness and faithfulness." No sacrifice was too great for his Lord and Master.

POLK. Gainesville, Texas. Membership doubled in two years. One child. Now visiting in the east, and may settle here.

RANKIN. Died June 5, 1894, at Baltimore. Born May 24, 1866. Graduated at La Fayette, 1887. At Pine Grove, Pa., June, 1890–Nov. 1893. Called to the La Fayette Square Presbyterian Church, Baltimore, and had begun a most promising pastorate. Very large audiences. Salary increased. Seventy accessions in seven months. Taken sick May 31, with acute pain in abdomen. Found to be appendicitis. Operation performed Monday; seemed better, but at night unfavorable symptoms set in. He knew the end had come, but talked hopefully, triumphantly looking to his "Heavenly home." Died at 1:15 A. M. on Tuesday, from chronic appendicitis. Rankin, although one of our youngest members, was dearly beloved by all, and his end is particularly sad, as there seemed so much promise in his life. He left a widow and three children. Wylie and your secretary attended the funeral services, which were very impressive.

REMINGTON. Holyoke, Mass. New church in prospect, costing $15,000. All subscribed for.

F. H. SMITH's letter should be printed in full, but space forbids. Tart and witty. Largest audiences in Cambridge, Mass. Attacked Harvard athletes who used main thoroughfare for a running track. Called them "living pictures." Aldermen investigated, and now they run in middle of street, properly clad. Checks umbrellas, summers in Maine. Exchanges so much that his sign is "three balls." Married. "Have a man, who sits on a rug and prays for the flock, when needed." If any of the class are near him, just yell "Smith—three loaves, please."

WARNE. Moderator of New Brunswick Presbytery.

WHITAKER. Bushkill, Pa. Unmarried.

The rest of the boys are moving on in the "even tenor" of their way at the same places, as recorded in the printed record of 1892, copies of which can still be obtained of the Secretary, free.

Nine members gathered around the festive board at Princeton, on May 6th, viz.: Whitaker, Trompen, Wylie, Parker, Levingood, Warne, Oates, Paton and Everitt. Mrs. Trompen was also present. The Secretary read a report of the Class, arranged according to age, and then each fellow told of his work and experiences. Our circle lessens on earth, but widens in Heaven.

F. B. EVERITT, *Secretary.*

SUMMARY.

Present membership	53	Deaths	3
Married	34	On Foreign field	4
Children	34	Home Missions (West)	5
Widower	2	City Missions	3
Engaged	1		

SECRETARY'S REPORT,
CLASS OF '90, PRINCETON SEMINARY,

Read May 3d, 1892.

"*Novos amicos dum paras veteres, cole.*" "Whilst you seek new friendships, cultivate the old," or in Gardner's laconic style, freely translated, "Whilst you are tackling new men, guard well the old ones."

Classmates, we have been out in the world these two years, trying new friendships, but come back to-day to the old shades, to renew, to make fast the old ties. We have found pleasure in the new, but delight in the old. Doubtless in our wanderings, Princeton reminiscences have so crowded our memories and Princeton theology our minds, that we have said with Addison,

" For wheresoe'er I turn my ravished eyes,
Gay gilded scenes and shining prospects rise,
Poetic fields encompass me around,
And still I seem to tread on classic ground."

Now, if he had been a little less amplitudinous, and had only left the "ground" off, so that it would read "tread on classic(s)," then we can see Bob Rankin smile as he recalls how he ventilated his Latin on Dr. Patton, but the ominous "translate it," ventilated something else.

Of course, we have all kept up our Catechism and have discovered the fallacies of the composite character of some of our questions, e. g. " How many Gods are there?" Now, anybody can see the compositeness of that, having a little of Catechism but more of ———.

Then "Wellhausen" has been a wonderful help to us. It fits in so nicely after the introduction and remarks about the weather. And for an after dinner talk, nothing is quite so analogous as the "Hebrew Feasts."

We really tremble for Princeton. Not for her orthodoxy—oh, no, not as long as our beloved Dr. Green and his associates live; not for her financial endowment ; not for her increase of students, for the class of '90 promises to do her share ; not for the magnificence of her buildings, as one after another arises to beautify these lovely grounds ; not for the worth of her sons, as Honor crowns their brows ; but really—for the demure character of the campus, since one by one the boys of '90 laid aside their field regimentals and put on their broadcloth. Did you not see a "paling of the green" when Warne hung up his knickerbockers, Seelye handed over the "racquet that never came," John Moore laid aside his "bloody shirt" (football blood), Gardner pulled in his mascot and Phraner pulled up his war horse? But those days of campus frolic are over, and long will they abide, as morning dew, in our memory.

We are here—and I am ashamed of the whole set of you, for, like Jim Williams, you all swore that any place was better than Jersey. And like the Israelite of old, you fled as if from bondage, when—the Directors said you could go. And here you are back again, and we only ask a tarrying long enough in this "intermediate State" to learn from the past how to prepare for the future.

Seriously, my classmates, we have been truly blessed of our Father, and we can all honestly "thank God and take courage." Death has spared its reaping from our immediate ranks, though it has crept very sorely into our brothers' homes, while from the old familiar faces of Stuart Hall there have gone no less than three—Drs. Moffat, Hodge and Aiken. No spokesman can speak the feeling of the class, as our loss is not collective but individual. Their impriut on our individual lives is unmistakable. Genial in the home, faithful in the class-room, and earnest in their labors, they proved themselves "workmen that needeth not to be ashamed, rightly dividing the word of truth." Their memories are ours, their work is ours, may their glory be ours.

For these afflicted ones, and our own good brothers, Phraner and Carrington, so recently bereaved in the loss of their wives, our prayers should to-day arise. May the Lord's uplifted countenance be upon them, and the rainbow of His promises embrilliant their overhanging clouds.

The circular of your Secretary is familiar to all, and, for matters of reference, we will review the replies in alphabetical order.

CROFTON CRAIG ADAMS.

Well, the class of '90 should be the most blessed class that ever went out of the Old Chapel. For her first man was born in Eden (Ohio) and his name is Adam(s). But Adam fell—notably into the hands of matrimony—"and all mankind, descending from him by ordinary generation" &c., notably Rankin, the soonest married and Nelson the most "wanted to be married" man in the class. Craig is the same old fellow, for he is the only fellow in the whole class that tried to get off a pun in his letter. We all remember his embryonic efforts in that direction. He is Pastor of the First Presbyterian Church of Smyrna, Del., being installed there by the Presbytery of Newcastle on June 12, 1890. In the line of special study, he has devoted himself to "Miracles and Parables," while "monuments and mummies" also occupy some of his attention. To keep up with the linguistic qualifications of Arthur Glenn Adams (born Sept. 21, '91), he is pursuing assiduously Greek, Hebrew, French and German. Just which of these languages the youngster talks now, or will talk hereafter, we are not told. And inspired by this self-same music in the house, he has started a music class in his church, himself the conductor. Adams is an occasional writer for the *Presbyterian*. Reports 500-700 pastoral calls a year. In the fall of 1890 (Sept. 9) he was married to Miss McKinney, daughter of Rev. W. W. McKinney, D. D., of the *Presbyterian*. Adams is not with us to-day, owing to special revival services in his church, begun recently by an evangelist. He has divided his membership into prayer-bands, and desires the prayers of his classmates for God's blessing on their labors.

WILLIAM ALLEN, JR.

Allen is located at Glen Moore, Chester county, Pa. He was installed over the Fairview Church, May 29, 1890. He was married Oct. 29, 1890, to Miss Lampen, of Philadelphia. He has adopted "serial preaching" for his evening discourses, taking different books of the Bible. He has received thirteen into membership.

NEAL L. ANDERSON.

Neal was from the "Sunny South," and at once returned to his former love, after graduation, having accepted a call to Marion, Ala. He was ordained and installed there on Nov. 30, 1890. In November, 1891, he received a call to the newly organized Central Presbyterian Church of Montgomery, Ala. He became its first Pastor on Feb. 14, 1892. His work in Marion was largely among the students of its famous educational institutions, and with the aid of an evangelist, a fellow-alumnus of Princeton, fourteen were added to his church on profession. Montgomery, his present location, is a town of 30,000 inhabitants, of remarkable beauty and growth. His church began with only thirty-three members, but has now doubled, is self-supporting and preparing to build a handsome, modern edifice.

On Aug. 14, 1890, he found a partner in Miss Nannie Faison, daughter of Major W. L. Faison, of Clinton, N. C., and one son shares their home life. We are glad to see that Neal has already booked him for the class of 1914, Princeton Theological Seminary.

WILLIAM A. ANNIN.

Who would think that Annin was a native of the Jersey Pines, being born at Cedarville. 'Tis true, that Senior sermon of his was rather *tar-tar-ic* and *highly-pitched*, but its theology did not *stick* after all in the cranium of Dr. Paxton. Whether or not that disgusted Annin, he gave up preaching for teaching and settled at once in the Kemper Family School of Boonville, Mo., where he has been ever since and "will likely be for some time to come." Its military character is well adapted to his stately bearing and we predict his success, the more so, because Annin is a fearfully conscientious fellow, and even anticipates all his debts. At least he forwarded your Secretary the handsome sum of one dollar. Annin is the first one of our boys to announce "not married, but engaged."

WILLIAM S. BANNERMAN.

How our hearts are stirred for the boys on the foreign field. We admire their self-sacrifice, and earnest devotion. Bannerman is the first one of our list to greet us from "over the line" (Canada.) No letter direct has as yet been received from him, but a recent letter is published in the May number of the *Church at Home and Abroad*. From it we gather the safe arrival of himself and wife at Gaboon, West Africa, their continued health, and their delight in the work. They are zealously learning the Pangwe and Mpongwe languages. The natives seem eager, yea, even impatient to hear the truth and the doors are, in very fact, wide open. Through Johnson, we learn that Bannerman has a young son.

HENRY C. BASKERVILLE.

Baskerville has the honor of being the "Patriarchus Maximus" of the class. Although coming to us only in the Senior year, he at once identified himself with our interests and affections. He is settled at Centre Hall, Pa., being installed in 1890 over the Sinking Creek and Spring Mills Churches. He was married before entering the Seminary.

SEELYE BRYANT.

From the oldest to the youngest is quite a jump. But, beg pardon, Seelye is not the youngest, although he liked to pose as such. He would liked to have been, yes, he would have been, had not Hedges and Sam Polk "stolen the march" on him. It was mean in them to do it, but then ! —

From his letters we gather that he is located in a worldly, Unitarian town of Massachusetts, Lancaster by name. He has returned to the faith of his fathers, being installed Oct. 1, 1890, over the Evangelical (Cong.) Church of that town. He has had good success, the church receiving more additions in his short Pastorate than in the "preceding two combined." He is President of their Local Union of Y. P. S. C. E. On May 12, 1891, he concluded, with the help of Miss Margaret Ferguson McLean, of the same town, that it "was not good for man to be alone." Well, Seelye, we hope your married life will be as joy-bringing to you as the presence of your "red, white and blue paradigms" (to quote Dunlap) were to us. We miss them—yes, and we miss you to-day.

KENT M. BULL.

April 19th is a great historical day. For then, in '75, fell the first blood of the Revolution at Concord and Lexington. Then, in '61, fell the first blood of the Civil war in the Baltimore riots, and on that very day Kent Bull added his noise to the melée, although not in Baltimore. From that day to the Freshman foot-ball game, there was a good deal of gore about Bull, but the climax was reached on the foot-ball arena, back of Edwards Hall, and Bull has been known ever since as a peaceable man. He is located at Nottingham, Chester county, Pa., being installed Pastor over that church on May 28, 1890. We fear Bull is "tackling too hard," for he writes that he has not been absent from his pulpit one Sabbath, and adds, significantly, "results are encouraging." On Dec. 2, 1891, he was married to Miss Mary Ann Pollock.

Henry M. Campbell.

In virtue of the last remark, we will now introduce Henry Campbell with his favorite song, "My Mary Ann." Those of us who had to endure that song at Burroughs' will appreciate this remark. Campbell came to us in Middle year, primed with Alleghany theology. He found Princeton fellows quite congenial, the Faculty more so, and the Directors most so, and he concluded to remain. When he left he carried to Missouri with him a good share of the esteem of his classmates. He entered upon his work, as Stated Supply, at Monett, Mo., in July, supplying two churches. In spite of many discouragements in that over-churched town, he held on till he was called to the Fourth Presbyterian Church of Kansas City, as successor to your Secretary. There he was installed Oct. 5, 1891, and the work has grown slowly but surely. As to matrimonial prospects, he writes "expect to be married soon."

Richard J. Campbell.

Campbell showed the utter fallacy of that Brown Hall joke, perpetrated on him as the "late" Mr. Campbell, by sending in his reply promptly. He came to us in Senior year, fresh from the sea isle of Ireland. He writes "went straight to Joseph, Ore., where I labored in the Presbyterian Church till last summer, when I took a run through other parts of Oregon and Washington and stirred up some weak mission churches, and they were anxious that I should remain wherever I went. I then went to the Puget Sound country, Washington, but not falling in love with that country, I came to California and took to Menlo Park and it to me. This place is in the center of a very wealthy part of California, popular by reason of many millionaire's residences here and about. Also, it is within half an hour's walk of the famous Stanford University, where I can hear the best men of the day." He is there as Stated Supply over a church of thirty-three members, is boarding at a hotel, expects to attend the Portland Assembly, and is neither married nor engaged. So we leave him to head the "estate of single blessedness."

We are here face to face with the strange Providences of God. When two hearts have become one, and that one heart put into God's hands, how seemingly strange to have it torn by death. But the mystery of His dealings is beyond our ken, and we only wait the dispensation of the fulness of time, when "we shall know even as we are known."

Carrington was ordained June 17, 1890, as Evangelist to Brazil, and was married on Aug. 10, 1890, to Miss Clara Emery, of Washington. They sailed two days later for Sao Paulo, which they reached on Sept. 22. There they remained studying the language until March 12, 1891, when they settled at Rio Claro, 120 miles N. W. of Sao Paulo, a town of about 7,000 people. There they studied the language with the native preacher. At the August meeting of Presbytery, Carrington was appointed as Pastor interino of a portion of Mr. Dagama's field, with residence in Rio Claro. He began work there in September with six or seven preaching points, and continued with apparent success until all his work was stopped by the death of his wife. That scene is best described in his own words:

"I was called home by a telegram informing me of my wife's illness. I did not expect anything serious, as Rio Claro was some 2,000 feet above the sea-level, and exempt, as it was claimed, from the fevers which harass the low-lying coasts. I was agonized to find her almost at death's door, and with a fatal disease (yellow fever) whose name I had heard but never realized. Six hours after I left her on the 18th of December, her temperature leaped to the appalling figure of nearly 106° Fahr., while her pulse ranged between 135 and 140. In three or four days the fever subsided, the temperature settling below the normal. On the 24th hemorrhages set in, leading to facial meningitis. She was unconscious from the afternoon of Christmas day and died with scarcely a struggle at midnight of Saturday, Dec. 26, 1891. Her resignation in the presence of death to the will of her Saviour was sweet and trustful. She felt that God had called her to lay down her life there in His cause. She realized that every human means available had been exhausted and that her life's work was done."

"How blest the righteous when he dies" is all we can say; our hearts are bowed, our prayers ascend, God's will be done. A link that has bound us to the "Class home" has been broken, but, in the breaking, has linked us to the heaven-home. Our sympathies, our prayers, are with our bereaved brother, who with his little daughter, Clara Emery Carrington, (born June 14, 1891,) has returned to this country. Because of the Board's desiring married men in Romanist countries, he will not return. He is now Stated Supply over the Tacoma and Kensington churches, in the suburbs of Washington, D. C. His home address is 1334 Q, N. W., Washington, D. C. He returned on a vessel on which were eighteen cases of yellow fever and four deaths from the same, but he mercifully escaped the disease.

R. H. CARSON.

Carson entered our class in Senior year, and was one of the first to receive a call. He was installed Pastor of the First Presbyterian Church of Stillwater, N. Y., on May 11, 1890. He entered the work with his usual energy, and has almost broken down through over-work. Forty-three have been added to his church, thirty-five of them on Profession. He is Superintendent of his Sunday School and Bible Class teacher as well. He has been invited to preach at three different times in vacant churches, but declined. Not married, nor engaged, as "can't find a girl."

GEORGE M. CUMMINGS.

George has at last found a congenial clime, as he is in a place of acknowledged *short-comings*. For he has gone to the wicked region of the Black Hills, which Henry Campbell would call the "ante-room to hell." His first year was spent in preparation, we presume, in the City of Brotherly Love, where he had charge of the Educational work of the Y. M. C. A., and was also Secretary of the principal Philadelphia Centre of University Extension. Whether or not they tired of him or he of them, he gave up his work and entered the pioneer corps of frontier workers. He was ordained Dec. 27, 1891, and has now charge of the churches of Newcastle, Wyoming and Edgemont, S. D. His Wyoming church has six members, five of whom are women, and yet George declares he is a "bachelor with a vengeance." He would like the work if he could confine himself to only one field, but hardly thinks that he will remain there very long. His message to the class is in Luke 18 : 29, 30 : " There is no man who hath not left house, or parents or brethren, or wife or children, for the Kingdom of God's sake, who shall not receive manifold more in this present time and in the world to come, life everlasting."

JAMES W. DOUGHTY.

Doughty's reply reached us after the Reunion. He is at Yamaguchi, Japan, "studying the worst gibberish ever spoken by man." He has been teaching in the girl's school. The field is very promising, with a large native church and flourishing school. On June 12, 1890, he was married to Miss Brooks Cozine, and one child, Helena by name, graces the home. Our prayers are with you, dear brother, in your discouragements, as well as successes. (The Japanese hieroglyphics on the outside of the letter were interesting, but needed one of Ned Miller's *foot-notes*.)

E. P. DUNLAP.

Dunnie comes from the Buckeye State. Now, a Buckeye belongs to the genus "horse-chestnut." Draw your own conclusions, and for your help recall the story of the "ladders." But Hazlitt says, "Wit is the salt of conversation." That saves Dunnie from being styled fresh. For the "*bon mot*" ingredients in the Dunlap character are proverbial. Dunlap and Kansas City get along well together and he is there still, the Pastor of the Linwood Presbyterian Church. This is one of his own founding, and he never tires of telling of his first Sunday School there, "out under the trees"—the balmy trees—the breezy trees, &c. Then they went a little higher—there you are again, the "ladders"—and met in the third story of a "corner lot." (Now that sounds like Dunnie's Western rabbit story.) They entered their new and neat little church building on Feb. 1, 1891. They organized Oct. 12, 1890, with eighteen members, and now number fifty-eight. A very flourishing Sunday School is held. The first year the church raised for the Pastor's salary $600, and this year $650. He is not married and "no prospect, either immediate or remote." He is enjoying his work thoroughly, and from what we know by personal observation is very popular and successful. His occasional expeditions with the rod and gun meet his taste exactly, and he adds, by way of parenthesis, "long on funerals, short on weddings." My only regret is that Thompson did not sell Dunlap a typewriter.

GEORGE A. T. EDDY.

Eddy, Valedictorian of the Class of '86, Princeton College, and Classical Fellow of our class, is located at Beverly, N. J., being installed April 29, 1891. During the summer of 1890 he supplied the pulpit of the First Presbyterian Church of Washington, D. C. Then for one year he pursued his studies in Princeton, as Fellow in Greek. He was married June 4, 1890, to Miss Rose Gabriel, of Cleveland, Ohio, and "one vigorous" youngster, now ten months old, by name Alfred Gabriel Eddy, enlivens the home. He has not yet been entered at Princeton, but undoubtedly will be.

JAMES S. E. ERSKINE.

Erskine led the Anti-Revision forces on to victory in that wonderful "Mock Presbytery." He is located at Thompson Ridge, Orange county, N. Y., being installed Pastor over the Hopewell church on June 17, 1890. He was soon taken sick with malarial fever, and unable to preach for three months, dragged himself along for four months, then obliged to rest for three months. He resumed work in April, 1891, and is gaining in health, weighing about thirty pounds more than he did in the Seminary. He has received twenty-two on Confession. "The greatest awakening was when I was unable to do any Pastoral work or preaching." He is twelve miles from Thompson, and unmarried.

FRANK B. EVERITT.

Was ordained in his home church as Evangelist on May 9, 1890. On June 9 he left the home of boyhood and youth for "greater worlds to conquer." He lingered long enough at the great International C. E. Convention at St. Louis to report its daily proceedings to the New York *Tribune* and *Mail and Express*. He began his labors in Kansas City in the latter part of June, having charge of the Fourth Presbyterian Church and the Walrond Avenue Mission. To the former he was called as Pastor in the Fall, but in the Spring declined it, having received a call to a much more promising field in East Trenton, in connection with the Chapel of the First Church. During his stay in Kansas City his church nearly trebled in membership, mostly by letter. Since coming to Trenton on Aug. 1st he has received forty-five members, thirty-two of them on Profession. Our Sunday School numbers 550, prayer meetings large, audiences increasing, and interest constant. All kinds of industrial work are carried on in connection with the Chapel, as Drawing, Music, Military, Manual Training, Sewing and Kindergarten Classes. The church contributions have increased by nearly $1,000 in the past year. Prospects are good for a strong church. Study at a minimum, practical work at a maximum. His opinion of the West is tersely this, "A bad place for bachelors," of which he is most decidedly one. He is one of the Vice-Presidents of the State C. E. Union, and in Sept., 1890, he took a flying trip through Colorado and Utah.

Frank L. Fraser.

We are glad to chronicle that Frank is at last settled over a Pastorate, and near his Manitoba home at that, viz., at Hallock, Minn., as Stated Supply. After graduation he spent the summer in Dickinson, N. D.; then the winter in Boissevain, Manitoba, where he had charge of three churches. He preached three times a Sabbath, his afternoon service being eight miles out of town. He reports thirty-five additions on Profession there. They gave him a call there, but he declined, intending to go to the foreign field. He spent that summer at his old mission field along the sea, at New Brunswick, Can. In the fall he returned to Princeton to resume his studies. About the middle of January he accepted a call to the Presbyterian Church of Manchester, N. J. But he has since declined it, owing to the failure of the church to build a new manse. Fraser is engaged, he says, to "one of the sweetest girls in the country," but does not look for marriage yet for some time to come. Frank, look out for "the sweetness long drawn out."

Frank W. Fraser.

We came near missing this Fraser. But after several "tracers" we found him still "burning the midnight oil," this time under the elms of Harvard. He supplied the church of Langhorne, Pa., during the summer, but left on Sept. 25 for Yale, where he studied along the lines of Philosophy and N. T. Criticism, receiving the degree of B. D. on presentation of thesis on "The Encylical Character of Ephesians." On the strength of this he received appointment by the Harvard Faculty to the Divinity Fellowship. He went to Cambridge on Oct. 1st, where he has since been, especially investigating the Johannine question. He has now accepted a call to the First Presbyterian Church of Columbus, Ind., where he expects to begin work on July 1st. He is "most absolutely single," not even engaged."

M. H. GARDNER.

Gardner always was popular, but never more so than on the athletic field. His dignified bearing, his *persuasive* manner, were only too winsome. But leaving "flies" alone we will find him at the same place, Martinburgh (and listen—"Lock Box 31"), N. Y., where he is Stated Supply over the Martinsburgh church, and where he has recently organized the Glendale church with fifteen members. He was ordained by the Presbytery of Albany, Dec. 8, 1891. He has received, he says, "no effectual calls," and declares he is in "no imminent danger of a marital catastrophe." He finds fault with the census of your Secretary, because it does not afford the recording of such worthy deeds of his as "killing a black bear," &c. He scores Paton for writing "review articles filled with daghesh-fortes and like abominations." Altogether, Gardner, your letter is refreshing and shows that you are as tart as ever.

W. F. GIBBONS.

Gibbons describes his work as "plain, old-fashioned, square-toed preaching." We hope the last adjective does not describe the control that Miss Margaret Monaghan, of Westchester, Pa., assumed over him as his wife on May 22, 1890. Well, bring up Rebekah Monaghan Gibbons, age six months, in the same way, and some of '90's sons will be along after a while. He is located at Forty Fort, Luzerne county, Pa., amongst the miners, and is Pastor of the Stella church. He writes encouragingly of his work thus:

"For the last month there has hardly a meeting gone by when there was not some one who stayed to inquire of me privately the way of eternal life. These have been young men and heads of families." We all rejoice in such encouraging tokens of the Lord's blessing on our classmates.

JAMES HEANEY.

"Found at last" is the heading here, for only yesterday did we hear from him. He is at State College, Centre county, Pa. He will be installed there to-morrow. He went first to Danville, N. J., during which time (July 17, 1891), he was married to Miss Agnes Moore Huey, Carn Cullagh, Antrim county, Ireland. He returned and labored near Philadelphia, and about three months ago accepted a call to the above place.

CHARLES SUMNER HEDGES.

Hedges is, as far as age goes, the Benjamin of the class, being born March 6, 1867. He is the only representative in our class of the dusky sons of the South, and is honored by us as a faithful, earnest, reserved Christian student. He is now located at Augusta, Ga., as Stated Supply of the Christ Presbyterian Church. He is also engaged in the educational work of his church in that city, teaching several hours every morning, except Saturday. He conducted revival services last December and January with blessed results. He is neither married nor engaged. He has resigned his present charge, to take effect June 1st, so as to devote himself more exclusively to the educational work, which is quite prominent in that city.

WILLIAM JESSUP.

Jessup reached Syria on Nov. 29, 1890, and is stationed at Zahleh, at the American Mission, with a fellow-Princetonian. He has mastered enough of the Arabic language to converse, to hold family prayers, and make prayer meeting talks in it. He hopes soon to begin regular preaching in pure Arabic. He was married Oct. 15, 1890, to Miss Faith Jadwin, of Brooklyn, and rejoices in little Theodosia Davenport Jessup, of one month's activity. They live in a mud house in a city of 15,000 people, and challenge the world for a happier life. Their greatest trouble is with the Jesuits, and they are engaged in a struggle with the Government to keep their schools.

ANDREW F. JOHNSON.

Johnson spent only one year (Senior) with us. He is now at Kincardine, New Brunswick, Can. He was installed May, 1890, over the Melville church. It is a mission station in a Scotch colony. There are four preaching stations, with four Sunday Schools, four prayer meetings and two Pastor's Bible Classes. Thirteen additions. Nearly all the people attend church on the Sabbath. He is living with his mother, and as soon as he can provide a home for her, will marry (as engaged) and apply for work on the foreign field, perhaps in West Africa.

J. F. JUNGEBLUT.

You will find our postman at 738 Eleventh street, Milwaukee. His church is the First German Presbyterian, over which he is Stated Supply. He had the pleasure of beginning the German Presbyterian work in that city, and organized his church on May 3d, 1891, with twenty-eight members. Membership now is fifty. He began his Sunday School with only six children, now over 100. He was married to Miss Mary Stark on May 27, 1890, and Erna Irene came near being a "Columbia," being born Feb. 23.

J. C. LEVINGOOD.

No word has been received from Levingood, although several efforts were made to reach him. He has been stationed, since gradnation, at Lower Merion, Pa., but has now resigned and has gone to the Continent, presumably for study.

J. E. LYNN.

Lynn follows Baskerville closely in age. Is settled at Pottsville, Pa., over the Second Church, where he was installed Oct. 7, 1890. His membership has increased by thirty-two. Audiences doubled. He has held two series of revival services, but that plan does not seem to work with his class of people. Lynn was married before entering Seminary and has one child, Rachel Ida Bowman. He has had several invitations to preach in vacant churches but has declined.

JOHN MCMILLAN.

McMillan was another Senior entrant, coming also from the Emerald Isle. He seemed bent on seeing the world, for, after graduation, he pushed further Westward until stopped by the Pacific. He settled at Slaughter, Wash., being installed there Nov. 6, 1890. He also held a mission station at Green River. His Sunday School rapidly grew from fifteen to over 100. He is living with his brother-in-law, and has little prospects of marriage, as "no love for the Western girl."

JOHN B. MCCUISH, PH.D.

McCuish is best known as the only fellow who never missed a recitation in the three years. Good for you, Mac. We honor such faithfulness. After graduation he preached during the summer in Ottawa Presbytery, Canada. He declined the calls there, and in the fall entered the University of the City of New York, with McGinniss, to study for the Ph.D. degree. This was conferred on them on June 9, 1892. He was ordained May 2, 1892, and since Jan. 1st has been in charge of the Lee Avenue Presbyterian Church, St. Louis, Mo., a branch of Dr. Niccoll's. It is growing rapidly. He is unmarried and resides at 3746 Penrose street.

C. E. MCGINNIS, PH.D.

Another Doctor. McGinnis had a call early in his Senior year, which he accepted, to the Olivet Presbyterian Church of Lansingburgh, N. Y., over which he was installed as Pastor in May, 1890. He pursued, the following year, studies in the University of N. Y., for the degree of Ph. D. He is engaged and a secret I must tell. McGinnis is not with us to-day, for his mind and heart are on another very important event that is to come off to-morrow. Boys, hush.

P. S.—The following telegrams were exchanged on the day of the reunion. "To C. E. McGinnis, congratulations from the bachelors at Princeton. We mourn our loss."—Whitaker, Oates, Erskine, Everitt. Back came the reply, "Sympathy and greetings from the wise and otherwise."--McGinnis, Miller and Williams.

JAMES T. McLEAN.

"Pastor Presbyterian Church, Little Britain, Lancaster county, Pa." is the printed heading of McLean's letter. He was installed there on June 18, 1890. His church numbers 300 members and he has received 32 into membership. He has driven a lively trade in weddings, viz; 14, and a brisk one in funerals, viz; 39. He was married Dec. 3, 1890, to a western lady.

M. J. McLEOD.

Is a Canadian by birth but well Americanized. "He loves us and we love him." In his Senior year, he declined a call to a church in Newark, N. J. He accepted one to Toughkenamon, Chester county, Pa., and at its three preaching stations did good work. Was installed Oct. 14, 1890. He recruited for a month in January at Lakewood, N. J., and resigned his charge the same spring, because the climate did not agree with him. He is now stationed at Stated Supply at Albany, Mo., about seventy-five miles north of Kansas City. He began his work there (so Mason says) with a poem on the "Mid-Continent."

ROBERT W. MASON.

"Hello, did you want to see me?" comes from De Soto, Mo. Of course it is Bob Mason, just the same as when he came down the aisles of Stuart Hall. Mason introduces himself with the gilt-edged card of the De Soto Presbyterian Church, Rev. R. W. Mason, Pastor, over which he was installed Jan. 19, 1891. (We hear Bob is a gilt-edged preacher of St. Louis Presbytery.) He intended to locate at Hannibal but was changed to De Soto. He complains of "too many churches," although he has the leading Protestant Church. To the marital question he pleads "not prepared." Two openings were offered him last summer. We last heard of Mason delivering a temperance lecture, beginning with Adam. As he says, "All I want is a start, and let me go far enough back." Well, success to your momentum, Bob.

E. D. MILLER.

The best thing about Miller is, he is honest. He will return a book—or, at least, he says he will—loaned back in college days. Ned belongs to the fraternity of "graceful nonchalential frivolity," to use his own expression. He is stationed at Bethayres, with P. O. address at Huntingdon Valley, Pa., over which church he was installed Pastor, April 28, 1891. After graduation he preached four months in Westchester, Pa., then six months as a P. G. at Princeton, beginning work at his present field May 1st, 1891. He is boarding and single.

HUGH MILLER.

A Canadian, from Ontario, entered our class in the middle year. After graduation he spent four months in Pleasant Plains, N. Y. He then took a P. G. in Princeton, during the fall of 1890. From Oct. 2, 1891, to Feb. 21, 1892, he took charge of a mission at Cramer Hill, N. J., under the Second Presbyterian Church of Camden. He is now with his brother in Des Moines, Iowa, (1325 12th St.,) without a charge, but likely to enter mission work.

JOHN W. MOORE.

Moore is another Japanese by adoption, being settled at "Kochi, Japan, No. 37, Masugata." He arrived there on Oct. 24, 1890, and has been teaching four hours a day and studying. Does not preach much as yet. Married June 5, 1890, to Miss Ellie Reid. The next spring found John Watson Moore, 2nd, in the home. He is about 400 miles from Doughty. He is after Thompson and a typewriter. He claims the loveliest location in all Japan, with the people eager to hear, and if he and brother McIlvaine could only have the right kind of native helpers, that section would be christianized in five years. They have a province of half a million with two pastors and two evangelists.

WM. MURCHIE.

He is located at Birnscarth, Manitoba, Canada. Ordained May 29, 1890, and labored in St. John's Presbytery until November, 1890. Took a P. G. at Edinburgh, and became quite famous over an address on "Canada" delivered in the land of Burns. Began work in Birnscarth, Minnedosa Presbytery, on July 7, 1891. He is single.

WM. F. S. NELSON.

Nelson spent one year at Sturges, S. D., as Pastor-elect. While there twenty-seven united on profession. He also had charge of the Pleasant Valley Church, where twelve were added on profession. Two out-stations were also occupied by him. He left there November, 1891, on account of ill-health. He was installed Pastor over the Presbyterian Church at Langhorne, Bucks county, Pa., on April 20, 1892. He had a call to the Presbyterian Church of the famous Hot Springs, of Dakota, but declined. Nelson "stole the march" on the boys by being married April 10, 1890, to Miss Mary A. Henry, of Philadelphia; he claims the oldest "heir" of the class, Wm. Franklin Nelson, born Jan. 6, 1891.

LUTHER A. OATES.

Our most *extended* apology for a man, was born for a southern Colonel—only he came too late for the war. Since this opportunity was missed, he made good use of his height as a manager for our ball team and a target for Pach's best camera. Oates is here to-day as sure "as the Pennsylvania railroad goes." He supplied the Second Presbyterian Church of Charleston, S. C., during the summer of 1890. Then, a P. G. at Princeton. From June, 1891, to September, 1891, he supplied the Boundary Avenue Church, of Baltimore, Maryland. In December, he accepted a call to Delaware City, Del., where he was but recently installed. He is living in the manse with his sister and "not engaged that I know of." His present field affords him ample time for study, which is agreeable to his taste.

ALBERT G. PARKER.

He may be addressed at Pylesville, Harford county, Md., two miles from which is the newly-built Highland Presbyterian Church, over which he was installed Pastor on May 27, 1890. In the two years Pastorate, the membership has been increased by fifty-three additions. Parker was not long in becoming a Benedict, being married on May 21, 1890, to Miss Jessie Bewley, of Washington, D. C. On April 4, 1891, John Bewley Parker entered upon his years of preparation for Old Nassau, and long may he live to grace the Parker home.

A. McD. PATTERSON.

Patterson came near being "lost, strayed, or stolen." But he was finally found, complacently smiling at "Lock Box 94, Mechanicsville, Saratoga county, N. Y.," only one mile from Carson. He was installed Pastor of the First Presbyterian Church of that place on June 3, 1891. For six months after graduation, he preached in the First Presbyterian Church of Hamden, N. Y. In October, he entered "The National School of Elocution and Oratory," Philadelphia, Pa., taking his B. O. degree in June, 1891. He has had good success in his present charge and is much encouraged. He expects to be married in July.

LEWIS B. PATON.

Our only information from Paton is through his mother. He was ordained in the First Presbyterian Church of East Orange, N. J., on April 20, 1890. He then pursued his two years' course of study, under the Hebrew Fellowship of the Seminary, at Berlin, Germany. He has lately accepted a call to the chair of "Old Testament Exegesis and Criticism" in Hartford Theological Seminary, formerly occupied by Professor Bissell. He is unmarried; will return to this country in August and assume his new duties in September.

STANLEY K. PHRANER.

Is at Chieng Mai, in the Laos Country of Siam. He is in charge of a church with a native helper, and is beginning to use the language somewhat. He was married on June 9, 1890, to Miss Elizabeth Pennell, of Omaha, who died on their arrival at their field of labor on Feb. 12, 1891. Stanley was himself much broken down in health, but has recovered and is prosecuting his work with zeal and interest. The sad news of his affliction deeply stirred our hearts, and endeared us more than ever to our homes on the foreign field. Stanley was well-nigh ubiquitous on the campus, and his heroic perseverance abroad makes him carry well the worthy name he bears.

SAMUEL POLK.

Was the only man of his class who faced the crowned heads of Europe. Sam is the second youngest lad in his class, but oh, my! We all rejoiced in his trip abroad—not particularly to get rid of him, but for his own good—but when he came back and told us—well, we almost wished he had stayed at home. He went, after graduation, to Airville, York county, Pa., where on June 4th, 1890, he was installed over the Chanceford Presbyterian Church. As to matrimony, "lo, I have looked to the sea these seven times. The seventh time, behold! there ariseth a cloud out of the sea, like a man's hand." We trust ere this the cloud has become "abundance of rain."

ROBERT J. RANKIN.

Lives "next door" to Polk. Fortunately it is so, or it would be hard to find him. His railroad station is McAll's Ferry, his P. O. address is Sunnyburn, and his church is the Pine Grove Church. If that is not nearly "all the earth," it ventures well nigh to it. He is the first Pastor of his church, and has had perhaps greater spiritual results than have followed any of the rest of us. Without the assistance of any Evangelist, he has been privileged to gather into his fold 102 precious souls. The Lord be praised for the glory of his grace, and, brother, we rejoice most heartily with you. Because of his success, he has recently been elected Moderator of his Presbytery. He received the past year two very pressing calls to larger fields, but declined both. He was married May 15, 1890, to Miss Lizzie S. Peacock, of Berlin, N. J., and in April, 1891, Robert Leon brought joy to their hearts, while, to-day, we hear more music in that Sunnyburn home—this, a daughter.

A. W. REMINGTON.

Settled at Canaan Four Corners, N. Y., from which Pastorate he has but recently resigned. Was married on July 2, 1890, to Miss Mary Louise Kimball, of Milford, N. H.

FRANK HYATT SMITH.

Whether or not Smith belongs to the Briggs' categorical class, his answers are along that line. We have noticed his concise style in his "Golden Rule" articles, and we presume "Professor" Craig Adams would class him as "staccato." He accepted a highly flattering call to the North Avenue Congregational Church of Cambridge, where he was installed Feb. 8, 1891. Under the shadows of Harvard, he has been launching shafts of oratory at Princeton theology, &c. He has received four calls, and is engaged.

WILLIAM H. P. SMITH.

Is located at Stewartstown, York county, Pa., as Pastor of that church, installed June 11, 1890. Twenty-five additions. A new manse built, costing $2,700, and yet Smith is single.

JOHN H. THOMPSON.

Thompy has improved more than any one else of our class, especially in the line of spelling. Probably, this is due to a helpmeet, whom he took to himself on Sept. 4, 1890. He could not afford to "waist" life, and so entered into a partnership with Miss Sarah Cornelia Lansing for a "hunnymoon" on equal shares. They succeeded very well, spending the winter at home. He came to Princeton for a P. G. course but did not tarry long. In the spring he received calls to Hopewell, Pa., and Goodwill, N. Y., over the latter of which he was installed Oct. 15, 1892. His address is Montgomery, Orange county, N. Y. Hello, all ye marriageable men of '90, Thompy wants to see you. Take Erie Railroad from New York.

JACOB N. TROMPEN.

Entered in Middle year. He spent five months at Mausey, N. Y., then a P. G. at Princeton. In April, 1891, he began work at Ramseys, N. J., (Passaic connty,) where he was installed Aug. 19, 1891. His membership has increased from thirty to 100. Trompen has been married for many years and has a family of two children, Nicholas and Harry.

D. RUBY WARNE.

Warne still swings the racquet and preaches meanwhile at Kingston, N. J. He still enjoys his "love sets," for he married on June 12, 1890, Miss Margaret Jones, and Elsie, of six months' activity, "fathers the rattle and rattles the father." He was installed June 7, 1890. He enjoyed a stirring revival season in his church in the winter of 1890, and has a most charming country home.

CHARLES H. WHITAKER.

Our genial President, as benignant as ever, graces the churches of West Grove and Avondale, Pa., being installed in June, 1890. Twenty additions by Profession. Avondale church has been renovated at a cost of $1,500. He has been keeping house with his mother, but now is boarding. The Quaker community is rather slow for him, he says.

JAMES W. WILLIAMS.

Went to Ashland, Pa., where he was Pastor for eight months, being installed Oct. 21, 1890. He accepted a call to the Dunmore Presbyterian Church, of Dunmore, Lackawana county, Pa., whither he went May 1, 1891. He lives in a most beautiful manse but is not married.

S. B. WYLIE.

Was with us only during the last year. After graduation he spent five months on his native island (Ireland) and then took a P. G. at Princeton, during which he supplied the Deer Creek, Md., church. He is now in charge of the Kings Street Chapel, a mission of the Fifth Avenue Church of New York City, in which latter pulpit he has also revelled. He was ordained April 22, 1892, at Princeton. He is still single but hopeful (engaged).

This closes the record of our class, summarizing as follows :

Total,	56
Pastors,	35
Stated Supply,	7
Pastor's Assistants,	3
Without Charge,	3
Teachers,	3
Foreign Missionaries,	5
Widowers,	2
Married,	24
Engaged,	6
Single,	24
Fathers,	17
Children,	19

Letters were also received from Voorhies (Second Presbyterian, Trenton, N. J.,) Hudnut (First Presbyterian, Port Jervis, N. Y.,) and Coffin (Presbyterian College, San Fernando, Trinidad, British West Indies,) who, though not of us, have a large share of our affection and prayers.

Your Secretary has not, he trusts, been over frivolous in his record, but knowing that a little lightheartedness is sometimes good, even in our own profession, he has so indulged. We have nought but gratitude to express for the many mercies received, and only wait our Father's call to wider fields, or even to the higher field in His own home.

FRANK B. EVERITT,
SECRETARY.

TRENTON, N. J., MAY 3, 1892.

Theological Seminary

CLASS OF 1890.

TRENTON, N. J.:
SAMUEL MELLOR, JR., PRINTER.
1890.

TRENTON, N. J., September 26th, 1900.
DEAR CLASSMATES :

The Decennial Reunion has passed and around it linger many pleasant memories. On Monday evening, May 7th, 1900, at the residence of Mrs. Leigh, there gathered around the table the following members of the class circle, Adams, Mr. and Mrs. Everitt, Mr. and Mrs. Gibbons, H. Miller, Oates, Mr. and Mrs. Parker, Mr. and Mrs. Polk, Remington, Thompson, Mr. and Mrs. Trompen, Warne, Whitaker and Williams. Kenneth Everitt and Donald Parker were also present. After a delightful repast, the various members of the class responded to toasts, of both a humorous and serious nature. The Secretary was instructed to convey to Mrs. Wm. Henry Green the sympathy of the class in the death of her husband, our beloved Dr. Green.

The next class banquet will be in 1905.

The class history was ordered published and sent to the class. It has been unduly delayed, because of incomplete reports, and even now, members will doubtless discover errors in dates. If so, kindly notify the Secretary, that corrections may be made for future use. Members desiring printed reports of '92 and '95 can have them at mere expense of postage. They are of same size, so that they can easily be bound together. We hope, this will be done. The Treasurer would report that he has on hand $17.80, which may cover the cost of this issue, the price of which is 30 cents each. Those, who have not so paid, will kindly do so upon receipt of the history.

Now, fellows, get down the old class photo, and let us go over together the history and work of the boys of '90, praying ever for still greater blessings upon their labors.

Fraternally,

F. B. EVERITT,
Secretary.

Princeton Theological Seminary.

Class of '90 Decennial History.

ADAMS, C. C. Smyrna, Del., June 12, '90,-May, '95. With *Presbyterian*, '95-'96. Bedford, Pa., May, '97.—Famous health resort, Carlsbad of America. Married, Sept. 9, '90, Miss McKinney, daughter of Rev. W. W. McKinney, D.D., of the *Presbyterian*. Arthur Glenn, born Sept. 21, '91, and Harold Craig, Feb. 15, '95. Now County and District President of S. S. Work, and in charge of local Summer School. Still edits S. S. page in *Presbyterian*.

ALLEN, WM. Glen Moore, Pa., '90-'92; Ambler, Pa., '92-'94; Pennington, N. J., '94.—Married Minnie R. Lampen, Oct. 29, '90. Two boys, William, 3d, age seven years, and Louis Lampen, six years. About ninety on Confession. Declined call to Fourth Church, Phila. Church improvements at Pennington, $2,500.

ANDERSON, NEAL L. Marion, Ala., May, '90,-Dec., '91; Central Presbyterian, Montgomery, Ala., Dec., '91.—First and only pastor of this church. Membership now 273. Married, Aug. 14, '90, to Miss Anna H. Faison, of Clinton, N. C. Lucius Faison, born '91, died June, '93; Margaret Neal, Aug., '93; Neal L., Jr., '94; Ruth, '97; John Monroe, '99, died Aug., '99. Received 138 on Confession. Convener and Moderator, by appointment of Synod, of new Presbytery of East Alabama and Moderator of new Presbytery. Chairman of Presbyterial Committees on Foreign Missions, Colored Evangelization, and Christian Education; of Synodical Committee of Publication and Colportage, member of Southern Assembly's Committee on Colored Evangelization, 1899.

One of three original promoters of the Southern Conference on Race Problems, and author of the constitution of the society which is to hold these conferences. Author of present age of consent law in State of Alabama, raising age of consent from ten to fourteen years. Chairman of State "Steering Committee" on the dispensary law. Inventor of automatic return carriage for typewriters, sold 1898. Published Hand Book of Home Missions in Synod of Alabama; 2,000 copies issued by Synod. Also, "Recoil of Evolution's Assault on Teleology," published in *Presbyterian Quarterly*, 1899. Special Study, Life of Christ.

ANNIN, WM. A. Boonville, Mo., in Kemper Family School, '90–'99. Superintendent of Public Schools in same town, '99.—Married, June 27, '99, to Miss Anna Laura Wilkins. Pauline Elizabeth, born April 8, '00. His message to the class—" Move heaven and earth for 'no subscriptions to creeds.'"

BANNERMAN, WM. S. French Congo, West Africa, Gaboon and Corisco, '90–'95; Juneau, Alaska, '99.—Married to Miss Grace Mitchell, Aug. 18, '90. Harold, born Aug., '91; Mitchell, July, '95; Paul, March, '97. Received 150 on Confession.

BASKERVILLE, H. C. Centre Hall, Pa., '90–'95; Goodes Ferry, Va., in Home Mission work, '95–'96; Princeton, N. J. (as teacher), '96–'97; Camp Crook, S. Dak., '97,—over four churches, one, he organized. Married, '81, to Miss Emma Reed. Children are Emma R., Howard C., Charles E., William E., Robert W., Arthur P. Special study in philosophy. Declined in '97 a call to professorship in seminary at Danville, Ky.

BRYANT, S. Lancaster (Cong.), Mass., Oct., '90,-Jan., '96; Scituate, Mass., Oct., '96,-Sept., '99; Canton, Mass., Sept., '99.—Still in Congregational Church. Married, May 12, '91, to Margaret F. MacLean, who died Feb. 26, '93, leaving Agnes Lee, born Dec. 29, '92. Married Aug. 26, '97, to Kate W. Skeele, and Dorothy Emmons, born Sept. 2, '98.

BULL, K. M. Nottingham, Pa., '90–'95; Church Hill, Md., '95–'97, over three churches. Relieved of one in '98, when he moved to Kennedyville, Md.; same charge. Married, Dec. 2, '91, to Mary A. Pollock. Four girls and no boys, Helen, age seven and a-half; Annie, six; Harriet, three; and Mary, three months. One child, Kent M., a twin to Annie, died. Sixty on Confession. Two revivals.

CAMPBELL, H. M. Monett, Mo., '90–'91; Kansas City, Fourth, '91–'93; St. Louis, Cote Brillante, '93.—Married, Aug. 24, '92, to Nanne Wilson, of Belleville, Pa. No children. About 110 on Confession. Wife very sick, but in Adirondacks now and better.

CAMPBELL, R. J. Joseph, Oregon, '90–'91; Menlo Park, Cal. (near Leland Stanford University), '91–'92; Felton, Cal., '92–'94; Forbes Church, Portland, Oregon, '95–'97; Cosmopolis and Montesano, Wash., '97–'98; Centralia, Wash., '98–'00; Calvary Church, Tacoma, Wash., '00.—At Felton, church built. Calvary church, now self-supporting. 117 accessions. To Europe in '94. Have taken Paul's advice, "in whatsoever state I am, therewith to be content." So unmarried. Twice President of Tacoma Presbyterian Ministerial Union; Chairman Young People's Committee of Presbytery.

CARRINGTON, W. A. Rio Claro, Brazil, '90–'91; S. S. at Tacoma and Kensington, Md., June, '92,-Jan. '93; A. P. at Westminster Church, Elizabeth,

N. J., Jan., '93,-Oct., '93; Wyalusing, Pa., Oct., '93,-March, '98; Forest City, Pa., '98.—Organized at Wyalusing the Lime Hill Church, and built new church at Sugar Run. Married, Aug. 18, '90, to Miss Clara Emery, of Washington, D. C., who died of yellow fever in Brazil in '91. Married, Sept. 26, '94, Miss Nellie Stevens, of Wyalusing. Two children; Clara, age nine; Ruth, three. Revivals at Lime Hill, Wyalusing and Forest City. 135 additions in his two pastorates.

CARSON, R. H. Stillwater, N. Y., '90-'99; Grace Church, Brooklyn, N. Y., Dec. 1, '99.—Married Dec. 1, '97. Chairman S. S. work, Presbytery of Troy, six years. Eighty additions by letter and Confession, since going to Brooklyn. Wife very sick.

CUMMINGS, G. M. Y. M. C. A. work, Phila., Pa., '90-'91; New Castle, Wyoming, and Edgemont (Black Hills), S. Dak., '91-'95; Clarance, Iowa, '95-'98; post-graduate study at Princeton, N. J., and Chicago, '98-'99; Mt. Vernon, Ia. (Linn Grove Church), '00.—Married in '95. Two children; girl, born May, '96, and a boy. Revival in '95, adding sixty-seven on profession.

DOUGHTY, J. W. Yamaguchi, Japan, '90-'93; Hiroshima, Japan, '93.—On furlough, July, '99,-Nov. '00. Married, June 12, '90, to Brooks Cozine. Helena, born Apr. 24, '91; John Addison, Apr. 14, '93; Adaline, Dec. 5, '94; and Richard, Dec. 30, '97. Secretary of Mission five years. Also served as Moderator. Have translated a book on theology into Japanese, but not published it yet. Am publishing a monthly gospel paper in Japanese. "There are no revivals in Japan. The people are dead in trespasses and sins beyond anything you can understand without being here to see for yourself. We gather them in one by one. The missionaries are *never* pastors, but overseers and evangelists." His child, Adaline, is blind and has infantile paralysis. Hope for the latter malady, but none for former. She is left in blind institution in Columbus, Ohio. Doughty has sent photos of himself and native helpers.

DUNLAP, E. P. Linwood Church, Kansas City, Mo., '90-'92; Wood River, Neb., '92-'95; East Jordan, Mich., '96.—Married, March 27, '93, to Alice M. Swan, of Kansas City. Gaius, aged five years and ten months, and Dorothy, two years and six months. Chairman Committee on Foreign Missions. About 100 accessions. East Jordan self-supporting this year, and advanced salary $300. Offered lately one of the best churches in Michigan outside of Detroit and Grand Rapids—a church of 400-500 members—but refused, feeling his little church could not spare him yet. Benevolences in East Jordan have averaged $200 per year since he has had it. Gave nothing before. Lovely country and good trout fishing.

EDDY, GEO. A. T. Supplied First Church, Washington, D. C., six months after graduation; N. T. Fellow in Princeton Seminary, '90-'91; Beverly, N.

J., '91-'95; A. P. at Washington and Compton Avenue Church, St. Louis, Mo., '95-'97; Boonville, Mo. (South), '97.—Married, June 4, '90, to Rose Gabriel, of Cleveland, O. Alfred Gabriel, born June 10, '91; Catharine Eunice and Mary Priscilla, Dec. 29, '95. The latter died Dec. 13, '97. 121 additions. Delegate this year to G. A. at Atlanta, Ga.

ERSKINE, J. S. E. Thompson Ridge, N. Y., '90.—Married June 26, '95. No children. Chairman Temperance Committee. Revival in '94. Additions, seventy-eight.

EVERITT, F. B. Fourth Church, Kansas City, Mo., '90-'91; Trenton, N. J., '91.—The latter field was a mission of First Church, but organized in 1899, upon a self-supporting basis, with 344 members. Finished first year of independent organization with note and all debts paid and balance on hand. An institutional church, with large sewing school, cadet class, and other industrial classes. Married, Sept. 11, '95, to Sara Helena Van Dyke, and Kenneth Van Dyke born Oct. 16, '96.

FRASER, F. L. Dickinson, N. D., summer of '90; Boissevain, Manitoba, winter of '90; New Brunswick, Can., summer of '91; Princeton, N. J., as post-graduate, winter of '91; Hallock, Minn., '91-'94; Crookston, Minn., '94-'98; Marshall, Minn., '98-'00; Luverne, Minn., '00—a fine, large, new church. Married recently to the girl of whom he wrote nine years ago, "the sweetest girl in the country."

FRASER, F. W. S. S. at Langhorne, Pa., May–Sept., '90; P. G. at Yale, '90-'91, where he took degree of B.D.; Divinity Fellow at Harvard, '91-'92; Columbus, Ind., July, '92,-May, '96; S. S. at Morris, Can., July, '97,-May, '98; Crookston, Minn., '98 —Married, Oct. 17, '94, to Bertha Chloe Cooper, of Columbus, Ind. No children. Elected in '98 Stated Clerk of Red River Presbytery. Called to chair of Hebrew and Biblical Literature in Macalester College, St. Paul, Minn.

GARDNER, M. H. Martinsburg, N. Y., '90-'93; Horseheads, N. Y., '93.—Organized new church at Glendale. Stated Clerk of Chemung Presbytery. Additions, 111. Content with his trout fishing; no girl need apply.

GIBBONS, W. F. Stella Church, Forty Fort, Pa., '90-'97; Dunmore, Pa., '97.—Married, May 22, '90, to Margaret Monaghan. Rebekah Monaghan is now eight years; Eleanor Haller, six; and Margaret Randolph, four. Has written short stories for *Youth's Companion, Lippincott's, Chautauquan, Outlook, N. S. Times,* &c.

HEANEY, JAS. S. S. at Danville, N. J., '90-'91; State College Pa., '92-'95; Shamokin, Pa., '95-'99. Now without charge; address, 52 N. 21st St., Philadelphia, Pa. Married, July 17, '93, to Agnes Moore Huey. S. Spencer Heaney, age six.

HEDGES, C. S. S. S. of Christ Church, Augusta, Ga., '90–'91; Teacher in Haines Normal and Industrial Institute, '91–'93; S. S. of Ebenezer First Church, Rome, Ga., '93.—Married, Sept. '94, to Gwendolene Lyman, who died July, '95, leaving a child, Charles Lyman, now four years and eight months old. Chairman of Publication and S. S. Work, Knox Presbytery. About twenty-five additions.

JESSUP, WM. Zahleh, Syria, '90.—Married, Oct. 15, '90, to Faith Jadwin, of Brooklyn, N. Y. Theodosia Davenport, aged eight; Elizabeth Palmer, six; Helen Butchart, five; and Henry Harris, who died July 3, '97, aged nine months. Moderator Syria Mission, Dec., '97–'98. Pastor in general over large district with several native pastors. Was home on furlough, '99–'00, and was to return on May 19.

JOHNSON, A. F. S. S. at Kincardine, New Brunswick, Can., over four churches, '90–'92; Pine Ridge Indian Reservation, S. Dak., '92.—Married, Nov. 10, '92, to Louise Cornelius, of Halifax, N. S. No children. Published a Book of Forms in Indian tongue. Has three Indian congregations organized, with a fourth applying. Sunday School of eighty.

JUNGEBLUT, J. F. German Mission Work in Milwaukee, Wis., '90–Jan., '95; Meridan German Church, near Alexandria, Neb., Feb., '95–'00; Arcadia German Church at Breda, Iowa, March, '00.—Organized First German Pres. byterian Church of Milwaukee, and built new church and parsonage. Illness of wife compelled him to leave. She is now in good health. Married, May 27, '90, to Mary Stark, and Erna Irene, aged nine; Calvin, seven; and Edna Elizabeth Emma, five, now grace the home. Of books he says, " The Word of God is buried by books." True!

LEVINGOOD, J. C. Lower Merion Church, Gladwyn, Pa, '90–'92; travelled abroad, '92–'94; at Greenwich Church, Othello, N. J., '94–'00; Langhorne, Pa., July 19,–'00.—Married, Sept. 24, '91, to Carrie M. Lawrence. Sidney Lawrence, born July 4, '93, and Madeline Janette, Feb. 7, '97. Chairman Church Erection Committee. About 100 additions.

LYNN, J. E. Second Church, Pottsville, Pa., '90–'94; Bergen, N. Y., '94.— At Pottsville, doubled membership and renovated church, at a cost of $6,000. At Bergen, C. E. Society of 118 members. Studying for Ph.D. Married, July, '78, to Rachel Ida Bowman, and has one child, Lida Maud, fourteen years old. Chairman Temperance Committee. Twice to General Assembly. Seventy-two additions.

McCUISH, J. B. P. G. at Univ. of N. Y., '90–'91, receiving Ph.D. in '92; Lee Avenue Church, St. Louis, Mo., Jan. 1, '92,-Oct. 1, '93; Divinity Fellow at Harvard, '93–'94; First Church, Fulton, Mo. (South), July 1, '94,–July 1, '95; Westminster, Pueblo, Col., Aug. 18, '95,–Dec. 18, '96; North Church, Denver, Col., Dec. 20, '96,–Aug. 1, '99; First, Leadville, Col., Aug., '99.—

Married, July 16, '98, Anna F. Hulburd, Assistant Principal of Salt Lake Collegiate Institute. Stated Clerk of Denver Presbytery for two years. Twice offered a college presidency. Additions, 210.

McGINNISS, C. E. Olivet Church, Lansingburgh, N. Y., '90-'99; Whitehall, N. Y., '99.—Married, May 4, '92, to Charlotte Ida Judson. Only child, Helen, died Oct. 23, '95, seventeen months old. Took Ph.D. from Univ. of N. Y. in '92. Additions, 125.

McLEAN, J. T. Oakryn, Pa., '90. Membership increased from 200 to 600, and a country congregation, too. Married, Dec. '90, to Carrie Cooper, of Indiana. No children. Chairman of Home Mission Committee for nine years. Additions, 424. One revival, two years ago, resulting in 100 additions, and another last year in 114.

McLEOD, M. J. Toughkenamon, Pa., '90-'91; Albany, Mo., '91-'93; P. G. at McCormick Seminary, Chicago, '93-'94; Third, Chester, Pa., '94-'99; Prof. of Greek in Lincoln University, '99-'00. Has accepted call to Pasadena, Cal. (504 members), where he will begin work on Nov. 1. Married, June 27, '98, to Edith Norton Wilson, and Henry Blakely has seen nine months of this old world. Additions, 400.

McMILLAN, JOHN. Slaughter (now Auburn), Wash., '90-'96; P. G. at Princeton, N. J., '96-'98; taking M.A. Degree in University and B.D. in Seminary; Ocean City, N. J., '98-'00; Atlantic City, '00.—Now in a new work just begun at the famous " city by the sea." Granted vacation of eleven months by his western church, when he visited Europe. Unmarried.

MASON, R. W. De Soto, Mo., '90.—Unmarried. Chairman Y. P. Societies. More additions this year than ever.

MILLER, E. D. P. G. at Princeton, '90-'91; Huntingdon Valley, Pa., '91-'93; American Reformed Church, Newburg, N. Y., '93-'94; studying in Germany and traveling, '94-'99, taking degree of Ph.D. in '99 from University of Berlin. Spent last winter in Princeton, N. J., and is looking for position as teacher of Philosophy. Has been offered presidency of a college or two, but declined. Expects to spend another winter at Princeton.

MILLER, HUGH. S. S. at Pleasant Plains, N. Y., '90; at Camden, N. J., '91-'92; Grimes, Iowa, '92; Spring Grove, Minn., '92-'93; P. G. at Princeton, '93-'94; Ardmore, Pa., '94-'96; Port Kennedy, '96-'97. Now S. S. at Lansford, Pa. A bachelor still. Visited the South the past winter.

MOORE, JOHN. Kochi, Japan, '90-'98; Susaki, Kochi Kui, Japan, '98.—Tour among villages. All new fields. Time of seed-sowing, few converts but progress good and prospects hopeful. Troubled with Higher Criticism, but

John remains even firmer than ever for the old truths. He has three boys, John Watson, aged eight years; Boude C., two years; and Lardner W., one year, all of whose pictures were gladly received by your Secretary.

NELSON, W. F. S. S. S. at Sturgis, S. D., '90-'91; Langhorne, Pa., '92-'94; Ambler, Pa., '94-'99; assistant pastor Oxford church, Phila., '99 —Has full charge of the pastoral work, and is superintendent of Sabbath-school, which has seven departments, closely graded, and promotions by examination. Has also charge of the C. E. Society, which last year gave $1,800 to missions. Preaches only occasionally. Throat trouble forced him to leave Ambler. Expects soon to publish book of Helps for Junior Societies. Is writing S. S. lesson helps for intermediate grade. Married, Apr. 10, '90, to Mary A. Henry, and Wm. Franklin, born Jan. 6, '91, remains still the only child.

OATES, L. A. S. S. at Second Church, Charleston, S. C., summer of '90; P. G. at Princeton, '90-'91; S. S. at Boundary Avenue Church, Baltimore, Md., June, '91,-Sept. '91; Delaware City, Del., '92-'99; Falling Spring Church, Chambersburg, Pa., '99.—Unmarried, with about 300 girls in Wilson College; "have narrowed them down to less than a dozen." Stated Clerk, New Castle Presbytery, '99. Chairman, Committee on Supplies.

PARKER, A. G. Highland Church, Pylesville, Md., '90-'99; Stewartstown, Pa., April 19, '00 —Married, on May 21, '90, to Jessie Bewley, of Washington, D. C. Parker's family heads the list with *six boys;* John Bewley, Apr. 4, '91; Albert George, Sept. 6, '92; Edwin Graham, Apr. 29, '94; Malcolm Bruce, July 4, '96; Kenneth Lawrence, Feb. 8, '98; and Donald Dean, Oct. 3, '99. He succeeds, in his new place, W. H. P. Smith, of our class.

PATERSON, A. McD. Mechanicsville, N. Y., '90.—Married, Sept., '92, to Josephine Langford, and now Josephine Langford, with her six years, and Jean McDonald, with her two, make home happy. No remarkable revival, but steady work.

PATON, L. B. Berlin, Germany, as student, '90-'92; Hartford, Conn., '92,— as professor of O. T. Criticism and Exegesis in Hartford Seminary. Degree of Ph.D. from University of Marburg, Germany. Upon return from abroad, had calls to Oberlin, Princeton and Hartford. Has had articles in the *Journal of Biblical Literature, Journal of Semitic Languages, Presbyterian, Reformed Review,* &c. Married, Dec. 30, '96, to Suvia Davison, of Hartford, and has one child, Suvia Lanice, two years old.

POLK, SAMUEL. Chanceford, Pa., '90-'93; Gainesville, Texas, '93-'96; Edington, Pa , '96.—Married, Sept. 14, '93, to Mary Amos. Two children, Joseph Littleton, five years old, and Rebeka Amos, three years. Additions, 97. Has lately studied in Princeton.

REMINGTON, A. W. Canaan Four Corners, N. Y., '90–'92; Holyoke, Mass., '92–'98; Hyde Park, Mass., '98–'99; Beacon Church, Philadelphia, '99.—His present church is an institutional one, as was also the one at Holyoke. Married, July 2, '90, to Mary Louise Kimball. No children.

SMITH, F. H. North Avenue Congregational Church, Cambridge, Mass., '91–'95; P. G. at Princeton, '97; pulpit supply since then. Present address, Williamsville, Erie Co., N. Y. (near Buffalo). Married, Oct. 17, '93, to Elizabeth A. Breed, of New York City. No children. Smith's racy pen has been busy, writing for magazines. He honored Prof. Green in a little poem, beautifully written, and his address to the Teachers' Association was a revelation of wit and eloquence. He has lost none of his old power. He has been supplying Central Church, Buffalo.

SMITH, W. H. P. Stewartstown, '90–'99. Resigned Dec. 11, '90, and now settled on a farm of his own at Dale, N. Y., in charge of two country churches. Built new manse and new church at Stewartstown. Married, but no children.

THOMPSON, J. H. Goodwill Church, Montgomery, N. Y., '90—over as fine a country charge as you ever saw. Married, Sept. 4, '90, to Sarah Cornelia Lansing. No children. Thirty-four additions.

TROMPEN, J. N. Ramseys, N. J., '91; over Reformed Church. Son Nicholas is eighteen years, and ready to enter Princeton next fall. Other child, Harry, is twelve. Member of Board of Examination of the Theological Institution of the Christian Reformed Church at Grand Rapids, Mich., for five years. Trustee of same institution and also of Board of Domestic Missions and Heathen Missions. On Classical Committee in Classis for five years. Seventy-two additions.

VOORHIES, W. S. Elmer, N. J., '90–'92; Second Church, Trenton, N. J., '92.—Received honorary degree of D D. from Chicago University in '99. Married, Oct. 20, '90, to Elizabeth Rutherford Randolph, and has three boys, Paul Davidson, born Dec. 31, '91; Wm. Sinclair, Jr., Oct. 4, '93, and Robert Randolph, July 26, '98.

WARNE, D. R. Kingston, N. J , '90–'98; Ewing Church, Trenton Junction, N. J., '98.—Have done evangelistic work. Married, June 12, '90, to Margaret Anne Jones, and Mary Elsie was born Sept. 26, '91, and Helen Insley, Oct. 31, '96. Chairman S. S. work. Revival in '90, with fifty-three additions. In all, ninety-six additions. Supt. of Correspondence Dept. of N. J. C. E. Union, and on Transportation Committee for London, '00. He and wife sailed June 26 for a tour of Europe, taking in London C. E. Convention and Paris Exposition.

WHITAKER, C. H. Avondale and West Grove, Pa., '90-'93; Bushkill, Pa. (Reformed Church), '93-'00; S. S. at Bordentown, N. J., '00.—While at Bushkill, took a B.D. degree from Union Seminary, N. Y., and studied for Ph.D. at Columbia University, but degree not yet received. Revival in '94 with forty-five additions. About one hundred in all.

WILLIAMS, J. W. Ashland, Pa., '90-'91; Dunmore, Scranton, Pa , '91-'96; in travel, '96-'97; A. P. to Rev. Dr. Wood of Second Presbyterian Church, Philadelphia, Pa., '97.—Unmarried. Has published articles for various papers.

WYLIE, S. B. S. S. at Deer Creek Church, Harmony, Md., '90-'91; S. S. at Alexander Chapel, New York City, '91-'92; New Castle, Del., '92.—Married, Sept. 29, '92 to Minnie Pyper of Belfast, Ireland. Hugh was born Oct. 10, '93, and Jeannette, May 25, '97. His publications are "still in the press."

Letters have also been received from the widows of Bros. Rankin and Phraner. Mrs. Rankin is living at Ocean Grove, where her children are attending school. Their names and ages are Robert Leon, born Apr. 5, '91; Ella May, Apr. 7, '92, and Helen Ethelyn, May 15, '93. Mrs. Phraner is residing with Stanley's father, Rev. Dr. Wilson Phraner, in East Orange. Her two children are with her and in school, viz.: Wilson Westervelt, born July 29, '93, and Stanley Lansing, born Sept. 16, '94. Our prayers and interest will ever follow these families of our departed classmates. We count them as our own, and our family circle shall always include them.

SUMMARY.

Total	57
Died	3
Pastors	39
Stated Supply	2
Pastor's Assistants	2
Without Charge	2
Teachers	2
Post-Graduate	1
Foreign Missionaries	3
Home Missionaries	3
Widowers	1
Married	50
Single	9
Children—Boys	43
Girls	35
Deaths—Wives	4
Children	7
	— 11

Of children, four were boys, viz.: Anderson (2), Bull, and Jessup; and three were girls, viz.: Eddy, McGinniss and Moore.

BACHELORS.

R. J. Campbell, Gardner, Mason, McMillan, H. Miller, E. D. Miller, Oates, Whitaker, Williams.

ADDITIONS ON CONFESSION.

McLean, 424; McLeod, 400; Williams, 350; Everitt, 333; McCuish, 210; Heaney, 145; Anderson, 138; Carrington, 135; McGinniss, 125; Eddy, 121; Gardner, 111; H. M. Campbell, 110; Levingood and Whitaker, 100. In all, twenty-two report 3,854 accessions.

DEGREES.

Ph.D.—F. W. Fraser, McCuish, McGinniss, E. D. Miller and Paton.
B.D.—F. W. Fraser.
D.D.—Voorhies.

MODERATORS.

Trompen (3), Hedges (2), Whitaker (2), Anderson, H. M. Campbell, Eddy, Erskine, Everitt, Jessup, Levingood, McLean, Oates, Remington, Thompson, Warne, Wylie.

STATED CLERKS.

F. W. Fraser, Gardner, Oates, McCuish.

SAME CHARGE AS IN 1890.

Erskine, McLean, Mason, Paterson.

SPECIAL STUDIES.

Church History—Whitaker, Carrington.
Theology—Eddy, R. J. Campbell.
Greek—McLeod, Polk, F. W. Fraser.
Philosophy—E. D. Miller, Whitaker, McCuish, Oates.
Literature—Heaney, Williams.
Sociology—Gibbons, McCuish.
Archæology—Erskine.

PATENTEES.

Anderson, Whitaker.

INSTITUTIONAL CHURCHES.

Everitt, Remington.

REPORT

TWENTIETH ANNIVERSARY

CLASS OF 1890

THEOLOGICAL SEMINARY

PRINCETON, N. J.

NEWS PRINT, STEWARTSTOWN, PA.
1911

MINUTE.

The twentieth re-union of the class of 1890 was held at the Princeton Inn on Tuesday evening, May 10, 1910, with the following members and wives present: Mr. and Mrs. Bannerman, Mr. and Mrs. Erskine, Everitt, Levingood, McMillan, H. Miller, Parker, [and little daughter Beulah] Paton, Mr. and Mrs. Thompson, Mr. and Mrs. Warne, Mr. and Mrs. Whitaker, Mr. and Mrs. Williams, Wylie.

After a social hour in the parlors, a banquet was served, with our President Whitaker as toast-master. As our guests, we had Professor and Mrs. Davis, Professor and Mrs. Erdman, Rev. Dr. Wilson Phraner, and Wilson Phraner, the son of our deceased classmate, Stanley Phraner.

Interesting after-dinner talks were given by all present. The secretary read his report and it was ordered printed, together with such material as he might gather later.

At a late hour the Class separated, looking forward, with deeper pleasure, to another, and, we trust, larger gathering in 1915, our twenty-fifth anniversary.

F. B. EVERITT, Secretary.

FOREWORD

The annals of a Class are of interest, only as they deal with living principles and living personalities. The growth of an idea transcends the growth of a man. Only as we incarnate vital truths, do we impress the world. To discover, to discriminate, and to divulge those elements of character that have made for failure or success, in the lives of fifty men, thro' two decades, would be no mean achievement. Writing history would then be more than a pastime. It would be a privilege, worthy of the best, and a task, worthy of the mightiest. To watch the rise of some, swift-winged, because Heaven-born and Heaven-sent; to see others wend their even course, with scarce a hillock's rise; and to mark the fall of others, as if pierced by some sudden shaft, this is startling in its surprises, and often mystifying in its causes. It is not the part of your historian to trace individual destiny. Each must follow his own rule of interpretation. The standards of measurement are, after all, of our own making. We judge, with an individuality as marked as that by which we preach. Let that judgment be charitable. For

> "We live in deeds, not years, in thoughts, not breaths;
> In feelings, not in figures on a dial.
> We should count time by heart-throbs. He most lives,
> Who thinks most, feels the noblest, acts the best."

None of our weaknesses would we hide. Our strength is not in our achievements, but in our fidelity. Our virtue is "to love the true for itself alone." Humble ministering, in Jesus' name, is our only claim to be known. We pause at the end of these two decades. The impress of our ministry is now at its height. It is flood-tide with us. The market is now above par. Soon, the ebb sets in, the goods are marked-down. But let not the "dead-line," and the ecclesiastical bargain counter affright us. We are still men, men with iron in our blood and steel in our thought. Ring true in all we do. The only failure is to fail to be true to the best that is in us. Thoroughness is a spiritual gift.

Holiness is wholeness. Eternity is too short for a work well begun. Live as we have never lived before, love as we have never loved, and that coming glory of all service will be ours, when we can say, with Him of old.

> "*I have glorified thee on the earth. I have finished the work which thou gavest me to do. And now, O Father, glorify thou me with thine own self.*"

And wrapped in a glory divine, in the likeness of God himself, we shall stand before his throne, in ineffable light, in unspeakable joy.

To keep the lines of this Class together, is an increasing responsibility. For we are widening in our circle, as the next generation comes to the front. It is no great task to keep in touch with the actual men of the class,—poor correspondents tho' some of them are; their wives are better—but our hope is, to maintain in some degree the ties as well of the children of our families. For this work, we ask your sympathy and prompt co-operation, when sought. Let our children know, that there is a Princeton bond, that cannot be severed and it will go far toward strengthening their faith in, and thought of, the ministry We yield to no fraternity in fellowship, in sympathy in mutual helpfulness, that, as Princeton men in the Princeton spirit, we are glad to give to each other, in the bonds of holy love.

C. C. ADAMS   -   -   2229 Butler Place, Minneapolis, Minn.

Smyrna, Del, May '90-May '95; field Agent of Presbyterian,-April '96; Bedford, Pa.—Oct. '01; Missionary at Vesta & Wabasso, Minn.—April '02; field secretary of Albert Lea College for Women—March '03; Delhi, Minn. '08—now pastor Vanderburgh Memorial Church, Minneapolis. Built new church at Wabasso, costing $5000, and at Delhi, $8,000. President of City Ministerial Association. For sixteen years, has edited Sabbath School page of Presbyterian. Married. Two boys.

WM. ALLEN, JR.   -   -   Haddonfield, N. J.

Glen Moore, Pa. '90-'92; Ambler, Pa. '92-'94; Pennington, N. J. '94-'04; Haddonfield, N. J. '04—, where he has a new and handsome Memorial Church. Married. Two boys.

NEAL L. ANDERSON, D. D.   -   -   Winston-Salem, N. C.

Marion, Ala., '90-'91; Central Church, Montgomery, Ala., '91-'07; Winston-Salem, N. C. '08—A large church in a college town. Has an assistant. Convener and Moderator of New Presbytery of East Alabama. Active in Social Questions of the South. D. D. from Davidson College in 1904. Married. Two girls; three boys died.

WM. A. ANNIN   -   4050 Castleman Ave., St. Louis, Mo.

Teacher, Boonville, Mo. '90-'99; same, Supt. of Schools, '99-'03; Supt. Schools, Macon, Mo. '03-'09; now teaching Spanish in a St. Louis High School. Married. One boy, one girl.

WM. S. BANNERMAN   -   -   Titusville, N. J.

Missionary, Gaboon, W. Africa '90-'97; visiting the home churches '97-'99; Juneau, Alaska; '99-'01; Sitka, '01-'07. Titusville, N. J. '09. Married. Five boys.

HENRY C. BASKERVILLE   -   -   Royalton, Minn.

Sinking Creek and Spring Mills Churches, Huntington Pres. Pa. '91-'94; Evangelist & teacher '95-'97; Alzada, Mont. '98-'99; Camp Crook, S. Dak. '98-'00; Spearfish Valley '01-'04; Edgemont '05-'06; New London, Minn. '07; Harrison & Spicer chs. '08; Royalton, Minn. '09. Home Missionary to the Black Hills. Married. Four sons and one daughter.

SEELYE BRYANT   -   -   116 Bay St., Springfield, Mass.

Lancaster, Mass. '90-'95; Scituate '96-'99; Canton '99-'02; Middlefield '04-'06; Springfield '06. All Congregational churches and in Mass. Married twice. Two girls.

5

KENT M. BELL - - - Stewartstown, Pa.
Nottingham, Pa. '90-'95; Kennedyville, Md. three churches, '94-'01; Stewartstown, Pa. '01. Married. Four girls and one boy.

HENRY M. CAMPBELL, D. D. 379 N. 2d Avenue, Phoenix, Ariz.
Monett, Mo. '90-'91; Fourth, Kansas City '91-'94; Cote Brilliante, St. Louis '94-'01; Mesa, Pueblo, Col. '01-'06; Phoenix '06, Membership over 600. Teaches weekly Bible Class in Government Indian School. Many students members of his church. Expects to have an assistant. Has two months vacation and large salary. Best winter climate in the country. Married. No children.

R. J. CAMPBELL - - - - Lockport, N. Y.
Joseph, Oregon '89-'91; Menlo Park, Cal. '91-'92; Felton, Cal. '92-'94; Forbes Ch., Portland, Oregon '95-'97; Cosmopolis, Wash. '97-'98; Centralia, Wash. '98-'99; Calvary, Tacoma '99-'01; Mendocino, Cal. '01-'04; Blasdell, N. Y. '05, Lockport Second, '11. As to wife and children, he says: "None that I know of."

W. A. CARRINGTON - - - - Galeton, Pa.
Missionary, Brazil '90-'92; Kensington, Md. S. S. '92; Hope Chapel, Elizabeth. N. J. '92-'93; Wyalusing, Pa. '93-'98; Forest City, Pa. '98-'00; Middle Granville, N. Y. '00-'06; Bainbridge, N. Y. '06-'08; Marathon, N. Y. '08-'10; Galeton, Pa. '10. A manufacturing town of 6,000. Married twice. Three girls.

R. H. CARSON - - - - Brooklyn, N. Y.
Stillwater, N. Y. '90-'99; Grace, Brooklyn, '99. Large and wealthy church, with membership over 650. Married; one son.

GEO. . M. CUMMINGS 417 W. St. S. E., Washington, D. C.
Educational Dept. Y. M. C. A., Phila. '90-'91; New Castle, Wyo. and Edgemont, S. Dak. '92-'93; Clarence, Iowa '93-'98; P. G. Princeton and McCormick '98-'99; Mt. Vernon, Iowa '99-'01; Ida Grove, Iowa '01-'05; Garden Memorial, Washington '05. Married. Two boys, two girls.

JAMES W. DOUGHTY - - - Williamsbridge. N. Y.
Missionary, Japan, at Yamaguchi '90-'92 and at Hiroshima '93-'02; Sec. N. Y. Bible Society '02-'06; Member Ceylon Commission (British) '06-'08; now lecturer and political campaigner. In business, stocks and bonds of the clean, high-grade type. Married. Two boys and two girls. (one girl, in school for blind.)

EDWARD P. DUNLAP - - - Holly, Mich.
Linwood Ch., Kansas City, Mo. '90-'93; Wood River, Neb. '93-'95; East Jordan, Mich '96-'02. Since then, he has been in business, traveling for his brother's firm, Grosset & Dunlap, 52 Duane St. N. Y. City. Has purchased property at Redlands, Cal., and expects to develop that in the next five years, and eventually to live there. Married. One boy and one girl.

GEO. T. EDDY - - - - - N. Y. City.
P. G. (N. T. Fellow) Princeton '90-'91; Beverly, N. J. '91-'95; Asst. P. Washington and Compton Ave. Ch., St. Louis, Mo. '95-'97; Boonville, Mo. '97-'01; First, Huntingdon, N. Y. '01-'09. Now in Astor Library, N. Y. City. Married. One boy and one girl.

J. S. E. ERSKINE - - Thompson Ridge, N. Y.
Thompson Ridge, N. Y. '90 to present time. Married. No children.

FRANK B. EVERITT - - - New Park, Pa.
Fourth Ch., Kansas City, Mo. '90-'91; East Trenton, N. J. '91-'01; Minister in Charge, Y. P. Association Work, of Fifth Ave Pres. Ch. N. Y. '01-'03; New Park, Pa. '03. Married. Two boys and one girl.

FENWICK W. FRASER - - 82 North St., Massillon, O.
P. G. at Yale '90-'91 and Fellow at Harvard '91-'92; First Ch., Columbus, Ind. '92-'96; Morris, Manitoba, '97-'01; Jackson, Mich. '01-'10; Second Ch., Massillon, Ohio '10. Married. No children.

FRANK L. FRASER - - - Kennewick, Wash.
In Canada '91-'92; Hallock, Minn '92-'94; Crookston '94-'98, Marshall '98-'00; La Verne '00-'03; Los Gatos, Cal. '03-'08; Blue Earth, Minn. '08-'10; Kennewick, Wash. '10. Found that Minnesota climate did not agree with him after living in California. So moved last April to above address, where he has regained his health. Married. One son and one daughter.

MURRAY H. GARDNER - - - Brewster, N. Y.
Martinsburg, N Y '90-'93; Horseheads, N. Y. '93-'95; Brewster '05. Unmarried.

WM. F. GIBBONS - - - Clark's Summit, Pa.
Forty Fort, Pa. '90-'96; Dunmore '96-'09. Now recuperating, while assisting in the International Correspondence School of Scranton. Married. Four girls.

WM. JESSUP, D. D. - - - - Zahleh, Syria.
Missionary on the same field for twenty years. 4200 pupils under his care in his district. Must have FOUR good, strong men at once. D. D. in 1909. Married. Four girls, one boy died in infancy.

ANDREW F. JOHNSON - Pine Ridge, S. Dak.

Kincardine, N. B. Canada, '90-'92; Pine Ridge Indian Reservation, S. Dak. '92. Now District Missionary to Sioux Indians. Married. One son, with an Indian name, Maga Ska. He certainly should follow in his father's footsteps.

J. F. JUNGEBLUT - - - - - Lodi, Cal.

First German, Milwaukee '93-'95; Alexandria, Neb. '95-'00; Arcadia, Iowa '00-'01; Alexandria, Neb. '01-'03; Eureka, S. D. '03-'04; Hope German Reformed, Lodi, Cal '04. Married. One son and two daughters. He is the only man from whom we did not hear directly, but was located and history found, through other sources.

J. C. LEVINGOOD - - - - Wayne, Pa.

Lower Merion, Pa. '90-'92; studied in Germany '92-'93; Greenwich, N. J. '94-'00; Langhorne, Pa. '00-'03; Greenway Ch., Phila '03-'06, when, at his suggestion, it was consolidated with the Westminster Church, since which time he has been Assistant Pastor of the organization. Both church properties were sold, and a handsome, new church built at cost of $89,000, free of debt. Married. One son and one daughter.

J. E. LYNN - - - - Berlin, Ont., Canada.

Second Ch. Pottsville, Pa. '93-'94; Bergen, N. Y. '94-'07; ill-health '07-'08; Berlin, Can. '08. Married. One girl, of special musical ability.

J. B. McCUISH, D. D. - - - Newton, Kas.

P. G. Univ. of N. Y. '90-'92; Lee Ave. Ch., St. Louis, '92-'93; Fellow at Harvard '93-'94; Fulton, Mo. '94-'95; Westminster Ch., Pueblo, Col. '95-'96; North Ch., Denver '96-'99; First, Leadville '99-'07; professor of Philosophy and Ethics in Westminster College, Denver '07-'09; First Ch., Newton, Kas. '09. Fine, large church. Men's Bible Class of thirty-six members. Married. One boy (four years old, who recites the Greek alphabet and knows about thirty Greek words), and two daughters.

C. E. McGINNISS - - - - Whitehall, N. Y.

Olivet Ch., Troy, N. Y '93-'99; Whitehall '99. Married. Lost their only child, Helen in '95

J. T. McLEAN - - - - St. Petersburg, Fla.

Little Britain, Pa. '90-'01; Fourth, Chester '01-'02; Green Hill Ch., Wilmington, Del. '02-'05; Crystal River, Fla. '05-'08; Lakeland, Fla. '08-'09; St. Petersburg, Fla. '09. Tourist city. Married. No children, but adopted son.

M. J. McLEOD - - 151 Central Park West, N. Y. City.

Toughkenamon, Pa. '90-'91; P. G. McCormick Seminary '91-'93; Third Ch., Chester, Pa. '93-'99; professor in Lincoln University, '99-'01; Pasadena, Cal. '01-'10; St. Nicholas Collegiate Ch., N. Y. City '10. In Pasadena, had what was called the finest church edifice in America. Over 1300 members. Now has one of the richest, the church of Roosevelt, Mrs. Sage and Miss Helen Gould. Enjoys the city problems of the metropolis. Married. One son and one daughter.

JOHN McMILLAN - - - Atlantic City, N. J.

White River, Wash. '91-'93; P. G. Princeton '96-'98; Ocean City, N: J. '99-'00; Westminster Ch., Atlantic City '01. Unmarried.

E. D. MILLER, Ph. D. - - Gerrardstown, W. Va.

P. G. Princeton '90-'91, Huntingdon Valley, Pa., '91-'93; American Reformed Ch., Newburg, N. Y. '93-'94, since which time he has been studying in Berlin, Edinburgh and Princeton. Unmarried.

HUGH MILLER - - 1616 N. 16th St., Phila,. Pa.

P. G. Princeton '90-'91; Camden, N. J. '91-'92; Grimes, Iowa '92; Spring Grove, Minn. '92-'93; P. G. Princeton '93-'94; Port Kennedy, Pa. '94-'98; Lansford, Pa. '99-'03; Florence, Kas '05; Carversville, Pa. '05-'09. Now without charge. Unmarried.

JOHN MOORE - - - - Sherman, Texas.

Missionary, Kochi, Japan '90-'98; at Susaki Machi, Kochi '98. At above address on furlough, a little ahead of time, because of nervous troubles of his wife. Will educate his children there, and travel for the Board. May have to remain several years. Married Six sons, [youngest named after our Mason,] and one daughter.

W. F. S. NELSON - - Santa Maria, Cal.

Sturgis, S. D. '90-'91; Langhorne, Pa. '92-'95; Ambler, Pa. '95-'00; Assistant pastor, Oxford Ch. Phila. '00-'04; Clayton, N. J. '04-'10; Santa Maria, Cal. '10. Most promising field in Santa Barbara Co., in the greatest oil, sugar and bean district in the country. Married. One son, the "Class Baby," now going into business.

A. G. PARKER - - - - Olney, Ill.

Highland Ch., Street, Md. '90-'00; Stewartstown, Pa. '00-'04; Evangelist, Berwyn, Md. '04-'07; Olney, Ill. '07. Married, and holds the record still in family, with eight sons and one daughter.

A. McD. PATERSON - - Newburyport, Mass.

Mechanicsville, N. Y. '91-'08; First Cong. Ch., Shelburne, Mass. '08-'09; Old South Pres., Newburyport, Mass. '09. Founded by Geo. Whitefield in 1742, whose bones lie under his pulpit. Whitefield's desk is in the study of the church. Many tourists visit the spot. Only 35 miles from Boston. Married twice. One boy and four girls.

LEWIS B. PATON, Ph. D., D. D. - Hartford, Conn.

Fellow of Princeton at Berlin '90-'92; teaching in Hartford Seminary, as Instructor '92-'93, as Associate Professor '93-'00, as Professor since 1900, all in the Dept. of Old Testament Criticism. In 1903-4, leave of absence to take the directorship of the American School of Oriental Study and Research in Jerusalem. Married, but wife died by accident while in Jerusalem. One daughter.

SAMUEL POLK - - - - Colora, Md.

Chanceford, Pa. '90-'93; Gainesville, Texas; '93-'95; Eddington, Pa. '95-'04; West Nottingham, Pa. '04. Connected also with private Academy. Married. One boy and one girl; one boy deceased.

A. W. REMINGTON - - - Mt. Vernon, N. H.

Canaan Four Corners, N. Y. '90-'92; Grace Congregational Ch., Holyoke, Mass. '92-'98; Pres. Ch., Hyde Park, Mass. '98-'99; Beacon Ch., Phila. '99-'05; Freehold, N. J. '05-'10. Has resigned and is now resting at his summer home in New Hampshire. Married. No children.

FRANK HYATT SMITH, D. D. 29 Huntington Ave., Buffalo, N. Y.

North Congregational Ch., Cambridge, Mass. '91-'95; P. G. at Princeton '97. In 1905 he became lecturer on English Literature at Buffalo University, which position he still holds. Is in great demand at Chautauquas, at "$100 per." Married. No children.

W. H. P. SMITH - - - - Wyoming, N. Y.

Stewartstown, Pa. '90-'99. Stated Supply at Orangeville and Johnsonburg, N. Y. in 1900, and since then, on his farm, with occasional supply work. Married. No children.

J. H. THOMPSON - - - Montgomery, N. Y.

Goodwill Ch., Montgomery, N. Y., only pastorate '91. Lives on fresh air and contentment. Married. No children and no troubles.

J. N. TROMPEN - - - Aurora, Col.

Christian Reformed Ch., Ramseys, N. J. '91-'07, which church became the First Presbyterian. Now Congregational Home Missionary for Colorado. Married. Two boys, one grandson, Milton J. Trompen.

W. S. VOORHEES, D. D. - - Thompsonville, Conn.

Elmer, N. J. '90-'92; Second, Trenton '92-'02; Milford, N. J. '04-'09; Thompsonville, Conn. '09. Married. Three boys.

D. RUBY WARNE - Trenton, N. J. R. F. D. No. 1

Kingston, N. J. '90-'98; Ewing Ch., near Trenton, N. J. '98. Historic, formerly called Trenton, First, church. Married. Three girls.

CHAS. H. WHITAKER - Bordentown, N. J.

Avondale and West Grove, Pa '90-'93; Lower Walpack Reformed Ch., Bushkill, Pa. '93-'00; Bordentown '00. Papers announce his recent resignation from Bordentown. Married. No children.

JAS. W. WILLIAMS - - - Abington, Pa.

Ashland, Pa. '90-'91; Dunmore, Pa. '91-'95; Assistant pastor, Second Ch., Phila '97-'04; Abingdon, Pa '04. Married. No children.

S. BEATTIE WYLIE - - - New Castle, Del.

P. G. Princeton and supplying Deer Creek Ch., Harmony, Md '90-91; Alexander Chapel, Fifth Avenue Ch., N. Y. City '91-'92; only pastorate, New Castle, Del. '92. Married. One boy and one girl.

Addenda

"*Mark now, how plain a tale shall put you down.*"

"*The deepest truths are best read between the lines.*"

DEPARTMENT OF HEALTH AND HYGIENE

Foremost among our blessings are those of health and physical ability to do our work.

"*Non est vivere, sed valere vita.*"

The best assets in life are a sound character and a sound body. And, of all men, the preacher should have them. Physically speaking, sermons should not be born of sighs, nor prayers of pains. The smart and the ache make poor initiative and still poorer momentum, and both are needed in the ministry.

As a rule, our Class has enjoyed good health. Some, as Whitaker, have not missed a day thro' illness, while, to others, has come the usual breakdown through overtaxed nerve and strength. McLeod had a six months siege of insomnia. Henry Campbell suffered in 1904 a similar period of typhoid fever. Lynn suffered a serious break-down in 1907 and went to Canada for recuperation, where he is still located, regaining health. Fenwick Fraser was out a few months, with the grippe, while Nelson lost time in 1891, and Cummings in 1899. Carson is a sufferer from chronic throat trouble, and his people have the grace each year of sending him to the Bermudas or elsewhere. Gibbons is at present out of active work, ill-health compelling his resignation last year; but a long trip to Palestine, and light work for a few years, promise ultimate recovery. A nervous break down forced me to relinquish in 1903 a most promising work in N. Y. City, in connection with the Fifth Ave. Church, but these years "in the open" have greatly benefitted me. Probably we would all fare better, if we followed the Medo-Persian rule of Remington to relax every ten years and take a prolonged rest at least a year, which rest he is now taking in his country home in New Hampshire.

Some of our men are having anxious times with the loved ones, who have stood so faithfully by them. Our prayers and sympathies go out now to brothers Henry Campbell, Carson, and Levingood, watching by the side of invalid wives. Mrs. Campbell has been very ill for ten weeks with tubercular trouble. May the watching moments be brightened with the faith of the poet, as he wrote.

"Behind the dim unknown,
Standeth God within the shadow,
Keeping watch above His own."

DEPARTMENT OF SINGLE CUSSEDNESS!

Oh! beg pardon! but how else shall we describe the hopeless celibacy of a few! Our terminology is limited, our temper merciless.

To call the roll is enough:

R. J. Campbell, Gardner, McMillan, E. D. Miller, H. Miller.

These never sighed for love, nor sang from love's returns. With quiver empty and bow unstrung, hapless hunters they, in the quest of this world's good! No fruitful vine by the side of their house, no olive plants around their table! *Requiescat in*———

Murchie died unmarried. The rest of the class have long been in the "luxury of living," altho' a full decade passed by before Mason, Oates, Whitaker and Williams found the ones chosen for them.

Of the class, Bryant, Carrington, Paterson and Phraner have been twice married. Paton remains a widower.

DEPARTMENT OF TRAVEL.

There is little of the hermit in this Class. With Tennyson, it says,

"I cannot rest from travel; I will drink
Life to the lees."

Our feet have pressed the soil of every continent. And when that Martian air-line is established, methinks some Bohemian in our ranks will be first aboard. Perhaps Bannerman occupies first place as a peregrinator; Africa, France, Italy, Switzerland, Alaska, Canada and United States are a few points in his itinerary. And to think that he has finally stopped near Trenton, and midway between the county workhouse and the State Asylum! Nelson has spent at least a month, often two months, every year since graduation in travel. Has been three times to Europe, and in all its countries; in all but about five states in this country and all through Canada. Carrington has touched three continents in Brazil, the British Isles and his own "dear, native land." Remington has braved the rugged peaks of Sinai, as well as covered Egypt, Palestine, Turkey, Greece and Italy. R. J. Campbell, the "lone traveller," has been in Great Britain, Canada, Alaska and all over these states. His airship is liable to alight anywhere. Warne, in 1897, toured the United States and in 1900, Europe. Paton was a year in Jerusalem, as Director of the American School of Oriental Study and Research and therewith traveled extensively in the Holy Land and Egypt. Gibbons has just enjoyed a pleasant trip to Europe and the Holy Land, thro' the kindness of his people. Because they came this year a month apart, he had two Easter Sundays, one in St. Peter's, Rome, where he saw the Miracle of the Holy Fire. Was in Rome, when "Teddy" turned down the Pope. Was in Dr Tipple's study, when he dictated his historic cablegram to Bishop Hartzell. Was in Egypt when the murderer of Boutrous Pasha was on trial and saw "Young Egypt" in its wildest mood Saw the Moslem "Feast of Moses," a parade from Jerusalem to Jericho and return, occurring only once in fourteen years. Saw 600 S. S. children parade the very streets of Stamboul in Constantinople, singing "Onward, Christian Soldiers," where less than twenty years ago, 17,000 Armenians were massacred Even the Turkish police saluted the Christian flags. Was also at Oberammergau. Frank Fraser has traversed the trackless plains of the west, back and forth, now in Minnesota and now in California, with Canada as a side line. Whitaker, in 1905, visited England and France. Doughty and Moore, of course, have been in Japan and the Orient, and Jessup all over Syria, and the lands between.

The rest of us have been content with our own little land, and have watched afar and dreamed. But do not judge us narrow, if as yet our horizon covers only familiar lines.

DEPARTMENT OF STUDY AND RESEARCH.

Our class may not all be specialists, but we have persevered in study. The class-room habit still lingers. Only now we study men as well as books. Cummings keeps company yet with his lexicon, and nibbles on Greek roots, as a rat does on cheese. He has declined one professorship in Greek in a western college and has substituted, in the same, in Howard University, Washington. McCuish and McLeod have also taught Greek in Colleges. Theology has been the field of Baskerville's penetrative mind, and his several exploitations therein have found their way thro' the religious press, notably the "Presbyterian." Philosophy and history have engaged McCuish, McGinniss and Whitaker, who revel in degrees of that line, while Ed. Miller is our recognized American authority on Kantian Ethics He eschews everything else but Kant, but Kant! No cow ever enjoyed her cud more than Ed, the delicious morsels of Emmanuel Kant. Who would have thought that Erskine would have taken up with such mundane matters as Archaeology, Astronomy, and geology? or Doughty, with American policies? or Gibbons, with fiction? Yet each has been successful in his line, Doughty, taking high rank as a campaigner for the Democratic party, and Gibbons, with utter abandon, scratching high place on the roll of fame, as the author of short stories and "Those Black Diamond Men." The Gibbons home is of the literary type, his wife also being a writer of no mean repute. Carson delves into church History as a specialty, while Carrington chooses English History and Literature. Anderson inclines to Civics and Social Studies, which have also claimed largely the attention of your Secretary in his institutional work in large cities. Nelson has also made special studies in criminology, with personal investigation of prisons and dependents, and the study of French and English specialists. Lynn has taken up Extra-mural work in Wooster University, and received the degree of M. A. from that institution.

For actual research, Paton undoubtedly leads, as he also does in literary output. His special field is Oriental Archaeology and History, holding, as he does, the professorship in Old Testament Exegesis and Criticism, and instructor in Assyrian, in Hartford Seminary, Conn. The following is a list of his published books. The Early History of Syria and Palestine, Scribners, 1902; Jerusalem in Bible Times, Univ. of Chicago Press, 1908; the Commentary on Esther in the International Critical Commentary, Scribners, 1908; Recent Christian Progress, Macmillan, 1909. He has contributed also numerous articles to Dictionaries, Encyclopoedias and the press. As a celebrity, Frank Hyatt Smith can keep pace with Paton, his lectures on English Literature being popular at all Chautauquas, and his tribute to Shakspeare, being honored with a place in the archives of the poet at Stratford. Bannerman and Johnson have been contributing to philology, the former in helping to reduce the Fang language of West Africa to writing and the latter has studied the Sioux language and published "Forms for special occasions for Indian Pastors."

But for real, artistic English, with life in every word, McLeod is peerless. We commend most earnestly to all the Class, those gems in sermonics: "A Comfortable Faith," "The Culture of Simplicity," "Earthly Discords and How to Heal Them," and "Heavenly Harmonies for Earthly Living." The latter has passed thro' six editions and two of the others, thro' three. For a spiritual tonic, they are unequalled.

Adams has for sixteen years peeped out of the pages of the Presbyterian every week on the Sabbath School page. Nelson has been on the staff of the Board of Publication, while occasionally some of the rest of us venture—even into poetry.

The lecturer is akin to the student and the author; and we have Doughty in politics, Frank Hyatt Smith, in English Literature, R. J. Campbell and Gibbons on travel, Remington, with the best illustrated lecture on Sinai in America, from original photographs, while Frank L. Fraser is a spell-binder on Missions, his three lectures, being "The Romance of the Missions" (California,) "The Indians of the Southwest," and "The Customs of the Hopi Indians."

Here also we should tabulate our unclassified *Literateurs;* Annin, teaching Spanish in a St. Louis High School. (The only heretic in the Class. How kind providence is!!); McCuish, teaching Xenophon in Bethel College in his town, and Polk, teaching Bible in the Academy in his parish. Eddy is ruminating in the Lenox Library, N. Y. City, classifying and translating. Thompson, still with visions galore, and cobwebs in the brain—oh, no, far from it—is travailing in pain to bring forth—a book. When it comes, he promises to lockstep with Annin in revolutionizing the Church. The only difference between the two, is, Annin is destructive, while Thompy is constructive. At any rate, the latter thrives under it, being still *incomparabile* the

"fat, round, oily man of God"

of the Class, and, incidentally, as bald as he is round. R. J. Campbell has been pushing Normal Class work, his class taking a full hundred per cent in the examinations of the State S. S. Association of New York.

DEPARTMENT OF POLITICS.

And here we show our polyglot character. A more wriggling mass of larvae never squirmed under the biologist's lens, than did this class, under cover of the question of their political faith. Cummings and Polk frankly avowed that faith as "unknown," Frank Hyatt Smith posed as a "composite," while R. J. Campbell, in very despair, said, "Proho-demi-publican," to which class Warne also shows a tendency in his affiliation with both Prohibition and Democratic parties. In fact, all of our independents as Adams, H. M. Campbell, Carson, Everitt, F. W. Fraser, McLeod, Paton, Remington, may be so classed. Doughty and Eddy like the term "Independent" none too well, and so affix "Democrat" to it. Still there are some "true blue" stuff politically yet in the class. Anderson, Baskerville and Wylie swear still by the Democracy, Carrington by Prohibition, while the G. O. P. [now known familiarly as the Get Out Party] has warm defenders in Amin, Bannerman, Erskine, F. L. Fraser, McCuish, McGinnis, W. H. P. Smith, Voorhies, Whitaker and Williams. Frank Fraser and Williams—the West and the East—write, "strong for Teddy." McCuish says, "still a true-blue Presbyterian Republican." The rest of the class pass the question by in significant silence, believing there are others than politicians who live

"to clutch the golden keys,
To mould a mighty state's decrees,
And shape the whisper of the throne."

HONORES HONORIFICIS.

As Frank Hyatt Smith says, "there are degrees in glory, but no glory in degrees," but Frank wears a D. D. McLeod has been offered a D. D. several times, but always declined it. Others are not so wary of honors. Anderson, H. M. Campbell, [Wooster 1919] Jessup, McCuish, Paton and Voorhies are "doctored with divinity." Paton also carries a Ph D. from the University of Marburg, Germany, while McCuish and McGinnis hold it from American universities. Baskerville, Fenwick Fraser, McMillan and Whicker have won a B. D. thro' special study.

Two men have graced the Moderator's chair of a Synod, viz. McCuish, of Colorado, in 1903, and Johnson, of South Dakota, in 1906.

Only two men, as reported, have attained to Stated Clerkships, viz, Gardner and Thompson, the former, however, by removal to a new charge, being now out of the office. [Thompson is opposed to the Executive Commission, and why not?] Cummings is Permanent Clerk of Washington (D, C.) Presbytery. He also preached, this year, the annual sermon before the Y. M. C. A. of St. John's College, University of Maryland. Doughty has been General Secretary of the New York Bible Society, and also, for two years, a member of the British Ceylon Commission.

This does not, by any means, exhaust the honors of the Class, but only touches those, which, in all modesty, the members have been willing to name.

THE COMING MEN!

How blessed we are, in our families! With the exception of Henry Campbell, Erskine, F. W. Fraser, Remington, Frank Hyatt Smith, W. H. P. Smith, Thompson, Whitaker and Williams, our married men rejoice in those fresh-grown petals that hold the sweetness of life, children. Of these, death has claimed eight, leaving to bless us still, sixty-one boys and forty-eight girls. What a goodly company! God bless them all. Especially are we interested in the fatherless ones, S. Spencer Heany, Chas. Lyman Hedges, Robert Judson Mason, Robert Luther Oates, Wilson and Stanley Phraner, and Robert, Ella and Helen Rankin. Our prayers shall ever follow them in life, and all others in our class similarly bereaved, and whenever they need a helping hand or a comforting thought, let them turn to the nearest member of their father's class, who, for the father's memory, can be naught but kind and true to the one that bears his honored name.

Ye bachelors,—not of divinity—the other thing——think of the eight boys and one girl of Parker, the seven boys and one girl of Moore, the five boys of Bannerman, the four boys and one girl of Baskerville, the four girls and one boy of Paterson, and the same of Bull, and the four girls of Gibbons! And then bewail your lockstep with misery, and be good!

Some of these "hopefuls" are well along in life's preparation. Trompen is the only one who claims to be a grandfather, although we surmise Baskerville is also. The latter has a son, ordained in 1909 to the ministry, who took that year a fellowship in Princeton. He also has two sons Juniors in McAlester College, preparing for the ministry. In the same institution is also Arthur Adams, with like inclinations. Fine! that three of our sons, in one institution, should tread the path, the fathers trod. That Western climate must be better than the Eastern, for ministerial proclivities. Harold Bannerman is a Junior in LaFayette, winning honors as an athlete, being a champion wrestler and boxer, altho' as a boy in Africa, he suffered serious illness. He is studying engineering, which profession is also calling Paul Voorhies to Wooster Technology. Lawrence Levingood, after leading his High School class in Philadelphia, has entered Princeton University. Rober. Rankin has chosen his father's *Alma Mater*, and is entered, a Freshman, at LaFayette, while his sister Ella is in Wilson College. John Watson Moore. Jr. is in Davidson College, to which college Bro Oates left the bulk of his fine library. Parker has three sons in Park College, or the preparatory schools connected therewith, two of whom are preparing for the ministry—another tribute to the West. Gibbons' oldest daughter is a Sophomore in Bucknell University, and Eleanor, a Freshman, in Wooster. It rejoices us all to know that the latter has there joined the Student Volunteer Band, and given her life to the work abroad. Vassar is claiming two of our girls. Theodosia Jessup, and Helena Doughty, classmates, if we are not mistaken. Mary Elsie Warne has graduated from the State Normal School at Trenton and is teaching school. Nelson's son is entering business.

And now we call the roll of the boys and their sisters, according to their ages as nearly as we can make it. (Some exact dates of birth are not on record.)

BOYS

Chas. E. Baskerville	
Wm. E. Baskerville	No ages given.
Robert W. Baskerville	
Nichola. Trompen	
Henry Trompen	
Wm. Franklin Nelson	Jan. 6, 1891
John Bewley Parker	Apr. 4, 1891
Robert Leon Rankin	Apr. 5, 1891
John Watson Moore	1891
Alfred Gabriel Eddy	June 10, 1891
Gordon Harold Bannerman	Aug. 24, 1891
Arthur Glenn Adams	Sept. 21, 1891
Paul Davidson Voorhies	Dec. 31, 1891
Albert George Parker, Jr.	Sept. 6, 1892
William Allen, 3rd.	Jan. 31, 1893
Calvin Jungeblut	1893
John Addison Donghay	Apr. 14, 1893
Sidney Lawrence Levingood	July 4, 1893
Wilson Westervelt Phraner	July 29, 1893
William Sinclair Voorhies, Jr.	Oct. 4, 1893
Hugh Wylie	Oct. 10, 1893
S. Spencer Heaney	Aug. 1, 1893
Edwin Graham Parker	Apr. 29, 1894
Louis Lampen Allen	Aug. 11, 1894
Gains H. Dunlap	Aug. 29, 1894
Stanley Lansing Phraner	Sep. 16, 1894
Harold Craig Adams	Feb. 5, 1895
Norman Mitchell Bannerman	July 29, 1895
Charles Lyman Hodges	1895
Malcolm Bruce Parker	July 4, 1896
Kenneth Van Dyke Everitt	Oct. 16, 1896
Paul Stewart Bannerman	Mar. 22, 1897
Bonde Chambers Moore	May 13, 1897
Richard Donghay	Dec. 30, 1897
Kenneth Lawrence Parker	Feb. 8, 1898
Gardner Wilson Moore	May 20, 1898
Henry Blakely McLeod	June 27, 1898
Robert Randolph Voorhies	July 26, 1898
Albert Baldwin Cummings	Aug. 15, 1898
Donald Dean Parker	Oct. 3, 1899
Arthur Marling Bannerman	May 26, 1900
Elmo Franci Parker	July 17, 1901
Wallace Henry Moore	July 20, 1902

Edward C. Bull   Nov. 8, 1901
Harold Greig Cummings   Nov. 8, 1901
John Wilkins Annis   1902
James Murdock Polk   Oct. 26, 1902
Robert Judson Mason   Feb. 5, 1903
Donald Newland Carson   June 18, 1903
Robert Luther Oates   July 29, 1903
Norman Neil Parker   Jan. 31, 1904
Maga Ska Johnson   Aug. 25, 1904
James Hugh Fraser   Jan. 24, 1906
Allan Paterson   June 21, 1906
John B. McQuish, Jr.   June 22, 1906
James Donald Everitt   Sept. 24, 1906
James Erskine Moore   1906
Henry Foster Bannerman   Jan. 18, 1908
Mason Edwards Moore   1908

AND THE GIRLS!!

Emma R. Baskerville   }
Lida Maud Lynn   }   No ages given
Helena Doughty   Apr. 24, 1891
Clara Carrington   June 14, 1891
Mary Elsie Warne   Sept. 26, 1891
Rebekah Monaghan Gibbons   Oct. 22, 1891
Ruth Paterson   Nov. 24, 1891
Erna Irene Jungeblut   1891
Ella May Rankin   Apr. 7, 1892
Theodosia Davenport Jessup   1892
Agnes Lee Bryant   Dec. 29, 1892
Helen Bull   Jan. 19, 1893
Helen Ethelyn Rankin   May 15, 1893
Margaret Neal Anderson   Sept. 1, 1893
Eleanor Haller Gibbons   Oct. 22, 1893
Anna Bull   Apr. 18, 1894
Josephine Langford Paterson   Sept. 28, 1894
Elizabeth Palmer Jessup   1894
Adaline Doughty   Dec. 29, 1894
Helen Butchart Jessup   1895
Edna Elizabeth Emma Jungeblut   1895
Catharine Eunice Eddy   Dec. 29, 1895
Margaret Randolph Gibbons   Jan. 9, 1896
Florence White Cummings   May 27, 1896
Rebeka Amos Polk   Oct. 26, 1896
Helen Insley Warne   Oct. 31, 1896

Enid Anderson	Jan. 9, 1897
Madeline Jeannette Levingood	Feb. 7, 1897
Harriet Bull	Mar. 6, 1897
Ruth Horton Carrington	Apr. 6, 1897
Jeannette Wylie	May 25, 1897
Dorothy I. Dunlap	Jan. 2, 1898
Jean McDonald Paterson	Jan. 2, 1898
Sovia Lanier Paton	April 24, 1898
Dorothy Emmons Bryant	Sept. 2, 1898
Mary Bull	Jan. 21, 1900
Pauline Elizabeth Annin	May 25, 1900
Elsie Paterson	July 26, 1903
Frances Patterson Gibbons	Sept. 31, 1901
Helen Gladys Everitt	May 4, 1903
Sibyl Hubbard Fraser	July 26, 1903
Helen Catharine McCuish	Sept. 21, 1903
Jean McLeod	Feb. 9, 1904
Ellie Reid Moore	1904
Margaret Louise Warne	June 1, 1904
Beulah Jean Parker	Dec. 20, 1905
Elizabeth Pauling Carrington	Jan. 13, 1908
Margaret Agnes Cummings	June 7, 1909
Anna Margaret McCuish	Sept. 3, 1909

IN MEMORIAM.

Death has been unusually active in our ranks, so we are told. Not many classes have had seven men fall in twenty years. The grim reaper has cut relentlessly. Brothers, wives, and children have all gone to the other side. Work was but begun when the call came. But no man faltered. And the brave widows have taken up the struggle with a man's heart and faith. It has been a pleasure to keep in touch with these families of our deceased ones, and, we trust, there may ever be the closest link between us. They are still of us, and we give herewith their residence and work.

MURCHIE.

The first to fall. After a P. G. course in Edinburgh, he labored at Birnscarth, Manitoba, June 1891-Dec. 1892. Taken ill at that time, he was a year in hospital, St. John, and died of tuberculosis, May 21, 1894. Unmarried.

RANKIN.

A month later and Rankin was called. He had had a most successful pastorate of three years at Pine Grove, Pa., when he was called in Nov. 1893 to the LaFayette Square church, Baltimore. The work was most promising, when, on June 5, 1894, he laid down his work with a true Christian triumph, after only four days of illness from appendicitis. His widow, with her three children, Robert, Ella and Helen, have since been living in their own home at Ocean Grove, N. J. They are now temporarily at Berlin, N. J., her former home, while Robert is in LaFayette College, Ella in Wilson College, Chambersburg, Pa., and Helen in the Haddonfield, N. J. High School.

PHRANER.

On Jan. 15, 1895, Phraner passed away after four years of service in Siam. A true missionary, who counted not his life dear unto himself, if he might "finish his course with joy." Twice ordered home, but declined. At last started, but died in Singapore hospital, after operation for hepatic abscess. Phraner was twice married, his first wife dying soon after arrival in Siam. His second wife returned to this country with her two boys, Wilson and Stanley, and resided with her father-in-law, Rev. Wilson Phraner, D. D., in East Orange. There she died on March, 4, 1903. The boys are still with their grand-father, who writes, that they are in the East Orange High School, "preparing for Princeton, and, I hope, for the ministry."

HEANEY.

On Sept. 8, 1904, James Heany died in Philadelphia, where he had been living since 1898. His pastorates at Danville, N. J., '90-'91, State College, Pa., '92-'95, and First Church, Shamokin, Pa., had been successful. Ill health compelled him to relinquish work for a season, and he had just accepted a call to a church near Orange, N. J., and had moved his goods, when he was stricken with typhoid fever, and died within a week in the Presbyterian Hospital. His widow, Agnes M. Heaney, still resides in Philadelphia, at 1322 S. 52nd St., while her son, Spencer, is in the High School, in the Manual Training Course, and will likely prepare for engineering.

MASON.

The next to follow was our beloved "Bob," always genial and happy. He was doing a splendid work in Salida, Col., in the heart of the Rockies, where he had built a new church, and where he was officially connected with the State C. E. Union, as it's Supt. of Personal Work. Mason was above all else a soul-winner, and his last illness proved it. He had been planning, with the Methodist minister, for joint Evangelistic services. After he had lost his power of speech on Sunday, Feb. 19, he motioned for paper and pencil, and on his knees and elbows in bed, he wrote out detailed instructions as to these meetings. Early Monday morning he became unconscious, and died Tuesday, Feb. 21, 1905. Interment was in Cincinnati, beside his father. His only other pastorate was De Soto, Mo., where he spent ten years, '91-'01, to which place and former home his widow returned, with Robert Judson, two years old, whom both parents dedicated to the foreign mission field, by the honored name of Judson. Robert was baptized by Rev. W. S. Faris, of China, is a healthy child, with his father's bright and active mind.

HEDGES.

Chas. Sumner Hedges, the only representative of the colored race in our class, fought a hard battle against tuberculosis. From '91-'92 he preached at Augusta, Ga., and taught in the Haines Normal and Industrial School. From '93-01 he did the same at Rome, Ga., being also principal of the Public School. Ill health forced him to give up his work, and he became a mail carrier in Houston, Texas, where he died on May 23, 1906, and was laid to rest in Olivewood Cemetery, of that city. His widow is now Mrs. Lizzie H. Johnson, and lives at 504 N. Pine St., San Antonio, Texas. His son Lyman, is living with his uncle in South Atlanta, Ga., is fifteen years of age, a Christian boy, and attends Clark University.

OATES.

Another is sadly missed at all our gatherings. For Luther never missed a reunion, if he could possibly get there. He was fond of his class and the old associations at Princeton. After a post-graduate course there, he served as pastor of the church at Delaware City, Del., '92-1900, then of the Falling Springs Church, Chambersburg, Pa. '00-'03 and finally of the First Church, Bridgeton, N. J., in 1903. There, he suffered long with pernicious anemia, induced by splenic poison. For several weeks, he was in the Medico-Chi Hospital in Phila., where the end came peacefully on Nov. 15, 1909. Almost his last words were these: "I shall soon be in the august Presence, viewing sights unseen." He was laid to rest in the cemetery at Bridgeton, the last services being conducted by our classmate, Wylie. His widow, Ethelinde Dennis, with their only child, Robert Luther, have located at Princess Anne, Md., near relatives, in a new home, "Rosemary Cottage." "Little Bob" has begun his school career and is a strong, promising child, whom, we shall follow, with all the others, with loving interest.

In addition to the above, Mrs. Clara Carrington died of yellow fever in Brazil in 1894; Mrs. Margaret Bryant, Feb. 26, 1893; Mrs. Elizabeth Phraner, Feb. 12, 1891, and Mrs. Eliza S. Phraner, Mch. 4, 1903. Mrs. Josephine Paterson and Mrs. Mary Ellie Moore have also passed away. Mrs. Suvia Paton died, in a sad accident, while traveling with her husband in Palestine Mar. 20, 1904.

Of the children, the following died in infancy, Helen McGinnis, the only child of Bro. McGinnis, Oct. 23, 1895; Mary Priscilla Eddy, Dec. 29, 1895; Kent M. Bull, Jr., Apr. 22, 1894; Lucius Faison Anderson, June 1893; John Monroe Anderson, Aug. 1899, and Robert H. Carson, Jr., Margaret Jean and Lydford McIlvain Moore.

Joseph Polk suffered a severe accident from fire, endured a long period of suffering and died of peritonitis in 1906, at the age of fifteen. Howard C. Baskerville was killed, April 19, 1909, while in the ranks of the insurgents in Persia.

Of all these, we may well say, with Tennyson:
"God's finger touched him, and he slept." And with Him, we leave our dead, "until the day-break and the shadows flee away."

FADS AND FANCIES, FOIBLES AND FOLLIES.

The side-lines of the Class! Modesty has kept most of the boys silent on this score. Probably, they feared being classed with the poodle-dog crowd. But some are frank enough to answer, and there is not a genealogist among them!! Bryant says, he never regretted selling Hodge's Systematic Theology to buy a tennis racquet: only now, [since he is so far from Warne] he has laid aside the racquet for golf, which he conscientiously plays every Saturday afternoon, and, next to "dynamiting orthodoxy," is his chief dissipation.

Williams plies a motor-boat and auto, while Wylie is satisfied with the former. McCuish dabbles in politics, and was urged four years ago to be the Mayoralty candidate in Leadville, on the Republican ticket. Thompson also takes a hand, now and then, in political matters, and has taught the "ring" of his county a few pointers on how to carry an election.

Your secretary believes in the open air, and has somewhat solved the vacation problem for a family of children, and moderate means, by possessing a comfortable camp outfit, and betaking himself each season to some water resort, where we "take to water, like ducks," the whole set of us.

Anderson and Whitaker are more commercial in their tastes, and each has put on the market, patented products, that pay. Anderson has a good thing in his return type-writer carriage, made and sold to the Underwood people. It has now reached the manufacturing stage, and numbers are in use all over the country.

Whitaker's foot-warmer for carriages has brought good returns, he, having sold his Canadian rights, but holding the rest.

Frank Fraser is plucking fruit and health by working between times, a fruit ranch, a mile from his home, in one of the greatest fruit belts of the country, on the Columbia river, Washington.

The Questionaire.

Theology

Question 1. Any change in theological convictions?

Reject with heart, soul, strength and mind, theology of the liberals. Adams.
Ultra-conservative. Reject teetotally all liberal theology. Anderson.
Growing broader all the time. Annin.
"Reformed theology for me." Baskerville.
"Still believe in the Atonement" Carson.
"Liberal Conservative—no sympathy with destructive criticism. Carrington.
"Princeton position is the only safe and sure one." Eddy.
"Not quite as stiff, more in sympathy with men and their need of a saviour.
F. L. Fraser.
"Have discovered that the Presbyterian church is the true church." Johnson."
"Trifling less rigid." McGinnis.
"Still conservative, still believe every word of the old Book." Nelson.
"Progressive Conservative." Paton.
"Old truths are best." Remington.
"Old Jerusalem gospel, Hodge-flavored, Princeton taught—nothing like it."
F. H. Smith.
"Old-liner." W. H. P. Smith.
"Same old Bible and same old creed." Voorhies.
"Newer criticism has proved little." Whitaker.
"Not quite so stiff." Williams.

Personal Convictions

Question 2. What convictions have grown stronger in the twenty years?

"That creeds should be re-stated every 25-30 years and subscription to creeds relegated to the dark Ages, where it originated." Annin.
"Traditional orthodoxy stronger." Baskerville.
"The over-ruling hand of Providence." R. J. Campbell.
"Need of preaching the old supernatural gospel, in humble dependence on the Holy Spirit, preceded and followed by an educational ministry." Carrington.
"The necessity of upholding Christ in every sermon and the advisability of preaching expository sermons." Cummings.
"One God and all men brothers; the spiritual beauty of Jesus; all religions divine in some degree." Doughty.
"That the great fundamentals are the articles of a standing or falling church, and that we must hold them as the most precious of possessions." Eddy.
"God guides His children still." Everitt.
"That God is gracious." F. W. Fraser.
"The divinity of Christianity." Johnson.
"Preach more sympathetic sermons." McLeod.
"That those entering the ministry should be men of intellectual vigor and spiritual earnestness. To reach men, we must have rare tact and sense." McCuish.
"God has called us to the most wonderful work in the world." Nelson.
"No possible substitute for the old Book and the old Gospel; Jesus Christ as the only Saviour of men has become bigger and more real." Paterson.
"The need to hold up Jesus as given in the Word." Remington.
"Stronger as to the needs of the Soul. Only the Cross." F. H. Smith.
"Stand more firmly on the simple bed-rock of the old-old Gospel. Care less for sectarian doctrine or government." W. H. P. Smith.
"All convictions have grown stronger." Thompson.
"The need of preaching the pure gospel with all of one's God-given powers. Must have Christ a reality and an abiding presence." Warne.
"Historicity of Christ, His deity, resurrection, power to regenerate, and our utter dependence on the Holy Spirit." Whitaker.

The Curriculum

Question 3. What is your attitude toward present curriculum of Princeton?

"Too conservative—not practical enough."

"Some practical correlation between its life and work and that of the Church. It does not fit men for the real work of the ministry."

"Should be less scholastic and more practical. Should know how to popularize doctrine and use it efficiently, how grade a sabbath school, how approach children, how apply the principles of modern business to church work."

"Needs more practical fitting for work."

"More practical courses needed."

"Emphasis on the practical side. Men with pulpit power is the great need to-day."

"Needs more practical teaching. HOW to preach and HOW to be a pastor."

"Study of sociological questions, the need of all Seminaries."

"Needs more emphasis on the sociological relations of the church and life."

"Too much Hebrew! Not enough Human."

"More juicy meat given out, not so much dry bones."

"Emphasis should be on religion rather than theology; that God's omnipresence should be taught, not as a verbal theory, but as a living fact."

"No serious fault to find."

"All right—the undergrads have swelled heads."

"Good enough as it is."

A Communication.

We insert here, properly, we think, the response of Prof. Erdman, given in accordance with the request of the Class at the banquet, that he should furnish a brief outline of the practical work, now done at the Seminary. In view of a somewhat critical attitude along this line, in our Class and all over the country, he, with us, desires a wide circulation of these facts:

"In my chair of Practical Theology, I devote three hours a week to instruction in the English Bible, in which classes I endeavor to suggest those passages of the various books which are best adapted to expository preaching, I also take up, in my course of Pastoral Theology, the methods of modern church life and organization. I also have a course entitled "Methods of Christian Work," in which, among the subjects treated, are Sabbath School work, Individual work for individuals, Evangelistic work, and Church Societies. There has also been added to the curriculum a required course in Christian Missions.

Each member of the Middle Class makes six visits to New York and Philadelphia to investigate, first-hand, various lines of Church and Mission Work.

At the regular Tuesday evening meeting, the students are addressed on practical topics by eminent leaders in Christian work.

For two days in the Fall, all work is suspended, while a Conference is in session on all questions, touching the practical work of the ministry."

Present Condition of the Church

Question 4. What is your view of the present condition of the Church?

"Hopeful gain in man-power; confusion of belief in pulpit." — Adams.

"Awakening of the Evangelistic spirit gives hope. The Presbyterian Church has lost the vision of the multitude in America." — Anderson.

"Church needs more prophets and fewer priests, and is greatly handicapped by encouraging the opposite. Change must come by abolishing creeds." — Annin.

"Too much subjectivity. Need more attention paid to the historic and objective features of Christianity." — Baskerville.

"Pessimistic, but some hope. Church needs to exercise discipline." — R. J. Campbell.

"She is seeing her best days, and better still to come." — Carson.

"Increasingly useful." — Carrington.

"Our own denomination better spiritually than ever before, for two reasons: evangelical spirit pervasive, and increasing interest in missions. Saddest feature is, so few candidates for the ministry, due wholly to financial outlook of the minister, his meagre salary, and his being laid off in the height of his usefulness." — Cummings.

"Far below what it ought to be, but making progress." — Doughty.

"Apprehensive. We are moving in perilous ways." — Eddy.

"Never more active and aggressive, and yet sadly unspiritual. Fault lies with both pastor and people; with the people, in *crowding* their minister with executive and other duties, and with the pastor in yielding so readily to the cry of the times." — Everitt.

"Hopeful." — F. L. Fraser.

"Growing much stronger among the Indians." — Johnson.

"Never better." — McCuish.

"Optimistic." — McGinnis.

"Never greater, never doing better work." — McLean.

"Too much delegated responsibility on the part of the pew; too much dependence on the purchasing power of money." — Nelson.

"Church drifting from the workingman. General situation bad, need great revival. People Lock to hear a man of conviction with twenty minute sermons." — F. H Smith.

"Suffering from materialism, but essentially as strong as ever." — W. H. P. Smith.

"Excellent." — Thompson.

"Very critical condition, getting away from old faith, and losing its hold." — Voorhies.

"Getting away from the Bible and Christ." — Warne.

"Transition. No firm grasp on fundamentals. Tendency toward better things." — Whitaker.

EXCERPT

From the Secretary's response for the Class at the Alumni dinner, printed, because it gives a resume of some important facts, not otherwise noted.

"The Class of 1890 comes to its twentieth anniversary with all the feelings of a man, just about to attain his majority. We feel we are now coming into that period of our ministry when our mental and spiritual possibilities are at their best and when our years entitle us to be heard. This Class has run the gamut nearly of all callings. We have men in Metropolitan pulpits, and men in Metropolitan business. We can write sermons, we can write fiction. We have spell-binders, on the political and lecture platform as well as on the sacred.

We are nothing, if not migratory. We have but two men in the home field who have been in the same charge the whole of their twenty years, both country pastors, and with no children to educate. But thirteen in all have lived out a decade in one charge. The average length of pastorate for the class is less than seven years. Our "wandering Jew" has the record of ten pastorates in twenty years. This is of interest, not merely in reflecting the restlessness of the age, but in suggesting another thing, that success is being considered in terms of quantity rather than quality. The short pastorate for quantity, but the long one for quality. And is not the church losing, in the shifting of the emphasis from quality to quantity, from the substantial solidity of time taken, time tested thoroughness to the ephemeral flash of a one-night stand, howling tho' its success may be. A work well-done is a life twice-lived, and the man who has grit to hold on is the man, who will have grace to win out.

Our somewhat vagrant tendencies have resulted in a most startling fact, viz: that one out of every four of our class is out of the active pastorate, and that, in the very prime of life. Brethren, we hear much about the failure of young men to enter the ministry. Here is a more startling fact, that there is a tremendous loss at the other end. The old ship is leaking fore and aft. Our men are not demitting the ministry, they are demitting the pastorate. It fills us with alarm. Where did the cog slip, in the mental and moral processes of the man, or in the ecclesiastical processes of the church? It is an anemic condition, but who has the anemia?

From the replies of my classmates, I have a word to say, as to the preparation this Seminary gives its students. There is a widespread belief in our class and out of it, that our Seminaries are not adequately meeting the needs of the ministry to-day. The awakening of the men in the pew is calling more than ever for the awakening of the man in the pulpit. We must train men for the problems of the twentieth century rather than the solving of the isms of the tenth. The minister of to-day cannot afford to be a man of the cloister but must be a man of the crowd. Socialism has in it less to fear than scholasticism, if by socialism, we mean, the full, fair facing of the moral and social questions of to-day.

Again the practical has the call to-day. Where one man goes out of these walls, trembling as to what he believes, there are ten men to go out, trembling as to HOW to do things. The spectre of defeat lies not in our exegesis, but in getting seventy per cent work out of a people that has been accustomed to give only thirty.

A third call to-day, is for the prophet in public life. Modern problems challenge the prophetic office anew. 'Passivity and a priestly cult are the diabolism of the present century. The voice of old, with prophetic accents alone can save the day. But let me close with a more cheering word. We are one in our loyalty to the Princeton type of theology. Only one man rebels and the Lord has taken good care of him, by keeping his mind and heart in the teaching profession We hail it as no small achievement, that we have weathered the gales of as caustic criticism of the Book as ever blew upon it. But at the mast-head, still flies the old, red banner of the Cross, in whose folds, let sinners rest and heroes die. Princeton theology is something more than traditionalism. Certitude in fundamentals is not dogmatism; belief in the essential verities of an organic, living faith, with joints fitly framed together, is not conservatism; assent to a compact formulae of federated and related truth, call it what you will, is not mediaeval. It is what the world wants, not to speak of its needs.

We believe still in the Princeton type, clean-cut, well defined and, above all, visualized in the life of the preacher. This type may or may not be *sui generis*, but whatever it is, it is our confidence to day, that in this staunch, unflinching type of belief lies the hope of the church, and its mightiest bulwark, against which no powers of hell can prevail, nor flood of criticism overthrow. The Calvinism of the Cross as Princeton-taught, is *facile princeps* the inherent power of the Christian ministry and, as such, shall ever be the glory, in the life and service, of the sons of '90.

SILVER ANNIVERSARY HISTORY

CLASS OF 1890

PRINCETON SEMINARY

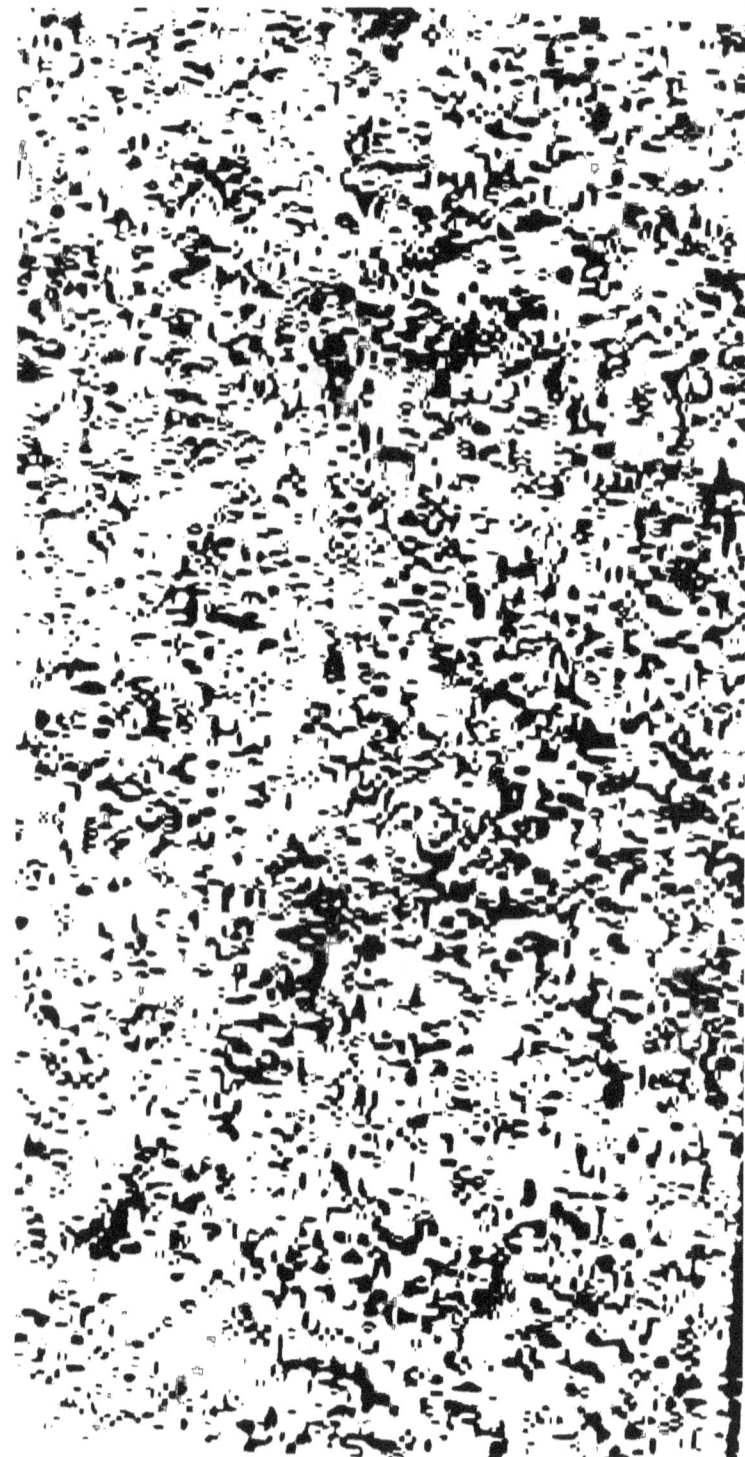

SILVER ANNIVERSARY
HISTORY

Impensa monumenti supervacua est; memoria nostra durabit, si vita meruimus

CLASS OF 1890
PRINCETON SEMINARY

MINUTE

In response to the call of the Secretary, the following members, and wives, of the Class of 1890 assembled for the Silver Anniversary Dinner of the Class at the Princeton Inn, on the evening of May 3, 1915, viz: H. M. Campbell, Mr. and Mrs. Everitt, Gibbons, Levingood, Mr. and Mrs. Polk, Thompson, Warne, Mr. and Mrs. Whitaker, and Williams. Messrs. Sidney Levingood, of the Senior Class in the University, and Robert Baskerville, of the graduating class in the Seminary, both sons of the class, were also present. A telegram was received from McLeod, regretting his inability, thro' illness, to be present and represent the class at the Alumni Dinner. Thompson was thereupon selected to fill the vacancy.

The Secretary read his report, which stated that all had been heard from or located, and he was instructed to issue, in printed form, the history of the class. He was also instructed to send the sympathy of the Class to Erskine, seriously ill, and to Gardner, in sorrow for the recent death of his sister, who made her home with him as his housekeeper.

Arrangements were made for taking the photo of those present, for insertion in the history. (Mr. and Mrs. Bannerman, and Wylie also appear in the photo, being present the next day).

The Secretary also presented his report as Treasurer, showing total receipts of $90.17, including twenty-one subscriptions to the History, and a balance on hand of 71 cents for Expense account. (The Class contributed four dollars for the same at the dinner).

With our President, Whitaker, presiding, interesting reminiscences were given until a late hour. The next re-union will be held in 1920.

F. B. EVERITT, *Secretary.*

CLASS ROLL

(*Numerals indicate number of years in their present location and work*)

Adams, Crofton Craig—202 W. Second St., Crosby, Minn. .... 2 yrs.
Anderson, Neal L.—Winston-Salem, N. C. .... 7 yrs.
Annin, Wm. A.—2844 Accomac St., St. Louis, Mo. .... 6 yrs.
Bannerman, Wm. S.—Titusville, N. J. .... 6 yrs.
Bryant, Seelye—So. Attleboro, Mass. .... 2 yrs.
Bull, Kent M.—Kennett Square, Pa. .... 1 yr.
Campbell, Henry M.—Phoenix, Ariz. .... 9 yrs.
Campbell, R. J.—168 Blose Ave., Toronto, Can. ....
Carrington, W. A.—Akron, N. Y. .... 2 yrs.
Carson, R. H.—744 Putnam Ave., Brooklyn, N. Y. ....16 yrs.
Cummings, Geo. M.—1333 Valley Place, S. E., Washington, D. C. ....10 yrs.
Doughty, Jas. W.—Williamsbridge, N. Y. .... 2 yrs.
Dunlap, Edw. P.—Holly, Mich. ....13 yrs.
Eddy, Geo. T.—Wyoming, N. J. (or N. Y. Public Library, 42. St.
   and 5th Ave., N. Y. City) .... 6 yrs.
Everitt, Frank B.—Glenside, Pa. ....
Fraser, Fenwick W.—Massillon, O. .... 5 yrs.
Fraser, Frank L.—Albany, Oregon ....
Gardner, M. H.—Brewster, N. Y. ....10 yrs.
Gibbons, Wm. F.—Clarks Summit, Pa. .... 4 yrs.
Jessup, Wm.—Beirut, Syria .... 1 yr.
Johnson, A. F.—Pine Ridge, S. Dak. ....23 yrs.
Jungeblut, J. F.—Lodi, Cal. ....11 yrs.
Levingood, J. C.—Wayne, Pa. .... 4 yrs.
Lynn, J. E.—Berlin, Ont., Can. .... 7 yrs.
McGinniss, C. E.—Hoosick Falls, N. Y. .... 2 yrs.
McLean, J. T.—Gulfport, Fla. ....
McLeod, M. J.—151 Central Park West, or St. Nicholas Coll. Ch.,
   N. Y. City .... 5 yrs.
McMillan, John—Atlantic City, N. J. ....14 yrs.
Miller, E. D.—Gerardstown, W. Va. ....
Miller, Hugh—1703 N. 16th St., Phila. ....
Moore, John—Susaki Machi, Kochi Keu, Japan ....17 yrs.
Nelson, W. F. S.—Santa Maria, Cal. .... 5 yrs.
Parker, A. G.—517 Hecox St., Peoria, Ill. .... 3 yrs.
Paterson, A. McD.—Newburyport, Mass. .... 6 yrs.
Paton, Lewis B.—Hartford, Conn. ....15 yrs.
Polk, Samuel—Lawrenceville, N. J. .... 3 yrs.

Remington, A. W.—Mt. Vernon, N. H. .... 5 yrs.
Smith, Frank Hyatt—Kenmore, N. Y. .... 2 yrs.
Smith, W. H. P.—Wyoming, N. Y. ....15 yrs.
Thompson, J. H.—Montgomery, N. Y. ....24 yrs.
Trompen, J. N.—Aurora, Col. .... 8 yrs.
Voorhies, W. S.—Thompsonville, Conn. ....6 yrs.
Warne, D. Ruby—Trenton, N. J., R.F.D. 1 ....17 yrs.
Whitaker, Chas. H.—815 Preston St., Phila., Pa. .... 4 yrs.
Williams, Jas. W.—Abington, Pa. ....11 yrs.
Wylie, S. Beattie—New Castle, Del. ....23 yrs.

    By this it will be seen that the longest present pastorate is that of Thompson, with 24 years, followed closely by Johnson and Wylie, each 23 years. The others over ten years in their present charges are Moore and Warne, 17; Carson, 16; McMillan, 14; Jungeblut and Williams, 11; Cummings and Gardner, 10. Paton has been teaching at Hartford 15 years, and W. H. P. Smith has been farming the same length of time. Dunlap has been in business 13 years. All the rest of us are comparatively new at our present tasks. Erskine has the record of the longest continuous pastorate, having been, at his death, twenty-five years in his only charge.

    In geographical distribution, 29 are now in the East, five in the Middle West, three in the far West, three on the Pacific Coast, two in the South, two in Canada, and two on foreign field.

OUR AUXILIARY ROLL

It has ever been our custom to keep in touch with the families of our deceased brothers. The loving interest of the Class of '90 shall ever follow the widow in her sorrows and in her joys, and the children in their rise and usefulness in life. For we hear the voices of fathers, speaking thro' the children, and their interests are our interests still.

We are, therefore, glad to include in this history the following reports from these families:

ALLEN.—Mrs. Minnie L. Allen still resides at Haddonfield, with her two sons, William, age 22, and Louis, age 21.

BASKERVILLE.—Mrs. Emma R. Baskerville is still at 15 Vanderenter Ave., Princeton, N. J. She was left with five children, one daughter having died in 1907, and the oldest son Harold, being killed in a sortie for food, when besieged in Tabriz, in 1909, whither he had gone as a missionary teacher, intending to return to complete his studies in the Seminary. The remaining children are: Mrs. Julia Hensel (widow), teaching in Albert Lea College, in Minnesota; Charles, Class of 1909, Princeton Seminary, Vice President of Bellevue College, Neb.; Ernest, Class of 1911, Macalester College, St. Paul, in business in Spokane, Wash.; Robert, Class of 1915, Princeton Seminary, just installed at Strasburg, Pa., and Arthur, in Senior Class, High School, Princeton.

ERSKINE.—Mrs. Esther G. Erskine may not reside longer at Thompson Ridge, altho that was her home. Her present plans are unknown to the Secretary.

HEANEY.—Mrs. Agnes M. Heaney is at 918 S. 48th St., Philadelphia. Spencer, the son, is a mining engineer, located at Wilkesbarre, Pa. He is following in the father's footsteps, being deeply interested in religious work, at present, Asst. Supt. of his Sabbath School.

HEDGES.—The address of Mrs. Hedges, now Mrs. S. A. Hedges Johnson, is 504 N Pine St., San Antonio, Texas. A dressmaker by trade, she, however is in poor health. Her son, Lyman Hedges, is finishing his course in Knoxville College, Tenn. He finished his trade of tile and iron works at Tuskegee last term, and is in good health.

MASON.—Mrs. Belle F. Mason is at her old home in DeSoto, Mo., where Robert—twelve years old—is in the seventh grade in school, and often talks of the years to come when "he can tread the same paths his father trod toward Princeton. He is a bright lad, full of health, measures four feet and seven inches in height, weighs about seventy-five pounds and is beloved by everybody."

McCUISH.—Mrs. Anna H. McCuish will remain, in accordance with her husband's wishes, at least for a year in Newton, Kansas, his last charge, where the oldest child, Helen, twelve years of age, is finishing her grade work and will take part of High School work this year. John B. is nine years old, and Anna Margaret, age six, enters school for the first time this Fall.

MURCHIE.—Died unmarried.

OATES.—Mrs. Ethelinde D. Oates resides at Princess Anne, Md., and writes thus interestingly of her son, Robert Luther: "Bob is in the seventh grade, stands well with very little study, being no plodder. It comforts me to see how much of mind and character, he has inherited. He even has his father's skill with tools. I have built him a shop in our back yard, where he built a fine boat, holding four people, and many other less ambitious things. He whistles and saws away, until it seems that the dear father must have come back." Mrs. Oates herself is in better health, and we shall watch with interest this promising builder. Robert is now twelve years of age.

PHRANER.—The widow died in 1903. The oldest son, Wilson, aged 22, lives with his uncle at 385 Jefferson Ave., Brooklyn, and has a position with the U. S. Trust Co., New York City. Stanley, age 21, is now in Senior Class, Princeton, and expects to enter the Seminary in preparation for the missionary field, probably Siam.

RANKIN.—Mrs. Elizabeth Rankin has been living at her old home in Berlin, N. J. for three years. Her son Robert graduated from Lafayette College in 1914, and is now teaching science in the Pingry School, Elizabeth. Ella, thru ill health, was compelled to leave college. An operation has failed to restore entirely her health and she is still at home. Helen is a Senior in the College Dept. of Beechwood, at Jenkintown, Pa. She has completed there the course in Domestic Arts, which she expects to teach next year. She, too, was in the hospital, undergoing an operation for appendicitis, but has entirely recovered.

Classmates, the world is large, the struggle fierce. It is your privilege and mine to stand loyally by every son and daughter of the Class, and to take the father's place to these fatherless ones, in kindly word, prayerful solicitude, and wise counsel. Go out of your way, if necessary, to encourage and help. And may every mother know assuredly that, in the father's classmates, they have those

> "Who heart-whole, pure in faith,
>   Once written friend,
> In life and death are true,
>   Unto the end."

FAMILY DATA

PARKER must at last divide the honors with MOORE. For each have a school of their own in their nine children each. Parker's are rated, eight boys and one girl, while Moore's are six boys and three girls. John, we hope this is right. Distance has somewhat lent mystery to your family tree, and, the more we investigated, the more mixed we became. And several letters from your relatives in this country, read at the Class Dinner, only the more bewildered us, until the Class voted to take your word for it, and call it nine.

Bannerman, Bull and Paterson can each claim five, while Gibbons has four. Bannerman's five are all boys, and Gibbons' four, all girls. Say, can't we bring these families together? Bull and Paterson also might match up, except that the sexes are the same in each, viz: one boy and four girls.

"Pity 'tis, 'tis true," that Anderson (three died). Bryant, Carrington, Gibbons, Jessup (one died), Lynn, Paton, Warne have no boys to discipline, while Adams, Allen, Bannerman, Trompen and Voorhies have no girls to caress.

The childless homes are those of Henry Campbell, Erskine, F. W. Fraser, McGinniss (who lost, in 1895, their only child, Helen), McLean, Remington, F. H. Smith, W. H. P. Smith, Thompson, Whitaker and Williams.

However, of these McLean has adopted a son, and Remington has taken a boy to educate, sixteen years old, with three generations of missionaries behind him, being a great-grandson of Rev. Isaac Bird, one of the earliest missionaries to Syria.

No new additions, since last report, save Katherine Bonde Moore, born January 29, 1911, and Bertha Loving Moore born May 27, 1913. One death has occurred, Margaret Agnes Cummings, in 1911, aged two years. This totals our family list as 59 boys and 50 girls.

DOUGHTY has one blind daughter.

WM. FRANKLIN NELSON, the "Class Baby" is larger than his father, and is studying bookkeeping and running a ranch in California.

MISS LIDA LYNN is on the staff of the Conservatory of Music, at Berlin, Ontario, giving piano instruction.

MAGA SKA JOHNSON, the boy with the Indian name, on Easter of this year, made his profession of faith in Christ, at the age of ten years.

HELENA DOUGHTY graduated in 1913 at Vassar, as honor student, with several Commencement appointments and a fellowship in history.

Received her Master's degree from University of Wisconsin in 1914. JOHN graduated as honor student at Perkiomen Seminary.

As yet, TROMPEN is the only one boasting of a grandson, altho rumors are coming in of some of the "family," following the matrimonial calling very ardently.

If no record appears here of the honors of your children, it is due to lack of information. We trust that by the next report all reticence and false modesty of parents may be overcome, and we may have a full account of what our sons and daughters are doing.

OTHER ANNIVERSARIES

The Silver Anniversary of the Class reminds us that other similar anniversaries are on the wing—and some will soon alight. Congratulations are in order for the following silver wedding anniversaries this year:

April 10, Rev. and Mrs. W. F. S. Nelson; May 21, Rev. and Mrs. A. G. Parker; May 22, Rev. and Mrs. W. F. Gibbons; May 27, Rev. and Mrs. J. F. Jungeblut; June 4, Rev. and Mrs. G. T. Eddy; June 12, Rev. and Mrs. J. W. Doughty and Rev. and Mrs. D. R. Warne; July 2, Rev. and Mrs. A. W. Remington; August 14, Rev. and Mrs. Neal L. Anderson; August 18, Rev. and Mrs. W. S. Bannerman; September 9, Rev. and Mrs. C. C. Adams; December 3, Rev. and Mrs. J. T. McLean.

These, with those of Allen, Carrington, Moore, Phraner and Rankin, seventeen in all, were the matrimonial ventures of the year of 1890. We are sorry that this history will reach the Class too late for extending any congratulations on the very occasion, but they all have our best wishes, our heartiest congratulations.

> "When I read tales of married woe,
> Among the stale newspaper jokes,
> I simply smile and think of you,
> Two very happy married folks."

To the two widows, whose silver wedding thoughts this year caught up a tangle of broken, sombre threads, we express the hope:

> "We'll catch the broken threads again,
> And finish what we here began;
> Heav'n will the mysteries explain,
> And then, ah! then, we'll understand."

Forget not, the "rarest hues of human life are rainbowed out of tears."

For the anniversaries of others, see printed history of 1900. Lynn and Trompen are so far ahead of us, we have lost all count, and R. J. Campbell, Gardner, McMillan, Ed. Miller and Hugh Miller are so far behind us—hopelessly behind—tearlessly behind—bachelors *in maledictione et malodore*—that we don't care. Bryant, Carrington, Jessup, Moore, Paterson, and Paton have each ventured twice on the matrimonial seas. Since last report, Jessup was married on November 14, 1913, to Miss Katharine Prime, of Yonkers, daughter of Mr. and Mrs. Ralph E. Prime. And Paton was married on June 30, 1915, to Mrs. Loraine Seymour Calhoun, a widow, with one daughter, of an old friend of his, and who for four years has been his private secretary.

Only Henry Campbell remains a widower. Phraner was also married twice, each wife dying.

And other anniversaries there are! "Dead line?" Oh, no! just golden anniversaries of ripened age. These cross the fifty-year-old line this year, in following order: McLeod, Wylie, Carrington, Anderson, F. W. Fraser, R. J. Campbell and McMillan. While the following have but one year of grace, when they, too, will cross in this order, Levingood, F. L. Fraser, Everitt, Moore, Johnson, Bryant and Polk. Then all will be "fifty years young," and over. Polk and Bryant bring up the rear in age, while Lynn and Frank Hyatt Smith are the "venerated fathers." The average age of the Class is now about fifty-three.

PRESENT VOCATIONS

1 Pastors—All except those named below—in all 28
2 Pastor's Assistant—Whitaker 1
3 Home Missionaries—Johnson, Trompen 2
4 Foreign Missionaries—Jessup, Moore 2
5 Missionary Secretary—Everitt 1
6 Without charge—R. J. Campbell, E. D. Miller, Hugh Miller, McLean,
7 Secular pursuits
   (1) Teaching—Annin, Paton
   (2) Business—Dunlap, Gibbons
   (3) Librarian—Eddy
   (4) Welfare Work—Doughty
   (5) Farming—W. H. P. Smith 7

   Total 46
Deceased 10

   Total 56

BY THE PRINTED PAGE

LITERARY PRODUCTIONS SINCE 1910

The Deacon—a Plea and an Appeal—an address before the Laymen's Missionary Convention, Chattanooga, 1912 more than 10,000 copies printed by Assembly's Committee on Publication.—Anderson.

Article in Bibliotheca Sacra, of July, 1914, on "Paul's Doctrine of the Logos."—Cummings.

Several leaflets on Men's Work.—Everitt.

Form of Government, Book of Discipline, and Directory of Worship, in Sioux language.—Johnson.

The Unsearchable Riches (1910); Fragrance of Christian Ideals (1911); Letters to Edward (1913), first two books published by Revell.—McLeod.

The Early Religion of Israel, by Houghton Mifflin, Boston, 1910; Series of articles on the "Hebrew Idea of the Future Life" in the Biblical World, 1910; several articles in Hasting's Encyclopedia of Religion and Ethics; series of articles on Modern Palestine and the Bible, in Homiletic Review, 1911; series of articles on "Archaeology and the Book of Genesis; in Biblical World, 1915; series of articles on "Archaeology and the Old Testament, in Pilgrim Teacher, 1915.—Paton.

My Church and I.—F. Hyatt Smith. (Copy promised to each member of Class).

History of Abington Presbyterian Church in book form, 1914. Also some historical pamphlets of same.—Williams. (Church 200 years old last year).

BY WIRELESS

OR MESSAGES FOR THE CLASS, AS PER QUESTIONAIRE

"My love to all the boys. When you meet I shall be in the midst of a union evangelistic meeting, with slight resources, little spiritual support, in a worldly community, shot thro' with every known sort of unbelief. Won'r you all pray for us?—Adams."

"My personal message of love is a confession of my own deep need of grace—the grace obtained only through humble, patient, self-sacrificing service and daily fellowship with Jesus Christ.—Anderson."

"My soul's sincere desire is that we may all have a growing love and loyalty for all of God's kingdom—the truth.—Annin."

"'Be not drunk with wine but be filled with the Spirit,' and ye shall have the power of the Spirit coming upon you.—R. J. Campbell."

"May your shadow never grow less, and as you grow older, grow also in love with the fundamentals of our holy religion, and be found, standing for construction, and not destruction.—Carson."

"May the closing years of our ministry be the most earnest in the King's business and the most fruitful in results.—Cummings."

"Love to all the men in attendance. Still interested in all of them.—F. W. Fraser."

"Do not allow too much worldliness to get into the church. Better a small membership and loyal than a most disloyal to God.—F. L. Fraser."

"I realize more than ever the divineness of Scripture, and the Divinity it reveals.—Johnson."

"Contend earnestly for the faith, once for all delivered to the saints. Hit harder than ever. Oh, the havoc wrought by the critics on the lop-sided faith of so many weak ones.—Moore."

"Be more earnest. Time passes. Let us work.—Nelson."

"Cling to fundamentals. Sunday is a winner because he cuts off the frills of doubt. Ministry needs a compact brotherhood. Masons far ahead here. Every man needs some side line. I lecture and write. Could have been a Christian Science lecturer, if willing to bury my common sense.—F. Hyatt Smith."

"The old-fashioned gospel is good enough for me. Stop preaching about every new thing under the sun and preach the gospel.—W. H. P. Smith."

"Schlafen sie wohl (we pass it on to Jungeblut).—Thompson."

"A message of good cheer. Christ is King, and the Kingdom is coming. After this war is over, there will be a better world, and greater opportunities for service than ever before.—Whitaker."

"Greetings to the Class.—Dunlap, McGinniss, Doughty, Parker, Remington, Trompen."

RELIGIOUS CONDITIONS, FREELY EXPRESSED

At least, so the questionaire called for. About one-half expressed anything. Perhaps they are not weighing heavily on their mind—or too heavily to warrant any diagnosing. Analyzing the replies, we find several storm centres. *E. G.*—Billy Sunday and his work. Lynn cries out for a "Billy Sunday revival all over Christendom." Carrington notes it as a "reaction toward Christ and the Church," while Anderson and Annin are sceptical. The former writes, "desperate need of preaching the old Gospel in the terms of modern life by trained men of deep spiritual life. Peril is to be found in cold intellectualism on the one side, and emotional religion on the other. It is of vital importance that the spirit of world revival should be directed by men not only of consecrated purpose, but cultivated brain and clear discriminating judgment." Annin is more definite in his criticism. "The years strengthen my conviction that God works slowly thru the ages, and not spasmodically. Hence, follows evolution necessarily, and the democracy and divinity of all truth, and all men. All men are God's children, therefore brothers. A consciousness of this sonship increases and is increased by self-respect and results in a constant increase of man's powers. This development of man is a slow growth, as the development of the world has been, taking ages for its accomplishment. So, in the individual, right character results from discipline in wildernesses, from learning lessons, from struggles, from victories. It still consists, as Christ expressed it, 'in loving God and man.' Saving souls, then, is not accomplished in a night, a day, or a year, by a mountebank, an irreligious demagogue, a mesmerist, who runs off with $50,000 in his pocket. Truth is the food of the soul, and only sincere souls who love all truth, are loyal to all truth and thus to Christ."

With this explosive, yet interesting, thesis of Annin's, it will be hard to get many of his eastern classmates to agree, who have worked in the Sunday campaigns, and cannot discount the tremendous power for good—permanent good—that is done by Billy Sunday. But my own personal word is, "Woe to the man who tries to imitate him. He is unique, the Lord is using him mightily, but not as an 'ensample to the flock.' No greater mistake can be made. Only in his earnestness, his old gospel, and his overpowering singleness of aim, would we follow in his steps."

The critics, of course, are another storm-centre, altho Cummings—Billy Sunday-like—dismisses them with a toss of his hand, saying: "Higher Criticism on its destructive side, is dead. The majority of our ministers preach the true gospel." On the other hand, Paton declares, "Progress in religious knowledge has been enormous in the last twenty years and the prejudice against the scientific study of the Bible has well nigh disappeared, at least in New England. (He might have added also, in vicinity of New York). The progress in religious education is most encouraging. A fine type of men is now entering the ministry, men that are animated by the highest ideals."

But several others shy at the shadow of the critics. Adams sees the "battle on between real and false faith for the possession of the church, and a mighty purging at hand for the shameless unfaith and bad faith of certain who sit high in the synagogue, and preach a gospel of anathema." Nelson says, "The greatest need is for clear-cut theology and protest against fads," with which W. H. P. Smith agrees: "The world wants the gospel in its purity or not at all. A diluted apology for it, it has no use for. It wants the Bible in its entirety and not an expurgated edition of it." So Remington believes the "world is wearying of philosophical cobweb and more ready than ever for the solid truth," while Voorhies sees a "serious need evident in the church to get back to old standards of teaching and training."

But, with it all, Williams raises another question, an administrative and serious one. He propounds two questions. 1. In the near future, at the present rate of change and new demands, will there be any need of theological seminaries, as they now exist? 2. Is the future minister to be a pastor, a preacher for souls, or a mere manager? A man of excellent executive ability, capable as an organizer, and a sport of sufficient athletic twist to run all side-shows that a modern community demands? Dunlap assures us that the photo-play, automobile and other developments in our social life have greatly complicated our ministry. Perhaps this is in the mind of Frank Hyatt Smith, when he says, "whole church needs staying up—restless." He, however, classifies himself as "severely orthodox," while Doughty wants to be put down as "liberal and progressive."

All in all, the minor strain is in the minority in the Class. Eddy says, "Outlook very dark. We are witnessing a collapse of modern civilization, but it may lead to a signal divine intervention. (Luke 21:28-31)." Frank Fraser calls the times serious, "Approaching the fulfillment of phophecy as to Christ's second coming." With which R. J. Campbell agrees, "The terrible time of suffering is hastening after which Christ will come again, and set up

His Kingdom." Campbell is studying at first-hand the Pentecostal cult, and finds them nearer the real N. T. spiritual life than any other.

Fenwick Fraser looks at it thru true-blue spectacles, sees a "time of religious decay, a recession from doctrinal position of Princeton, with Presbyterianism scarcely retaining its traditional ascendency." Be that as it may, Carson says, "present discouraging outlook due to preaching men's theories and the 'thus saith the Lord' forgotten."

But the optimists see all this, and a little more; and that's the difference. They see a way out. Bryant is incurably optimistic "in spite of war and Billy Sunday." Carrington notes, "A much greater activity in giving and in Missions." Gibbons, "Never greater revival activity and more Bible Study than at present." McLean, "A wave of revival is going on over the world. Thy day is at hand." Whitaker is broad-minded enough to see "a general improvement in business, social and religious life. The Kingdom is making progress in all these lines." Warne reiterates, "in spite of all we see, hear and endure, God is imminent in the world and the time is coming when the crooked places shall be made straight, etc." Thompson's pen (or brain) wearied by the time he reached that question and he replied, 'Bad, but on the mend.'"

Thus writeth the Redactor. His task was easy. The hard work is yours to redress the wrongs, to mobilize every faculty and power for action, to set the standards of faith high, and of personal living higher, that no man may call in question the ideals of your life, or stain the glory of your crown.

BE STRONG!

Say not the days are evil—who's to blame?
And fold the hand and acquiesce—O shame!
Stand up, speak out and bravely, in God's name

BE STRONG!

It matters not how deep intrenched the wrong,
How hard the battle goes, the day, how long,
Faint not, fight on! Tomorrow comes the song.

A SWING AROUND THE CIRCLE

OR THE HOME LIFE OF THE CLASS OF '90

Our journey begins in New England, with a visit to PATERSON, who takes us to his church in Newburyport, Mass., founded by Geo. Whitefield in 1742. He grows warm in historical reminiscence over the dry bones of Whitefield under his pulpit, and the dry bones on the top of Whitefield's desk in his study, in the shape of sermons—oh, no, beg pardon! Health fine, five children, but all other answers too brief for record.

Extremes often meet, so going west we come upon BRYANT at South Attleboro, Mass., deep in *new* work, having organized the Bethany Congregational Church on March 1, 1914, in the worst storm of the year. Two girls cheer his home-life.

Here we turn aside to Mt. Vernon, N. H., where we find REMINGTON at his summer home, Rencroft. Has been doing supply work for three and a half years, but has a call now. Fine physically, weighing 190 pounds. Special interest in a boy of sixteen he is educating, a missionary-bred young man.

Connecticut now claims us. At Hartford we greet PATON, newly-wed, with his ever-gracious presence and warm welcome. He has recently declined calls to the Chair of Oriental Languages and Literatures in the University of Michigan, and the pastorate of the Congregational Church at Litchfield, Mass. A popular teacher, a prolific writer, a fine fellow, the Class leave with him and his bride their very best wishes, and pass on to VOORHIES, at Thompsonville, Conn. Health excellent. Family scattering, one son married, another studying medicine, and a third in High School.

Crossing over into the Empire State we enter the nation's metropolis to find McLEOD on the hard job he was after, as pastor of the St. Nicholas Reformed Church on Fifth Ave. After a visit this year to his former $300,000 church at Pasadena, we could not but admire McLeod's spirit for the "hard job." His latch string is still out at 151 Central Park West, health fine, with a son and a daughter. A few blocks up Fifth Ave to 42nd St. we find EDDY in the alcoves of the N. Y. Public Library, in the Dept. of Sociology. He commutes to Wyoming, N. J., where he also has charge of the Presbyterian Church. Health excellent, and a boy and a girl in the family.

Crossing to the Borough of Brooklyn we find CARSON at home at 744 Putnam Ave. Health, "able to navigate," and family, like laws of Medes and

Persians, unchanged, i. e., one son. "Approached" several times with calls but prefers to remain in state of "grace." (Pastor of Grace Presbyterian Church). Moderator of Brooklyn Presbytery.

Crossing the Harlem, we seek out DOUGHTY at Williamsbridge, who is the chameleon of the Class; now in business, now the Welfare Secretary of the Citizens Union of N. Y. City, now preaching (which he does about twenty times a year) and now campaigning for democracy, which he did for Wilson in 1912. "Feel as young as I did twenty-five years ago, and not a grey hair on my head." Helena teaching, John in Cornell studying agriculture.

At Brewster we find GARDNER with home saddened by the death of his sister—a second one to die, upon whom he relied for the care and cheer of his home.

Over the river, amid the rich farms of Orange Co., is THOMPSON, the same, substantial defender of the faith as ever. Incidentally also, now a defender of ecclesiastical order, as Stated Clerk of Hudson Presbytery. Thompson's replies are too laconic for elucidation, and he deserves but passing notice. However, we manage to decipher as to health, "Might be worse." He looks it. (See photo). He had the nerve to send his wife alone to the Orient last year.

A trip up the beautiful Hudson brings us to Hoosick Falls, where McGINNIS is beginning his third pastorate. His replies are even briefer than Thompson's—must be climatic—but his health is good.

Westward, we find W. H. P. SMITH at Wyoming, N. Y., on his apple farm of 146 acres, recently bought in exchange for one of 82 acres. Evidently, farming pays—with Smith. Health good.

FRANK HYATT SMITH was recently installed pastor of the Kenmore Presbyterian Church, in Buffalo's finest suburb. "The most harmonious church in the Presbytery. 25 years old and no quarrels. Honey in the comb, land of Canaan." Health, "tip top." Crack a hickory nut with my teeth each New Year's to see how I am in order for cracking the odious Unitarian doctrines."

Coming to Akron, N. Y., CARRINGTON will probably meet us with his new auto, which, he claims, is the solution of the rural problem. Akron is a residential town of 2000, near Buffalo, and he serves two churches, six miles apart. Health good, he reports good revivals at all his charges, from 30 to 100 being received at one time. Three daughters.

Returning, we visit GIBBONS in his suburban home at Clark's Summit, near Scranton, where he is engaged with the International Correspondence School, in its Publicity Dept. Health too uncertain as yet to undertake a pastorate, yet much interested in a new church in his town.

En route to Philadelphia from Scranton all travellers read in glaring letters on the highest point, "Allentown—Dwell Here and Prosper." So your Secretary came, primarily to organize a new church—the second in his ministry. This he has done under considerable difficulty, as the city is strongly German. As side-lines, he has been the Field Secretary of Men's Work for the Synod, addressing and organizing Presbyteries, and he is in training with Thompson, as Stated Clerk of his Presbytery, for the position of one, Rev. Wm. H. Roberts, D.D., L.L.D. Health good, two boys and a girl. Enjoyed, with wife, this year, an extended trip to the Pacific Coast. He has just accepted the Executive Secretaryship of the Laymen's Missionary Movement for Eastern Penna., which includes all churches of all denominations east of Altoona, and part of New Jersey. His present work will be the directing of the big campaigns in Philadelphia, Reading, Harrisburg and perhaps Scranton. Headquarters, for the present, at Central Y. M. C. A., Philadelphia. Will resign here about October 1st, and reside at Glenside, Pa. near Philadelphia.

Philadelphia finds us WHITAKER, our genial President, dubbed at the dinner, the "French Ambassador" for his natty appearance, who is Assistant Pastor at West Hope Church, which gathers in about a hundred souls every year. Health "always good," and cares light, with a wife that looks after him well. Why worry?

A husky suburbanite is LEVINGOOD, living at Wayne, but pastor of the Trinity Church, Berwyn, with a son just graduated from Princeton University. HUGH MILLER you will find at 1703 N. 16 St., still supplying churches. Was regular supply at Forestville Church from 1912-1914. Health, fairly good. WILLIAMS, another suburbanite, at Abington, the 200th anniversary of which church was celebrated last May. Williams also will tour the country with you in an auto and house you in one of the most charming manses imaginable. Health, "only fair."

Nor must we forget New Jersey, with McMILLAN—last heard from at Atlantic City. But whether alive, semi-alive, or in love, "deponent saith not," for he is the only man from whom no word at all was received, altho four letters were sent.

And BANNERMAN, at Titusville, near Trenton, with other things, keeping track of those scattering boys, five of them. But health good. In an adjoining parish is WARNE at the old Ewing Church, in one of the most comfortable country manses to be found. He, too, meets the rural problem with an auto. Two years ago, fifteen young men united with the church. Health good, except for periodic headaches, for which no help. On the other side of Warne is the parish of POLK, at Lawrenceville, and you will find him solving the rural problem afoot, or on the beautiful golf links back of his house. Polk wishes all the Class to know that a trolley connects Princeton with Lawrenceville, and he welcomes all comers. He is fortunate to belong to a little coterie of the best clergy in Central Jersey, that meet to discuss timely questions.

Travelling southward, we visit BULL in his new field at Kennett Square, Pa., where he is pastor of the Toughkenamon and Unionville Churches, where McLeod began his ministry. We believe Bull also is inclined to farm, owning some land in that locality. The health of Mrs. Bull has not been good. Two daughters are teaching.

Delaware holds only one member, and that is enough. For WYLIE is now Moderator of the Synod of Baltimore, and the old New Castle Church assumes a new dignity—also, Wylie. How can that motor boat ever hold you now? He must have reached the state of eternal bliss, for he says, "No change, not likely to be any." Perhaps frozen fast! No, not in Delaware. Too hot. Health good.

On south we go, until the Capitol City finds us with CUMMINGS, in good health, with but one day's sickness—in how long, George? Hard field, but solaced by a clerkship in Presbytery (permanent) that helps out.

ED. MILLER is at Gerardstown, W. Va., after a brief stay in the State Hospital. Somewhat improved in health, and raising chickens.

ANDERSON we will find at Winston-Salem, the largest manufacturing city and business centre in North Carolina, and the seat of a splendid female college. He is a member of the Executive Committee of the Trustees of Davidson College, from which he received his D.D. in 1904. Declined call to First Church, Dallas, Texas, in 1909, then building a $200,000 church. Health better than in twenty years. One daughter graduated this year from Agnes College, another still there. In the seven years of his present pastorate 580 received, of which 306 were on profession. Church supports several foreign missionaries, and two ordained assistants to the pastor, for whom houses are being built at cost of $25,000.

Still further south we find McLEAN, at Gulfport, Fla., living in his own home near St. Petersburg, the paradise of Florida, where he was pastor for three years. From 1912-1915 he served the First Presbyterian Church of Clearwater, Fla., and now supplies the Bethel Presbyterian Church of Safety Harbor, and the First Church of Pinellas Park. Health good. Adopted son.

Returning to Ohio we greet FENWICK FRASER at Massillon, working to raise S. S. enrollment to 700—now past 400. But health "better than for years." About 100 received into church since 1912. Over in Michigan, at Holly, we may, or we may not, catch DUNLAP. For he is on the road most of the time, having demitted the ministry last Spring and travelling for his brother's firm in New York, Grosset & Dunlap, in whose New York office you may some time find him. In August he summers in a cabin on Pine Lake, in Mich., where he would "pile high the blazing logs" for any wayfarer of '90. Health, ordinary.

In Illinois, at Peoria, we visit PARKER, who, for three years has been pastor of the Bethel Church. Thirty-six received during the year. It will keep Parker busy, introducing to us his family of eight sons and one daughter —some of whom are on the way to the ministry.

A short trip to St. Louis, and ANNIN'S hospitable home at 2844 Accomac St. welcomes us. And we know whereof we speak, for we enjoyed that hospitality this summer. None better. Boys, don't pass Annin by, when within telephone distance. Hale him, and the doors swing open. For, altho' never ordained, Annin has much of the Princeton spirit yet, and loves his classmates still. He has just been advanced to the new High School building, and stands well as a teacher of Spanish and Latin. And John, thirteen years old, captured one of the prizes, offered by a local paper, for best original story.

Sorry, but we must take now longer sweeps in our journey. For we cannot reach ADAMS without the long trip to Minnesota. At Crosby we will find him nestled in a fine clump of twenty-seven pine trees, on the border of a fine lake, dotted with summer cottages. You can row, cycle or motor with him, on his itinerant trips to halls, school houses and churches, preaching from three to seven times a week. A sort of early itinerant missionary, it seems, "with indefinite parish, indefinite income, and indefinite duties of widely diverse nature; in a population speaking twelve languages, all of which are Greek to me." His only degrees, "the Thinning Thatch and the Silver Crown skilfully combined for my special benefit, by Father Time." Yet, health fine, still young, one boy in college, studying for the ministry, the other in business, both matrimonially perilous. Thanks, Craig, for that generous letter. Wish others were like you. No pick and axe needed to get your history!

JOHNSON, too, wrote a very nice letter, and deserves liberal space. For twenty-three years he has been on the Indian trail at Pine Ridge, So. Dakota. When he went there the Mission had three churches, two manses, one organized congregation and one native worker. They now have nine churches, nine manses for native workers, five Y. M. C. A. halls, twelve new stations, of which seven have become organized congregations. Present membership, 330. That many more have died, for the "death rate is shocking." And, listen, boys! From 60 to 75 per cent. of the male members can lead the prayer meeting creditably, praying, speaking. 25 per cent. of the women can lead the women's meeting. The Reservation has 7000 Indians, and claims, we believe, a larger proportion of Christian adherents than any other, altho Johnson says, "heathenism is a controlling influence." His health is good, notwithstanding an operation at Presbyterian Hospital in Chicago. His honorary degree is "Ciye," given by the Indians, meaning "Elder Brother." The work has become so large that the Board has divided it and assigned another man to the other half. He had, at this time, twelve native Sioux workers under his direction.

By way of Colorado, we come upon TROMPEN, at Aurora. Still Congregational Missionary for Colorado, altho has declined one call. Health perfect, and that of his wife and son, for whose health he went west, improving. One grandson.

CAMPBELL—modest, genial Henry—still has his "bow abiding in strength" in Phoenix, Arizona. And, again, we know whereof we speak. For it was our pleasure to supply his pulpit and mingle with his people for three weeks in June. And a more devoted people cannot be found! Whether he, or his people, are the "it," it is hard to tell. We are not surprised to hear that he was urgently sought for other pastorates, notably the First Church of Salt Lake City. Henry is one of the star preachers of the Class, and says frankly, that since leaving the Seminary, his pulpit preparation has been the one great thing in his ministry. Would that more of us had followed in his footsteps! He occupies a charming little bungalow of his own in that city, but is suffering from insomnia, and just now enjoying a long vacation east, and on Pacific Coast. He has two months off each year. After a long illness from tuberculosis of the spine, his wife died about three years ago. The Class were, we are frank to say, more pleased to see him at our dinner than any other—his first appearance with us since 1890. Strange to say, he had to be introduced. See photo (frontspiece) why?

And now we reach California, the land of Sunshine and Flowers! A "golden state" in every way, and happy the man that lives in it! Let us first look up NELSON—straight, angular Nelson—with as straight a gospel as his body. At Santa Maria we will find him, unless on his son's ranch. Nelson enjoys a summer course at the University of California, which this year enrolled 5000 students in those courses—and second only to Columbia in winter enrollment. His health is "fine, never better;" has built a new church and manse, the former at cost of $12,000, said to be the most beautiful small church on the Pacific Coast.

JUNGEBLUT is located still at Lodi, over German Reformed Church. This we know from minutes of his church and from a registered letter receipt. No reply to class letters since 1900.

The Northwest claims FRANK FRASER, who moved from Minnesota to Oregon for health reasons. Now at Albany, Oregon. Health good, save occasional breaks in voice, his weak spot. Was in apple-raising, but nothing said about it this time.

This completes the tour of our own country. We have swung from the Atlantic to the Pacific, from the cold of Minnesota to the tropics of Florida. What more can you ask, as a fulfillment of the injunction, "ye shall be witnesses unto me, both in Jerusalem, and in all Judaea, and in Samaria—"

But that is not all. The "uttermost parts" are not forgotten, altho we might cherish the hope that, when the final history of the Class is written, our sons and grandsons shall have done more than we have done to fulfil that final clause, to carry the name of Christ to all the world. May some familiar name of the Class of '90 shine out on the annals of every missionary field! Boys, girls, of the Class of '90, why not?

Over in Canada we find R. J. CAMPBELL at present recuperating from a nervous breakdown at the home of his brother and sister in Toronto. Since 1910 he has been pastor of Kanesack Church (Canada, we think). His eleventh charge, a missionary church at his going, but, in two months raised his salary $500, calling him at $2000. In three months the Sabbath School went from 75 to over 200 in attendance. He is now "open for a call."

LYNN is also in Canada for health reasons, at Berlin, Ontario. But now in very good health and has not missed a Sabbath for two years. Was Commissioner this year to their Assembly.

Across the seas now, first, to Syria, where, at Beirut, we find JESSUP, newly married, installed as Professor of Theology in Beirut Seminary, having persistently declined the presidency. Before leaving Zahleh, his people gave him, of their own meagre funds, a substantial reminder of their love and confidence. The war having called to the front all able-bodied Turks, men and boys, their families in Beirut were left without funds or work. The burden of their support fell largely on the Americans of the Mission and College. The city was divided into ten districts, and a woman visitor assigned to each district. Jessup and his bride have charge of a district in the old town and have 780 people dependent on them for food, and 220 others, dependent for work —a thousand in all.

Provisions are scarce, but a man in New York has generously given to the Red Cross for the work. American warships in the harbor assure peace. Jessup has three daughters in America, being educated for mission work, while two are with him.

And, finally, to Japan, where MOORE, graphically describes his case as "having the whole hog to scald." He, while on furlough, engaged in Home Mission work in Texas, from 1911-1913. His children, nine of them, are somewhat scattered. John Watson is a teacher in Winston-Salem, N. C. High School, where Anderson is; Boude and Lardner are at Austin College, Sherman, Texas; Wallace with his uncle in N. Carolina, and the other five in Japan. Conditions in Japan demoralized by gross immorality, in the church and out of it. War, commercialism, and revived idolatry, since Russo-Japanese war, at fault. Loose theology worse than ever. Yet a wonderful forward movement in the great centres.

In Memoriam

The Father's Voice came early into our Class, and MURCHIE was gone, after only four years in the ministry. (Tuberculosis, 1894, Canada, age 33). A few days later, RANKIN joined him in the home above. (Appendicitis, 1894, Baltimore, age 28). But a brief six months, and the Voice came to PHRANER in far-away Siam. Bravely he battled, but all in vain. The homeland shores of earth vanished, as a better homeland greeted him. (Hepatic abscess, 1895, Singapore, age 35).

The Voice spared us then until 1901, when HEANEY was called on the eve of a new home and pastorate. (Typhoid fever, 1901, Philadelphia, age 42). These four, strange to say, all died in hospitals.

Another lapse of years, and BOB MASON, always a favorite, heard the Voice far up in the heart of the Rockies. He, too, worked till the last, and then said, "Yea, Lord." (1905, Salida, Cal., age 50). HEDGES, our only colored classmate, also fought a losing game against the white plague. (Tuberculosis, 1906, Houston, Texas, age 39). The voice had had a wide reach, touching our Class in Canada, in Siam, in the Rockies, in the South, and once more it is heard in the East, when OATES responded, after another long and brave struggle. (Splenic poison, 1909, Bridgeton, N. J., age 44).

The fuller accounts of these men and their work are recorded in the printed record of 1910.

Since that report the following have died:

BASKERVILLE

On June 30, 1912, at the age of 62, Bro. H. C. Baskerville entered into rest, at the Mercer Hospital, Trenton, N. J., where he had been for six weeks. He had been a great sufferer for six months from intestinal cancer. A Virginian by birth, his pastorates yet covered a wide field, in the South, the West and the Northwest. He loved the Home Mission work, and the rugged life of the pioneer. His early legal training gave him a trained mind, that was ever at the service of the church in defense of the truth. He was a clear thinker, a strong writer, and a true servant. With us for only the Senior year, yet he made warm friends with us all. He received the degree of B.D. from Princeton Seminary in 1897, and of Ph.D., from Wooster University in 1903. He leaves a widow, with four sons and one daughter (married).

ALLEN

Allen was a Philadelphia boy. Unlike Baskerville, he never ventured far from home, his pastorates being at Glen Moore, Pa., '90-'92, Ambler, Pa., '92-'94, Pennington, N. J., '94-'04, and Haddonfield, N. J., '04-'15. The latter church had grown splendidly under his leadership and is recognized as one of the leading churches in South Jersey. The testimonials at his funeral service could not have been finer, and his popularity with his brethren was attested by the presence of over a hundred clergymen at these services. He had conducted services on Sabbath and Wednesday evening, his last message being, "Ye are my Witnesses." On Thursday he was unwell and remained at home. At seven-thirty that evening he was taken with violent pain in the chest and died of heart failure in a few moments. His age was 51. His pulpit ability was marked, and his warm, genial temperament made him beloved of all. His widow, with two sons, William and Louis, survive him and are, at present, at Haddonfield.

McCUISH

John B. McCuish is the second Canadian brother to be called home. Eight remain. He served as Stated Supply in St. Louis Mo., Fulton, Mo., Pueblo, Col., and Denver, Col. His first real pastorate was at Leadville, Col. He then became Professor of Ethics and Philosophy in Westminster College, Denver, from '07-'09; but in '09 he went back to the pastorate as pastor at Newton, Kansas. Of him, a co-presbyter writes: "He was one of the ablest and most scholarly, one of the most earnest and successful, one of the finest-spirited and best-loved ministers in the State. No one was regarded more highly or looked to more constantly in all the work of the Presbytery than he." He had been ill for five months, altho in his letter to the Secretary this Spring he made no mention of it, and evaded it in all his correspondence, maintaining his cheery disposition to the last. He took a heavy cold last January, which developed serious heart trouble. In May he rallied, but in early dawn of June 29th he passed to his reward, in the full confidence of assured victory. One of the last letters he wrote was to our Class, in these words: "Keenly do I regret my inability to be present with you as you are gathered at our Silver Anniversary Banquet. I assure you that I rejoice when I learn of any of you being attended by any degree of success in your labor in the Kingdom of our Lord."

He leaves a widow, with three children, two girls and one boy, which bears his father's name. They still reside in Newton, Kansas. McCuish received the degree of Ph. D. from the University of New York in 1892, and the degree of D.D. from Park College in 1908.

ERSKINE

James S. E. Erskine was born in LeClaire, Iowa, December 10, 1858. After a year in Alleghany Seminary, ill health laid him aside until he entered Princeton with us in 1887. His one charge was at Thompson Ridge, New York, in the Presbytery of Hudson. His ministry was featured by modesty, faithfulness and devotion. He was of a deeply religious nature and systematic and untiring in his efforts. His illness began a year ago with diseased glands of a cancerous nature. Radium treatment failed to heal. He was compelled to be often out of the pulpit, but he celebrated the 25th anniversary of his pastorate by preaching his last sermon on that day, May 9, altho he was unable to stand thro' the whole service. He passed peacefully away on August 9, leaving a widow. Thompson conducted the funeral service.

It may be of interest to know that in his earlier college days Erskine won a prize of $75 over Wm. Jennings Bryan, in an inter-collegiate oratorical contest. He was a descendant of the Erskines of Scotland, founders of the Seceders Church.

EXCERPT

EXCERPT OF RESPONSE FOR THE CLASS AT THE
ALUMNI DINNER

By Rev. J. H. Thompson

MR. PRESIDENT, FATHERS, BRETHREN, AND LADIES:

Never before have I been so impressed with the difference between a seventeen meter gun and a rifle. Nevertheless I offer no apology for appearing at this time, in behalf of the Class of '90, for I am reminded that it is the function of the infantry to take the trenches, after they have been shelled by the artillery.

If what Dr. Patton says is true—and I presume it is—that these Doctors and Professors are on the firing line, then I am convinced that the Presbyterian Church is in a like condition with Germany, in that she has no rear, for certainly the Class of '90 is on the firing line with the commissary department woefully weak, at times.

I may say of the Class of '90, that it is a very uniform class, and if I were not a member of the Class, I would say of uniformly high grade. We have no one man who towers so high above the others like Dr. Patton, that he forms a label for his class, and yet I am not unmindful of the fact that I have Wylie on my left, the notorious—I should say worthy—Moderator of the Synod of Baltimore, and Gibbons, an author of no mean repute. On my left is Campbell, from Arizona, who has given us one of our largest churches of the great West, and time would fail me to speak of Whitaker and Polk, and Warne, and Williams, Levengood, Bannerman, and Everitt, together with the many other illustrious members.

In representing the Class on this occasion, it affords me great pleasure to be able to announce that during the past twenty-five years we have not grown so good that we can dispense with an atonement wrought through the death and resurrection of a God Christ; that we have not grown so wise that the Book of Wisdom, the Word of God is no longer the Book of Books for us; that we have not become so powerful that we can instruct the Almighty as to what he may, and may not do; and above all, I am thankful to be able to say that we have not become so bad that we can eliminate his Satanic Majesty from the Universe, and account for all the devilishness in the world, by the pernicious activity of our own souls.

On the side—the Class has been manifesting, what is to me, an undue interest in the increase of the size of my waistcoat during the past twenty-five years. I have not told them the secret, but my friend Courtland Robinson over there knows it, and I am going to tell you. Twenty-five years ago, when I won my freedom from Dr. Davis, I resolved studiously and religiously to avoid all future association with Daghesh-lene.

NOTE.—It is only fair to say that Bro. Thompson was only chosen by the Class the night before the dinner. McLeod was the appointee of the Seminary Execrtive Committee, but was detained thru illness.

FINALE

The last word has been written, the last message read. Has it paid? Your Secretary cherishes two hopes, first, that his feeble efforts in this line may serve to keep burning the fires of devotion to the truth, as we learned it at Princeton, and perchance hold a little more steady our light, as the darkness presses, and a soul out of the night cries for help; and, secondly, that the Class Spirit may be so constant, so sympathetic, so broad, that every member may feel its warmth, and it be easier for every son and daughter of the Class to do right and harder to do wrong. And that the bonds of '90 be bonds for service, not self, for uplift, not censure, for truth and reality, not the false and unreal. Will you help? If a single fact in this history has evoked a thought of commendation, write the brother or sister to that effect; if it has struck a sympathetic chord in your own life and belief, tell the brother of it; or if you read between the lines, a message unexpressed, or hear a sigh unconsciously given, open your heart to that one, and pen at once your thoughts in language, Spirit-born. It all helps—oh, so much. And it costs—one stamp. We further trust that these several annals of the Class have so pleased you, that, to preserve them, you will wish them bound. If so, and a copy of the report of 1891, 1900, or 1910 is missing, you can have one *gratis* upon a postal request. Again, cost—one cent. God willing, it is likely that another edition of this History will be written in 1920 and possibly each decade thereafter. It may fall to the lot of others to write them. For your patience, your responsiveness, your co-operation hitherto, we thank you. May the only success worthwhile be yours, the success that consists in meeting God's expectations in God's way in God's measure.

> Forever haltless hurries Time,
> The Durable to gain.
> Be true, and thou shalt fetter Time
> With everlasting chain.

History

Class of 1890

Princeton Seminary

Thirtieth Anniversary

1890 - 1920

CLASS MINUTE

The thirtieth Reunion and Dinner of the Class of 1890 was held at the Orange Inn, Princeton, on Monday evening, May 3d, 1920. It was especially interesting to us, as the Inn, under the management of Miss Nisbet, is the old home of the "Rabbi." We lingered in our social hour before the dinner in the old familiar library. The following sat down at the two tables: Mr. and Mrs. Whitaker, Mr. and Mrs. Henry Campbell, Mr. and Mrs. Adams, Mr. and Mrs. Polk, Mr. and Mrs. Bannerman, Mr. and Mrs. Moore, Mr. and Mrs. Everitt, Mrs. Allen, Warne, Carson, Thompson, Gardner, Eddy, Frank H. Smith, Carrington, Parker, Levingood and Wylie—or 25 in all. The next day at Commencement there were present Mr. and Mrs. Fenwick Fraser who missed getting in the evening before. (At Assembly this year, were also McGinnis, McMillan and Paterson.) The Secretary read the history for the last five years and it was ordered printed. Each member was then called upon in order for some account of himself, and the discussion waxed so warm over some subjects that it was far past midnight when we left those hallowed walls for some needed rest. Whitaker presided as usual in his happy manner. The Secretary can only say that all present looked in the best of health and were keenly alive to the great problems of the present day. We were given no opportunity to speak at the Alumni dinner, a new rule being in operation that limited class responses only to the fifty-year men. Three other addresses upon living themes were given. Another reunion will be held in 1925. Get ready for it. Former copies of History of 1910 and 1915 will be sent gratis on application. Do you need any?

F. B. EVERITT,
Secretary.

CLASS REGISTER

Adams, Crofton Craig ....Underwood, Minn.
Anderson, Neal L..........................Savannah, Ga.
Annin, William A.........2844 Accomac St., St. Louis, Mo.
Bannerman, William S...................Titusville, N. J.
Bryant, Seeelye ....Saylerville, R. I.
Bull, Kent M........................Kennett Square, Pa.
Campbell, Henry M.....................San Jose, Calif.
Campbell, R. J. ....Foam Lake, Saskatchewan, Canada
Carrington, Wilmot A...............Holland Patent, N. Y.
Carson, Robert H.........744 Putman Ave., Brooklyn, N. Y.
Cummings, George M...1333 Valley Place, Washington, D. C.
Doughty, James W......908 Malone St., West Hoboken, N. J.
Dunlap, Edward P..........727 Church St., Ann Abor, Mich.
Eddy, George T..........................Wyoming, N. J.
Everitt, Frank B.........................Lewisburg, Pa.
Fraser, Fenwick W.........................Poland, Ohio
Fraser, Frank L........................Kennewick, Wash.
Gardner, Murray H.......................Brewster, N. Y.
Gibbons, William F....................State College, Pa.
Jessup, William ....Beirut, Syria
Johnson, Andrew F............Pine Ridge, South Dakota
Jungeblut, J. F..............................Lodi, Calif.
Levingood, J. C..............................Wayne, Pa.
Lynn, J. E..................Kitchener, Ontario, Canada
McGinnis, Charles E.................Hoosic Falls, N. Y.
McLean, J. T........................Gulfport, Florida
McLeod, Malcolm J.........151 Central Park West, or
 St. Nicholas Collegiate Church, N. Y. City
McMillan, John ....Atlantic City, N. J.
Miller, E. D........................Gerardstown, W. Va.
Miller, Hugh ....Phillipsburg, N. J., R. D. 2
Moore, John ....Susaki Machi, Kochi Ken, Japan.
 This year at Taylorsville, N. C.
Nelson, W. F. S.......................Santa Barbara, Calif.
Parker, A. G..............................Macomb, Ill.
Paterson, A. McD....................Newburyport, Mass.

3

Paton, Lewis B.................................Hartford, Conn.
Polk, Samuel ....Lawrenceville, N. J.
Remington, A. W.........................Mt. Vernon, N. H.
Smith, Frank Hyatt.......................Kenmore, N. Y.
Smith, W. H. P............................Wyoming, N. Y.
Thompson, J. H..........................Montgomery, N. Y.
Trompen, J. N................................Aurora, Col.
Voorhies, William S........................Garfield, N. J.
Warne, D. Ruby......................McConnellsville, Ohio
Whitaker, Charles H......815 Preston St., Philadelphia, Pa
Wylie, S. Beattie............................New Castle, Del.

SUMMARY

The following is our present status, as a Class in Vocations:

Teaching—Annin, Gibbons and Paton	3
In Foreign Field—Jessup, Moore...............	2
In Home Missions among Indians—Johnson....	1
In business—Dunlap	1
In farming—W. H. P. Smith..................	1
Supts. of Missions—Trompen, Nelson..........	2
Without charge—Bull, McLean, E. D. Miller, Remington	4
In pastorate—the rest	31
Total	45
Deceased	12
Total	57

CLASS HISTORY—1915-1920

The mantle of the prophet's office may have bene worth praying for, but not so, the historian's. For the chronicler of events can speak with little authority. The best he can do is to say with Scott:

"I cannot tell how the truth may be,
I say the tale as 'twas said to me."

All in all, the last half-decade of our career has been easy sailing. We have lost, by death, but one member, Williams. All have been located; some have found their way back into the active pastorate; and, generally speaking, all is well. Changes have not been so numerous, salaries have been increased, wedding bells of the next generation are ringing, why worry?

Your secretary has been near no Ouija Board, and ventures on no prognostications, but steers where the facts, not Fates, direct.

First of all, let us review our roster of honored names. We graduated fifty-seven in number. Twelve have passed on to their heavenly crowns in the following order: Murchie, after four years of service; Bob Rankin, after four; Phraner, after five; Heaney, after eleven; Bob Mason, after fifteen; Hedges, our colored brother, after sixteen; the beloved Oates, after nineteen; Baskerville, **patriarchus maximus**, after twenty-two; Allen, McCuish, and Erskine, after twenty-five; and Williams, after twenty-eight. The average term of these twelve in years of actual ministerial service is less than sixteen years. Two (Murchie, Hedges) died of the dreaded white plague, one (Allen) was called suddenly, the others passed away after days and weeks of weary suffering, that gave ample time for fullest witnessing to the power of sustaining grace.

Perhaps no better tribute can be paid these honored brethren than to reiterate our sincere interest in their remaining loved ones, and to give them the honored place in this brief chronicle of passing events.

Let us, therefore, with due reverence for these honored names, call the

AUXILIARY ROLL

or the families of our beloved dead. All these families have been heard from, except two; Mrs. Heaney, whose letter was returned undelivered, and she will now be hard to locate; and Mrs. Hedges (now Mrs. Johnson) whose letter to her former address at San Antonio, Texas, was not returned, nor has any reply been received.

ALLEN—Mrs. Minnie L. Allen is residing in her own home at 307 Kings Highway, East Haddonfield, N. J., which was her husbands last field, and in which church she is still most active. Of her two boys, William Allen, Third, is Factory Manager at the Abrasive Co., Frankford, Pa. He was confidential clerk in Gen. Scotts office at Camp Dix and was sent on special mission to Texas and North Carolina. Louis is in the banking business in New York, is married, and has one child, Samuel Clement, born Feb. 5, 1917.

BASKERVILLE—Mrs. Emma Reed Baskerville still resides at Princeton at 15 Van Deveneter Ave. Her family of four sons and one daughter are located as follows: Charles Vice-President and also Acting President of Bellevue College, Neb. He received the degree of D. D. last June, but is about to resign his work and take up the pastorate; William E. graduates this year from Princeton Seminary and goes out as Home Mission -y to Brookings, Oregon, on the far western coast, a true son of his father in his Home Mission zeal; Robert is a pastor at Conemaugh, Pa.; Arthur graduates from Princeton University this June and goes out under appointment of the Canadian Board to British Columbia for a year, when he will return and enter the Seminary, making in all five sons that this family has given to the ministry. The one daughter, Mrs. Julia Hensel, is Dean of Women in Monmouth College, Ill. Two children have died, one in missionary service in Persia.

ERSKINE—Mrs. Esther M. G. Erskine has purchased a home near the village of Pine Bush, N. Y., where she is engaged in various church activities, retaining her membership, however, in the church at Thompson Ridge, which her husband served for twenty-five years.

MASON—Mrs. Mason at first moved to her old home in De Soto, Mo., but four years ago moved to Oklahoma City, near which city her mother and sister live. She has just returned from hospital treatment. Naturally, her life is wrapped up in her only child, Robert Judson, now 17, with 5 feet. 6 inches of stature, and a weight of 119 pounds. "In expression and mind, he is like his dear father, but looks like his mother, they say." He has carried off the highest honors in his grammar grades, was made the editor of his High School paper the first year there, made all debate teams, and won the gold medal in the oratorical contest with seven schools. Also, an athlete, carries four solids at school, works in Carnegie Library after school hours and on Saturdays. Is at Estes Park, Col., for summer work, and aims to be "the best surgeon possible, and put the Mayo boys out of commission."

Well, success to you, Robert! You have the gifts and pluck of your noble father and our hats are off to the coming surgeon of America."

McCUISH—We regret to report that Mrs. McCuish soon followed her husband, departing this life on March 26, 1916, nine months after his death. Their three children are at 514 East Eighth St., Newton, Kansas, (his last charge) under care of a sister. Their names and ages are: Helen K., 16; a Freshman in Park College; John B. Jr., 13, in Eighth Grade, and Anna Margaret, 10, in Sixth Grade.

OATES—Mrs. Ethelinde D. Oates is at her old home in Princess Anne, Md. She was actively engaged in war work as a County Chairman. Her invalid mother passed away last year. Robert Luther is a student in Mercersburg Academy, Pa., preparing to enter the Engineering School at Lehigh University. He is a brilliant mathematician, and, like his father, with a mechanical bent of mind. Although only 16, he tops six feet in height, and so resembles his father that a visitor at the Academy, without knowing his name, identified him as an Oates.

PHRANER—The two boys sof Phraner are heard from. Stanley was a Lieut. in the Marine Aviation Service. Wilson was in the Navy, and spent most of his two years at Newport and Yorktown with the Atlantic Fleet, receiving his commission as Ensign, just before leaving. Stanley is at present Secretary of the Princeton Y. M. C. A. at Pekin, China, is married and has two daughters. Wilson is now in business in New York with his address at 385 Jefferson Ave., Brooklyn.

RANKIN—Mrs. Elizabeth Rankin still makes her home at Berlin, N. J.—her pre-marital home. Of her children, Robert is American Consul at Warsaw, Poland. Rejected physically during the war, he yet found service as a physician in the Bureau of Standards in Washington. Helen is teacher of English in the Livingston Park Seminary, Rochester, N. Y., and also this year, its Acting-Principal. Ella May will graduate this year from Millersville Normal School, Pa., to become also a teacher. Suffering from poor health, her life-work has been somewhat retarded.

WILLIAMS—Mrs. Harriet A. Williams is at present Secretary of the Riverdale Country School at Riverdale-on-the Hudson. Her home is at Ardmore, Pa.

THE CLASS

As to the living members of the class, we are glad to report that all have been located, although several have not been heard from—an inexcusable lapse of something more than memory, we fear. We can only say that Jungeblut is still at Lodi, Calif.; Bryant, at Saylersville, R. I.; McMillan at Atlantic City; R. J. Campbell at Foam Lake, Saskatchewan, Canada. These have been the notorious sinners as to answering class letters. We hope, when the trumpet blows, they will be on hand, but————————

Following our Questionnaire, we will review the responses in this order:

1—FAMILY DATA

ADAMS—One son, Arthur, at Assiout, Egypt, teaching, and Harold at Howard Lake, Minn.

ANDERSON—One daughter, married, with one child, named after his granddaddy, born March 26, 1919; the other Ruth, teaching in Junior High School, Savannah.

ANNIN—Daughter, a Junior, and son, a Freshman, in Washington University, St. Louis.

BANNERMAN—Harold, with aa C. E. degree from Lafayette College, is with an engineering firm in Princeton, and Trenton; Mitchell is in office of Bethlehem Steel Co.; Paul is in office of the Empire Rubber Co., Trenton; Arthur is a Sophomore in Lafayette. Harold and Mitchell are married and Bannerman boasts of one grandchild, Virginia, born on August 29, 1917. This little girl has the honor of being the first grandchild of the class, as far as we have it recorded.

CARRINGTON—Has one daughter married and two at home.

DOUGHTY—Has a daughter married, Mrs. Helena Paterson and a son, John C., married, with Adelina and Richard at home. John C. has one son.

EVERITT—Has son, Kenneth, graduated this year with third honors in Class of over 350 at State College, elected to Honor Fraternity, Phi Kappa Phi, and now a nomad for a year, working his way to the Coast, studying farming conditions throughout the country, to be a specialist in agriculture. Look out for him in Far West! Helen and Donald at home in High School.

GIBBONS—Has a houseful of girls, two of whom have been teaching at State College as has also the father. But Margaret is now bacteriologist at the Allentown, Pa. City Hospital. Eleanor is under appointment as missionary to India and ready to sail this Fall, if the proper papers can be secured by our Board. Margaret is also a Student Volunteer and hopes in time to also go to India. Frances is a student in State College. Rebekah has been teaching at State. Mrs. Gibbons has been through a very serious operation in a Philadelphia hospital, but is much improved.

JESSUP—Has a daughter, Theodosia, married to Rev. Edward J. Thompson, of Beirut. Jessup himself left Beirut for America, on March 12, 1919, with his daughters, Faith and Marie. Was taken ill with pneumonia in England, and at death's door. But reached New York May 18th. His weakness kept him at home, and fearing the cold American winter, he sailed for Syria on Sept. 30, arriving Nov. 6th, since which time he has been resting and recuperating. Although entitled to a year's furlough, after ten years of service, he was only able to take five months of it in America. His younger brother, (Fred) died in Persia, last December.

JOHNSON—Has the boy with the oddest name, Maga-Ska (or Julius).

LEVINGOOD has son in Graduate School, Princeton, preparing to teach, and a married daughter with one son.

MOORE—With his nine children tops the list. John Watson is married, and is Supt. of High School at Winston, Salem, N. C. Bonde C. is teaching in High School at St. Joseph, Mo.; Lardner W. is now a Middler at Union Seminary, Va., a graduate of Austin College, Texas; Wallace H. is a Junior at Austin College; Eleanor is at Salem Academy in Winston-Salem; James Erskine is in High School at Sherman, Texas, preparing to enter Austin College; Mason Edwards, age 12, Catherine age 9, and Bertha Loving, age 7, have been with the parents in Japan, and with them now at Taylorsville, N. C.

PARKER—Has four sons in the ministry, one a missionary in China.

POLK—Has a daughter, Rebeka, graduated from Mount Holyoke College, in 1919, and is teaching in Florida. James is in Fourth Form at Lawrenceville.

WARNE—Has one daughter married to Charles Kirsch, and one granddaughter, Margaret Warne Kirsch, born June 13, 1920.

WYLIE—Has son, Hugh, married Jan. 4, 1919.

Summing it all up, as far as reported, there are now fourteen children of the class married, seven sons and seven daughters, with nine grandchildren, five boys and four girls.

II—WAR WORK

ADAMS gave two boys to war service; Arthur was with the British "Y" in Palestine for a time. Now in Assiout, Egypt. Harold was in service a year and was wounded in camp.

BANNERMAN had one son who was in three major offensives, his troop, Second Cavalry, being the first to cross the Moselle, and first to reach the Rhine. He was in Coblenz with the Army of Occupation. Another son, Paul, was in Navy.

DOUGHTY had a son, John G., 2d Lieut. U. S. A. (Volunteers) and a son-in-law, Reuben Peterson, an Ensign in the Navy.

DUNLAP had a son for two years and three months in the navy.

EDDY had one son in the Aviation Mechanics Corps and a daughter who acted as nurse for seven months in Army Hospital at Colonia, N. J.

McLEAN had a son, an engineer, in the great March drive of 1918, and was in five of the great battles, coming home in October, 1919, without a scratch.

WYLIE had a son and daughter who risked their lives in work in the High Explosive Projectile Plate Works of Bethlehem Loading Co.

WARNE had a son-in-law in air service, about ready to go over, when peace came.

Of our own men, POLK was in "Y" work in France, and up in the firing-line. GIBBONS edited a paper for the Shipping Board one summer. WYLIE was chairman of Committee of One Hundred in a Liberty Loan Drive that won three Over-the-Top Flags and one medal. CARSON was a camp pastor at Camp Upton, N. Y.; ANDERSON was constantly in platform work. GARDNER was booked and passported for over-seas, when his duodenum got on a rampage, and put him on his back. NELSON was very active, especially in looking after enlisted men from his oil fields.

III—PUBLICATIONS

Our list of publications from the Class is pitifully small for this half-decade, unless the fellows are fearfully modest. GIBBONS has given out a work on the Study of English, and EDDY has edited various manuals of telegraphy in which work he is engaged as well as in preaching. F. H. SMITH issues thousands of a popular card, entitled "My Church and I."

IV—SPECIAL ITEMS

BULL, through an invalid wife, has held no pastorate for two years and sees little prospect of so doing in the immediate future. FRANK FRASER is on his fruit ranch, in State of Washington, near Kennewick, preaching erstwhile at Sunnyside Church, fifty miles from his home. The work is encouraging, he says, with a recent addition of seven new members and a prospect of sixteen more at the next Communion. He has had a salary increase of $300. GIBBONS, besides his regular teaching work at State College, is also engaged in Bible Study work at the Summer School and in "Y" Bible classes. McLEAN has erected a church building that would now cost at least $10,000 without ever asking for a cent of money and has maintained it ever since without ever asking support. W. H. P. SMITH is still sticking close to the farm, of about 146 acres with twelve milch cows to feed the babies of the city. He supplies occasionall nearby pulpits. Since we met in May, FENWICK FRASER has been installed as pastor at Poland, Ohio. Hudnut, one-time member of our Class, preached the sermon at his installation.

ED. MILLER is in the State Hospital for the Insane at Weston, W. Va. His general health is good, but little hope for improved mental condition. Is not violent, and goes there of his own volition.

MOORE is summering at Taylorsville, N. C., with his relatives. He expects to come north in the Fall and wants to visit as many of us as possible. He can give you a rattling good speech on Japan.

HENRY CAMPBELL is most pleasantly situated in San Jose, Calif., about thirty miles below San Francisco by trolley; has an Assistant, was Chairman of New Era Committee of Presbytery; came east to Assembly, but his brother-in-law and colleague to Assembly died en route east, and he had to leave Assembly to take the body back to Kansas City. He has been resting since at Wooster, Ohio.

NELSON has also a fine California home at Santa Barbara on the hillside overlooking sea and mountains and invites the Class to look in. He is now doing special work for the men in the oil fields of two counties; no organized churches, but preaches three times each Sabbath and each night in week except Saturday; has twelve preaching points, sometimes in dance halls, or in dining-halls, or in school houses. The men for whom he works have given him already two Fords and he has traveled in five years over 75,000 miles in them. As a side-line, he lectures on Art, and Travel. The Class Boy, William F. Jr., was in the army a year and is now working in Nevada for the S. P. R. R. Co.

ANDERSON is pastor of one of the oldest Presbyterian Churches of the South, the Independent Presbyterian Church of Savannah. Its organist of former years, Dr. Lowell Mason, has given the church some of its greatest hymns, as "From Greenland's Ice Mountains," and "When I survey the Wondrous Cross." His church is considered one of the four most beautiful churches in America. He was elected President of Austin, Texas, Theological Seminary in 1915, but found its financial condition misrepresented to him and he was released from that work soon after taking it up.

DOUGHTY after six years in Civic Work in New York among "the highbrows, dillettantes, officials and politicians," breathes once more the pure, free air of the ministry, in a Reformed pastorate in West Hoboken, N. J.

CARSON induced his congregation to pay off $15,000 of their mortgage on the 20th anniversary of his pastorate, and then they induced him to accept a check for $1,000 as a recognition of his splendid services.

McLEOD has been in deepest waters over his son's mysterious absence for two years, lost absolutely to everybody. He was recently found in Virginia, has been in hospital, and somewhat enfeebled, but is now at home with hope of full recovery. He received his honorable discharge before leaving hospital.

FRANK HYATT SMITH issued a volume of Shakespearian Studies that won an encomium from a Professor at Johns Hopkins "and I went on a Retreat as the Catholics say for ten days." He contributes a sermon each week to Buffalo papers, and is the joker of the Presbytery. A strong Mason, and a true-blue Princetonian. "Gave an obstreperous elder a dose of catnip and assafactida and he is milder than a Norwegian lamb. A word to the wise, etc."

EVERITT was for two months an organizer of five counties in the Interchurch drive last winter, he also organized Vocational Suppers for High School boys under Board of Education. He had Eastern half of Synod of Pennsylvania. Has had $500 increase of salary in last two years.

Only one death has occurred in the last five years. WILLIAMS, our "Jim," began to fail in health two or three years ago, through valvular heart trouble. On Jan. 3, 1918, he was seized with severe pain, was taken to Presbyterian Hospital in Philadelphia. He seemed to improve the first week, but then began to "slip from us." His suffering was intense, with no relief from morphia. After five weeks in the hospital, he passed quietly away on Sunday morning, March 3d. He was buried in the cemetery of the Great Valley Presbyterian Church, Chester County, Pa.

This closes the chronicles of another pentad. The Lord holds each year in His own hand. When that hand unfolds, we have but to receive. But blessed be His name! His purposes of grace are all and only for good. At our time of life, those purposes will no doubt ripen faster and faster. God grant we may keep step with the ripening, and our faces be ever, with increasing expectancy, unto Him.

Five-Year History

1920-1925

Class of 1890

Princeton Seminary

Read at the Class Re-Union Dinner at the Orange Inn, Princeton, N. J., Monday evening, May 11, 1925.

CLASS MINUTE

Once again, the home of the "Rabbi," our beloved teacher of old, Dr. Green,—now the Orange Inn—was the Mecca of our Class at its thirty-fifth re-union on May 11, 1925. Even a heavy rain did not dampen our spirits. It was a cheery gathering, happy over renewed fellowship. Some new faces appeared as R. J. Campbell, Alexander and Matthews. The rest showed but slight changes since last we met. We had the unique pleasure this time of welcoming two brides, Mrs. R. J. Campbell and Mrs. John McMillan, and no men in all the group were happier. And why not? It was a delight to welcome both the brides and the happiness.

We also were honored with the presence and words of Prof. and Mrs. Chas. R. Erdman—since elected Moderator of our General Assembly—, Prof. and Mrs. "Jack" Davis, and Prof. Smith. Mr. Dulles sent regrets. These are all the old faces left on the Faculty. Dr. Erdman met with us, not as a former teacher but as a former co-student. Bishop Paul Matthews—with us only in Junior year—now Episcopal Bishop of the Diocese of New Jersey, and living in Princeton—gave us his delightful and affable presence for awhile before the dinner, but could not remain.

At the tables, spread this time in the old Library of the Rabbi itself, Whitaker presided, and the following were present: Mr. and Mrs. Whitaker, Mr. and Mrs. Everitt (with their guests, J. Donald Everitt, Miss Laura Hetzel and Miss Emily Clingan, all of Lewisburg), Mr. and Mrs. John MiMillan, Mr. and Mrs. R. J. Campbell, Mr. and Mrs. Bannerman, Alexander (with us in Junior year only), Parker, Mr. and Mrs. Thompson, Wylie, Gardner, Levingood, Mrs. Allen and Paton.

The recital of experiences filled the hours until midnight. Donald Everitt entertained with musical selections on his saw. The Class History was read and ordered printed and sent to the Class. A report of the Treasurer is also herewith printed. The contributors of this year are entitled to a free copy of the History. If your name is not on that list, may we ask for a "gift of appreciation"—of any amount to keep the treasury filled until the next re-union in 1930. It is only to be expected that Death will begin more serious inroads now as we pass on into the "upper years", and it may be necessary to send out more notices than usual. This, the Secretary is very willing to do, if the Class provide the funds. He would appreciate prompt notice of any deaths of members of the Class.

No charges are made for the History. Your gifts are voluntary. Only once in five years do we call for funds. The Class again rallied to the work of our only missionary abroad, John Moore, and sent him $175 which he has gratefully acknowledged.

FRANK B. EVERITT, Secretary.

CLASS ROSTER, 1925

Name	Address	Occupation
Adams, Croften Craig	Maple Plains, Minn.	Pastor
Anderson, Neal L.	25 West Oglethorpe Ave, Savannah, Ga.	Pastor
Bannerman, Wm. S.	Titusville, N. J.	Pastor
Bryant, Seelye	20 Park Place, Pawtucket, R. I.	Editor
Bull, Kent M.	Kennett Square, Pa.	Retired
Campbell, Henry M.	278 Post St., (office) San Francisco, Cal.	Sec.
Campbell, R. J.	Poplar Plains Crescent, Toronto Can.	Evang.
Carrington, Wilmot A.	Woonsocket, R. I.	Pastor
Carson, Robert H.	744 Putnam Place, Brooklyn N. Y.	Pastor
Cummings, Geo. M.	1628 T St., S. E., Washington, D. C.	P.—S. C.
Doughty, Jas. W.	908 Malone St., West Hoboken, N. J.	Pastor
Dunlap, Edward P.	5264 Seaboldt, Detroit, Mich.	Business
Eddy, Geo. T.	Wyoming, N. J.	Pastor
Everitt, Frank B.	Lewisburg, Pa.	Pastor
Fraser, Fenwick W.	Poland, Ohio.	Pastor—S. C.
Fraser, Frank L.	Kennewick, Wash.	Retired
Gardner, Murray H.	Brewster, N. Y.	Pastor
Gibbons, Wm. F.	State College, Pa.	Teacher
Johnson, Andrew F.	Pine Ridge, S. D.	District Miss.
Jungeblut, J. F.	Lodi, California	Pastor
Levingood, J. C.	Wayne, Pa.	Pastor
Lynn, J. E.	Kitchener, Ontario, Canada	Retired
McGinnis, Chas. E.	Hoosic Falls, N. Y.	Pastor
McLean, Jas. T.	Gulfport, Fla.	Retired
McLeod, Malcolm J.	151 Central Park West, N. Y. City	Pastor
McMillan, John	239 S. Metropolitan Ave., Atlantic City	S. S.
Miller, Hugh	Phillipsburg, N. J., R. D. 2	Retired
Moore, John	Takamatsu, Kagawa Ken, Japan	F. Miss.
Nelson, W. F. S.	Santa Barbara, Cal.	H. Miss.
Parker, A. G.	Conneautville, Pa.	Pastor
Paterson, A. McD.	Newburyport, Mass.	Pastor
Paton, Lewis B.	Hartford, Conn.	Teacher
Remington, A. W.	Ivoryton, Conn.	Pastor
Smith, Frank H.	Garrison Road, Williamsville, N. Y.	Retired
Smith, W. H. P.	Wyoming, N. Y.	S. S.—Farmer
Thompson, John H.	Montgomery, N. Y.	Pastor
Trompen, John N.	Aurora, Colorado	Retired
Voorhies, W. S.	Eddington, Pa.	Pastor
Warne, D. Ruby	McArthur, Ohio	Pastor
Whitaker, Chas. H.	5 E. Asbury Ave., Oak Lane, Phila., Pa.	S. S.
Wylie, S. Beattie	2304 W. 11th St., Wawaset Park, Wilmington, Delaware	Retired

SUMMARY

In the Active Pastorate .... 23 (or 56% of Class)
Retired, with occasional preaching .... 8 (or 20% of Class)
In Missionary Work, Home or Foreign 3
In Teaching 2
In Business 1, Press Work 1, Farming 1 3
In Secretaryship 1, Evang. Work 1 2
       Total 41
Deaths, during 1920-1925—Annin, Jessup, E. D. Miller, Polk 4
Total deceased of Class .... 16 (or 28% of Class, as graduating)

CLASS HISTORY—1920-1925

The writing of history is no dull pastime. To some, it may be only the chronicling of facts; to another, the more interesting work of a Redactor. But, if so, there were famous redactors of old—so we are told—altho not in Princeton. With the archaeologist, the historian never knows what delightful surprises await him.

Speaking of archaeology, reminds me of the lines of Webster—no, not Noah, nor Daniel, but a better Biblical name, John—who said:

"I do love these ancient ruins,
We never tread upon them, but we set
Our foot upon some reverend history."

"Ancient ruins—reverend history." How suggestive. I can vouch for the latter—will you for the former? For ever since we laid claim, via the daghesh-forte route, to the title of "Rev.", we have been making "reverend history."

But 'those ancient ruins'! My vision of that has been knocked into smithereens by reading of Remington getting an increase of $500 in salary in his 62d year, and Trompen still going at the rate of a thousand miles a month in his Dodge car and adding 44 members to his church last year; and then, worst of all, two dyed-in-the-wool bachelors having the nerve to take unto themselves a wife when, as Remington says, "the sage tea has washed out of my hair." If you call that "ruins", please label them what age.

But we are out of the "grades",—yea, even beyond the Freshman stage, and we perforce must look upon ourselves as "grave, old Seniors." The words of Goneril to her tormented father King Lear are not amiss:

"I do beseech you, to understand my purpose aright,
As you are old and reverend, you should be wise."

Wisdom belongeth to years, and we need not be ashamed of the unconscious note of authority with which we are apt now to speak. Would that the world would trust a little more the sage advice of its fathers, (except certain ex-college Presidents who seem to have lost their bearings on the Prohibition question.)

But, with Jean Ingelow, let us say, in her winsome way:

"Show me your nest with the young ones in it,
I will not steal them away;
I am old, you may trust me, linnet, linnet,
I am seven times one today."

And we—'ancient ruins'—are seven times seven—and more. Who can distrust us? So do not challenge without cause my statements as to age, which I give on no better authority than Bro. Alford Kelley

(John, as we knew him) who has a penchant for dates. it seems—not the college kind, however, for he, too, with Gardner, loves "single cussedness"—and birds.

Kelley points out the fact that Baskerville (if he had lived) and Lynn are 75 this year, Lynn, passing his three-quarter-century mark on Nov. 23 of this year. Wonder if we can remember that long enough to "shower" him with good wishes, as leading us all to the century-mark. Mason, if living, would have been 70. Then comes a goodly host of 26 living graduate members, who are in their sixties, with Frank Hyatt Smith, leading them on, and McLeod trailing in the rear to see that none deny their age and fall out. Before the year is over, Wylie, Carrington, Anderson, Fenwick Fraser, R. J. Campbell and McMillan will have "toed the line." Of course, R. J. and John are very excusable for ageing so much the past year. Who wouldn't? The strain must have been terrible. And then there will be seven of us (Levingood, Frank Fraser, Everitt, Moore, Carson, Johnson and Bryant) to push on after the rest over the sixty-year line. But of all of you here to-night, it is only fair to say that Bishop Matthews is the Junior of us all, altho in one of the highest offices of his church.

For our regular class, 1866 was the banner year for births, with 1865, a close second. Baskerville was the oldest man when we graduated, at the age of 40, while Hedges, our colored brother, was the youngest at 21.

But, again the archaeologist in us speaks of some strange "finds." Adam (s) like his famous progenitor, was born, of course, in Eden (Ohio). Matthew(s) when joined with Paul is staggeringly Scriptural. Gibbons and Allen just missed by one day, being a New Year's gift. Numerous lights in the Class came near breaking into this firmament at the same time, but a merciful Providence saved the day, e. g., what an effulgence there would have been, if Moore, Rankin, and Carson had ever struck this mundane sphere at the same time, and yet they only missed it by ten days. Or what cataclysms of nature—infant nature. of course—might have occured,if Alexander, Jessup and Thompie could only have had a little confab in advance, and timed their appearance in this world for the same day. For they were only five days apart. Surely, after all this,

"There is a Divinity that shapes our ends,
Rough hew them how we will."

But here we are—'ancient ruins'—and I am here to testify that about every last one of you sent back to your Secretary, in reply as to your health, such expletives of over-abundant health as almost to force a new Thesaurus of. words. Listen!: "good, never better" (Adams); "never better" (R. J. Campbell); "Perfect, feel as young as ever" (Doughty); "first-class" (Lynn, at 75); "young at 68" (F. H. Smith); "excellent" (Cummings). Not a sick one on the whole list, nor even a tired one, as far as we can see. Not even any enthusiasm over the new Pension Plan. Either you are a mighty vigorous lot, or the biggest bunch of —Jesuits, we ever saw. Well, so be it. Praise God for good health. May the next pentad find you as buoyant and hopeful as now. It makes all the difference in the world, whether, at sixty, you are a Barzillai or a Caleb.

> "Grow old along with me.
> The best is yet to be.
> The last of life, for which the first was made.
> Our times are in His hand,
> Who saith: "a whole I planned,
> Youth shows but half; trust God,
> See all, nor be afraid."

Before proceeding further, it behooves us to pause a moment before some new-made graves in the last five years. The first to be called away after our last meeting in 1920 was our beloved Jessup, who died on Dec. 12, 1920, from acute bronchitis after thirty years of service in Syria, which was homeland to him. For he was born in Beirut, Syria, in 1862, his father, being the renowned missionary, Rev. H. H. Jessup. Our Jessup was one of the charter members of the Student Volunteer Movement, and went out to Syria in Nov. 1890. He began work at Zahleh, where he stayed until 1915, when he was transferred to Beirut as professor in the Theological Seminary. But the war came on, and theology as well as other studies had a slim chance for awhile. The Mission at Beirut was made the headquarters for Relief Work and Jessup was made the Secretary of that work. He studied Turkish law and represented the Mission with the Government. His executive ability at this time was invaluable, and he was looking forward to a great field of usefulness in training Syrian young men for Christian service. Jessup was twice married, his second wife, surviving him. He received the degree of D. D. from Temple University, Philadelphia.

Strange to say, our beloved brother Edward Demoss Miller passed away four years ago on Feb. 19, 1921. His death was not reported even to his Presbytery, and his name was still in the Minutes of the Assembly last year. But this can hardly be blamed to carelessness of Presbyterial clerks. Ed was on the roll of the Phila. North Presbytery but had been for many years, leading the life of a recluse at Gerardstown, W. Va., where he had some kind of a chicken farm. No one ever got a line from him. He died of tuberculosis at the age of 58 years, eight months, and 12 days. He is buried in the old Gerardstown cemetery. Ed was a most likeable fellow, but, as we all know, had a rather disappointing career. Of brilliant mind, he carried off the Classical Fellowship in Princeton College in 1886, and ranked high as a student in the Seminary. He had only one actual pastorate, at Huntingdon Valley, Pa., and that for only one year. Then he began that "walkfest" of his, in studying in the different universities of the world, a philosophic epicure, all the calories he cared for were the Kantian Categories, or the like. He became a great authority on Kant, but his mind and ministerial abilities were practically wrecked. He took his Ph. D. at Berlin, after long years of study there. He waited in vain for some Chair in Philosophy over here to invite him, but nothing came his way, and his mind broke almost completely, so that he shut himself apart from the rest of us, being cared for by kindly hands within his family circle.

On Feb. 26, 1922, our Classmate Wm. A. Annin passed away in his home in St. Louis after a nine days illness of pneumonia, leaving a widow and two children. Interment was at Rolla, Mo. Annin came to Princeton in 1879, entering the University as a Freshman, and made his profession of faith in the 1st Church here, while a Freshman. He went into teaching, after graduation, for several years, and entered the Seminary with us in 1887. He never was licensed or ordained, preferring to follow his chosen profession of teaching. He was supt. of Schools in Boonville, Mo., from 1899-1903, and of Macon, Mo., from 1903-1908. He then entered the High School work in St. Louis, and became one of the most successful teachers of that city. His high place in the hearts of both his sudents and fellow-teachers was shown in many ways during his illness. Once, during that illness, when some one said: "everybody loves Mr. Annin", he roused himself enough to say, "I would rather they should say that than that I was rich or famous." He was also Librarian of his school at the time, and had so over-worked his strength that he could not resist the disease.

But the saddest tragedy of the last five years came in the calling away of both Sam Polk and his wife within eighteen days of each other. Mrs. Polk was taken suddenly ill and was taken to Mercer Hospital on Dec. 15, 1922. An operation revealed a cancerous condition that was hopeless. She lingered for five days, and was then laid to rest at West Nottingham, Pa., their former parish. Sam seemed to bear up wonderfully well, but he had three funerals in succession. He had returned from a dinner at one of his parishioners, when his sister-in-law found him semi-conscious in his own kitchen. He never regained consciousness and died on Jan. 7, 1923. Interment at West Nottingham, Pa. These two deaths strike us most heavily, because both were always at our re-unions and the manse at Lawrenceville was a veritable "house by the side of the road" to the Class of '90, as they wended their way back to Princeton. Sam was described by one, as "the most loved man in New Brunswick Presbytery."

But the list is not complete yet. For what brings us sorrow as well as the death of classmates, is the death of their helpmates, who have so faithfully stood by them all these years. Besides Mrs. Polk, the following mistresses of the home have crossed the river since last we met. Mrs. Gibbons left an unbroken family circle on Oct. 2, 1923. In 1920, she passed thro an operation for tumor on the spine. Not fully restored to health, she, nevertheless, was able to do much good work with her husband, especially among the college girls at State College, Pa. Paralysis was setting in, and she consented to another operation in the University Hospital in Phila. Gibbons and his daughter gave a blood transfusion, but all in vain. Whitaker conducted the last services, much to the comfort of our dear brother, and the good wife was laid to rest at Oaklands, Westchester, Pa., by the side of her father and mother "in the sunset hour."

Mrs. Paton died Jan. 9, 1924 in her Hartford home after nine months of illness, the details of which we have not yet learned.

And only a few weeks ago, word came that Warne had been called to part with his companion. On March 17, she was taken to a hospital in Zanesville, Ohio, where two married daughters were living. On March 31, she was operated on for appendicit's, but peritonitis set in, and the end came on Apr. 6. She was taken back to her old home for burial, while loved ones wait "not as those that have no hope", but believingly.

Trompen has lost his second son, Harry, who passed away on Decoration Day, 1920 in his 30th year. McLeod's oldest boy has also "gone home." There may have been other deaths in the Class circle, of which we have not yet heard. We can only commend all the sorrowing hearts to the God of all comfort, assuring each one that the Class of 90 enters into their sorrows with more than formal feeling, with downright brotherly sympathy and love.

But shadows soon give way to sunshine. And the bells we hear are not all tolling bells. Some are wedding bells. Now, let the Band strike up "The Campbells are coming." For, sure enough, here they are; R. J. with his bride, and McMillan who was born near enough to Scotland to appdeciate the name, taking unto himself a Campbell. Both swear, by heaven and earth, that they have the salt of the earth, in wives, and, just to preserve peace, let no man dispute the claim. There is enough dust in the air without any further scraps.

But the children are stepping forward at a commendable pace. Within the last five years, Adams, Carrington, Cummings, Gibbons, Mrs. Jessup, Moore, Paton and Warne have all added a son-in-law or daughter-in-law to their circle. Long life and the real thing in happiness to each and every one of them. Some of the rest of us are merely watching developments, at times an interesting, and then again a worrisome pastime.

Up to the time of writing, only Gardner and Hugh Miller have held out against all the charms of the fair sex. They vow eternal celibacy, "tho the heavens fall." If Dunnie were here, he would jolt them with a continuation of the quotation ad libitum enlivened with suggestions of his thrilling ladder story.

The Class of 90 has not been afraid of innovations; one of which— yea, two of which— you see here to-night, viz, having our good wives and lady friends at our Class Dinners, and, for the first time in our history, inviting to join us the men who did not graduate with us, but who were with us for a year or so. As to the ladies, we can never say enough. "All we are and all we hope to be"—but then, Dunlap is not here and the quotation fails for words again. We can only say, that life would have been one long jazz but for the steady hand and word that broke up the syncopated music and brought harmony and real rhythm into existence. As far as we have heard, none have supplanted their husbands, and none have turned modernists. Some drive autos. while others still drive—their husbands. Some raise children and others raise the—roof! pardon me. But with all their idiosyncrasies, they know how to make good men, and it is an honor due them that we have them with us to-night. Some even gracefully wield the gavel, as does Mrs. Fenwick Fraser in the President's chair of the Ohio Synodical Missionary Society. And some handle as efficiently the by no means inferior task of the pen as does Mrs. Everitt in her position as the Secretary of the Penna. Synodical Society, the largest Woman's Missionary Society in our church, Others may have as important positions of which we have not heard. We are glad to chronicle this much among the honors of the Class.

But it is a new pleasure to us to-night to have at our table men who did not tarry long enough to carry away a Princeton diploma. But we hail them as "mighty good fellows" just the same. Alexander. and Matthews are here to speak for themselves. We heard from the following:

Alexander is Synodical Supt. of the Synod of Penna. (U. P. Church) with home at Crafton, Pa. Allison is student pastor at the University of Wisconsin. Has just toured the State in the interest of a denominational building on the campus, and is inaugurating, as a result, a "Paint-Presbyterian-Property" campaign, as he found so many Presbyterian churches, needing painting. He says, he thinks more of his job every year and would not change it for any other field. Barackman is pastor of the First U. P. Church of West New York, N. J. Bishop is in Evangelistic work, with headquarters in Phila. at 130 S. 56th St. Has had fine success along this line. Gulick is a retired Congregational clergyman living at 140 West Pomona St., Germantown, Phila. His impaired health forbids his attending such functions as these. He sends his greetings, especially to Dr. Erdman, who was his neighbor in that city. Heuver has written twice from Rockford, Ill., 90 miles west of Chicago. He has two children, secured a Ph. D. from the University of Chicago, and was last year Moderator of the Synod of Illinois. Hudnut, as you know, is pastor of the large and influential church at Youngstown, Ohio, and is a member of our Board of Foreign Missions. He not long since went, in their behalf, to visit our stations in Africa. Hudnut has one son studying for the ministry, now in Western Seminary. His other son is a Sophomore in the University here. He has one married daughter. His message is "better days ahead; work on." Macbeth is pastor of St. Paul's Presbyterian Church in Vancouver, B. C. He has developed into quite a writer of note, his letter-head announcing seven or eight books he has written. Is a leader in Canadian Presbyterianism. Matthews has risen to the Bishopric of the Diocese of New Jersey with home in Princeton on Bayard Lane. Penrose is President of Whitman College, in Walla Walla. Wash. Within the past two months, he has practically lost his eyesight, and can no longer recognize things or persons. He left us to attend the Yale Divinity School. Phillips is pastor of the First A. R. Pres. Church, Charlotte, N. C.

No word has come from Coffin, Hays, Lippincott, or Twinem. Nor was any letter returned, altho so requested by the postmaster of the place addressed. Hays' address is unknown. He went into army as a chaplain. Latimer and Ricketts have died.

But we must not forget our Auxiliary Roll, another feature of our Class history. This is made up of all the families of our deceased brothers. We still claim relationship to them, and keep them in our hearts and minds. The orphaned ones have first claim. Phraner's two boys are doing well. Wilson is Sec-Treas., and a Director of Baker and Williams' Bonded and Free Warehouses in New York City. He is an elder in the Central Presbyterian Church of Brooklyn, of which Dr. John F. Carson is pastor. He has a boy one year old. Stanley is one of the editors of the New York Bureau, editing the financial and foreign exchange page of that paper. He has two girls and a boy.

McCuish's children are living as follows: Helen is taking a nurse's course in the Presbyterian Hospital of Chicago; John B. Jr., is a Freshman in Washburn College, Topeka, Kas., preparing for the Foreign Mission field; Anna is in the Newton, Kas. High school where she is living with her aunt, who came to take care of the children after the death of their parents.

Rebeka Polk was married last June to Paul C. Dietz, once a Master in the Lawrenceville School, now teaching in the Principia in St. Louis, as professor of physics. James married Belle Barnes of Atlanta, who "contains in her one tiny personality ALL the feminine perfections—beauty, sweetness of character, industry and real old-fashioned goodness." Happily married, all of them.

The children of Jessup are reported as follows: Theodosia, a Vassar graduate, went as a Red Cross aid with the British Forces in their operations during the war in Palestine. In Jerusalem, she met the Rev. Edward Thompson, a British Chaplain from India. They were married in Beirut, he is now professor of Bengalee literature and language in Oxford University, England. Elizabeth, a graduate of Smith, married Kingsley Blake, a doctor with an important position in the radium department of St. Luke's Hospital, N. Y. Helen is in a sanitarium, recovering from over-work. She was published in the Yale list of American Junior poets. Faith graduates from Vassar this year, and with her younger sister, and step-mother, go to Syria for a year.

Of the others, we are sorry to be able to report only partially, as we have not been able as yet to get any replies from Mrs. Annin, Mrs. Baskerville, Mrs. Hedges, nor Mrs. Rankin. Second letters were sent, with return request. No letters came back, except one for Mrs. Heaney, nor did any further word come from these sisters. Mrs. Allen again graces our presence to-night, and can speak for her own two boys. Mrs. Erskine is living at Pine Bush, N. Y., with her brother, is in poor health, but busy in mission and church work. Mrs. Mason is living at 1329 E. 54th St., Chicago, where they have been four years while Robert was in the University of Chicago. He graduates this June. He also entered Rush Medical College in the Fall, has had almost three-quarters year of work and study along the line of his profession. He is much interested in church work, is a deacon in the Hyde Park Presbyterian Church, and active in the Young People's Work. He has many of his sainted father's sterling qualities. Her health is not the best and she may have to move from the city.

Mrs. Oates is the house-mother of 34 young ladies in a Seminary for Girls at Tarrytown, N. Y. Robert has been tunnel-building out in California with her brother, an engineer. He is in love with the West.

Mrs. Williams also has a position with a school, being Executive Secretary of the Riverdale Country School, at Riverdale-on-the-Hudson. She sends best greetings to all.

You no doubt thought us super-modern when we asked about your autos. To be strictly up-to-date, we should have asked about your radios. But the auto question revealed what we expected to find, viz, about every kind of car under the shining sun, with the Ford in the lead by all odds. Frank Hyatt Smith is authority for saying that the only car mentioned in the Bible is where David came to the Ford. His answer to said question was: "I despise the murderers." And a Mason at that, sworn to love, etc. We think our brother from Canada, R. J. Campbell, deserves the prize for nerve-running trips. For on only a few days training, he has driven his new McLaughlin car here safe and sound. Let him tell his own experiences. But they are no longer luxuries, they are necessities now to every wide-awake worker. It was no small jaunt for your Secretary to drive here today in one run of 215 miles. His nerves are on edge yet, and not even the tranquility of a scene like this can calm them down seemingly.

But a hasty glance at the returns:

ADAMS—Has changed to the Minnetonka North Shore group of three churches with address at Maple Plain, Minn. One son was married, and two grandchildren born, in the last five years.

BANNERMAN—Made an address at Lincoln University Commencement this year.

HENRY CAMPBELL—Has been for two years the Pacific Coast Secretary for Men's Work, with office at 278 Post St., San Francisco, and home at San Jose. Likes his work, and is on the road a good deal of the time. Is driving his third Buick car.

R. J. CAMPBELL—Has been in evangelistic work, with good success. Located at Lochnaw Cottage, Poplar Plains Crescent, Toronto. Canada. Four months tour of the States last year.

CARSON—Celebrated his 25th anniversary as pastor of Grace Church, Brooklyn, recently. Has paid off $57,000 of debt in sixteen years. 676 members. Fifth in Presbytery in benevolences and third, in gifts to the Boards. Church gave him an anniversary gift of $1300. His wife has been an invalid for 25 years and for sixteen of them has not stood on her feet, yet is brave and cheerful. Her poem, "My Patch of Blue" has reached 7,000 copies sold, most of the proceeds of which she has given to missionary causes.

CUMMINGS—Is Stated Clerk of Synod of Baltimore and Permanent Clerk of the Presbytery of Washington City.

DOUGHTY—Has a work very encouraging in Hoboken, N. J., with a fine group of young people developing.

DUNLAP—Says nothing about himself except to greet us in his old cordial way. He is in business as a traveling salesman for his brother's firm in N. Y., and lives at 5264 Seebaldt St., Detroit, Mich.

EDDY—Has just resigned charge at Wyoming, N. J. Would like field within 100 miles of N. Y.

EVERITT—Still in the college town of Lewisburg, Pa., with 150 Presbyterian students in Bucknell University to look after and a proposed Presbyterian Orphanage and Home for Convalescent Children on his mind made possible by the gift of a farm near that place by one of his parishioners. The whole matter is very much in embryo as yet, but plans are being laid to merge the Presbyteries of Central Penna. in support of the movement. There is only one Presbyterian Orphanage anywhere east of Ohio, the one in Phila., and that not under any ecclesiastical control whatever. The Lewisburg site is ideal, and if you have rich parishioners interested in the care of helpless children, here is your chance.

JOHNSON, A. F.—District Missionary to the Sioux Indians, in the Dakotas and Montana. Itinerates a good deal. Speaks the Dakota Indian language so fluently, that he is constantly consulted by them in their many problems. In good health. His son, Julius Kenneth (called by the Indians, "Maga Ska," or "White Swan") graduated this year from Hastings College, Neb. Fine, dependable boy, undecided as to career.

LEVINGOOD—Reports a sick wife, and one son teaching in Princeton University.

HUGH MILLER—Had two scratches on his reply: (1) as to coming, "very uncertain," (2) auto: "chevrolet". Nothing else. Reminds us of the minister's blanks "additions—none; losses—none; benevolences—none. Pray for us that we may hold our own." Hugh lives near Philipsburg, N. J.

MOORE—By all odds the best correspondent in the Class, altho the furthest away. Four letters are here for you, if you have time to read them. He is much disturbed over the theological situation on the foreign field. Has two sons out in Japan teaching now, and two other children with him. He wants us to especially know that he has nine children and is even with Parker. John got a D. D. from Davidson College, when home the last time on furlough, and weighs over 200 lbs. No special connection between the two facts. You might think the increase due to swelled head. He appreciates deeply the interest of the Class in him and his boys. As you know, John is the only one of the Class to name boys after his classmates, viz, Mason and Erskine, and so the Class sent him $135 five years ago to help on the education of those boys. This year, $175 has been raised for him from the Class or our churches which goes toward his gospel auto.

NELSON—Is in Home Mission work as Stated Supply of the Los Alamos church, Cal., and lives in beautiful Santa Barbara. He visits the oil fields also.

PARKER—Still has the edge on John Moore. Altho the same number of children—nine—Parker has three grandchildren against Moore's two. And Parker leads us all in sons on the mission field, having three in China, one in India, one in Switzerland, two in Tennessee, and two in Park College. Just think of that family mail—how interesting. He changed to Conneautville, Pa., in 1923.

PATON—Mourns the death of his wife (second) recently. His only child, Suvia Lanice, was married on Oct. 11, 1924, to Mr. Whittemore, a lawyer of Boston. He was called to the chair of Old Testament in Rochester Seminary but declined.

REMINGTON—Declined a call to Mass., and is settled at Ivoryton, Conn., over a Congregational church. Your Secretary and wife visited him in his summer home at Remcroft, N. H., last summer, with a mountain-top vista that can not be beaten. Do not pass him by, if you ever tour New England.

FRANK HYATT SMITH—Retired, at his old home in Williamsville, N. Y. "Preach and lecture, look complacently on the cloth, don't wear a Fosdick sweater, and young at 68." "Wife broke down in 1922, regained her health here, where no sisters annoy; I unload sermons where they like roast beef and not veal." Harpers asked him for a novel—honors enough.

TROMPEN—For twelve years the Congregational State Worker for Colorado. Now serving a church as Stated Supply.

VOORHIES—Lately moved to Edington where Polk once was.

WHITAKER—Is stated Supply over the M. Y. Smith Memorial Church near Phila., a growing field and his, the only Protestant church there.

Theologically, we have no heretics—altho two did sign the Auburn Affirmation. Denominationally, we have 29 listed as in the Presbyterian Church, North: two (McLean and Moore) in the Presbyterian Church, South: One (Anderson) in Independent Presbyterian Church; two (R. J. Campbell and Lynn) in the Canadian Presbyterian Church; four (Bryant, Paton, Remington and Trompen) in the Congregational Church; and two (Doughty and Jungeblut) in the Reformed Church.

106 children are reported, six of whom are on the foreign field. Incomplete reports show 22 grandchildren and a goodly number headed for the ministry.

We regret that postals, letters and printer's ink failed to get any reply from the following: Bull, Frank L. Fraser, Jungeblut, McGinness or Neson.

The problems just ahead of us are not those of old age and "ancient ruins," if we can think so. Pity tis, tis true, that the jingle that catches us at times is the following:

"It's not what you'd do with a million,
If riches should e'er be your lot;
But what are you doing at present
With the dollar and the quarter you've got."

But who should worry, with a new Pension Plan sure to be put over. Sixty-five never seemed so far away to some as it does now.

The problem before us is not the age-long scientific one. G. K. Chesterton in his recent book on St. Francis of Assisi, says: "a man in Voltaire's time did not know what miracle he would next have to throw up. A man in our day does not know what miracle he will next have to swallow." Trust God to reconcile all differences and bring His book thro the fires.

The problem is the one we have always faced: how to make real men and women out of the materials given to us by a kind Providence. Todays challenge is something more than that of character-building. It is even more than that of a saved-from-hell generation. It is making of men worth-while, with qualities for leadership and spiritual impression.

We can close with no better words than those of J. G. Holland:

"Wanted: Tall men, sun-crowned, who live above the fog,
In public duty, and in private thinking."

That's our job and let's to it, with the remaining years at our command. For the summons may come all too soon, with our task but just begun.

"Work while it is day; for the night cometh, when no man can work."

And whoever falls before we meet again, may Death be to them
"That golden key
That opens the Palace of Eternity"

And, with the Master at hand, may the latch turn easy, and it be said of that one, "He faltered not, but went in."

Frank B. Everitt,
Secretary.

EXCERPTS FROM CLASS LETTERS

ADAMS—Letter heading: "Community Churches, Crystal Bay, Long Lake, Maple Plain, Minn." Have been in new field a year and five months. A lovely manse, with modern comforts, one of the best. Three church buildings, one here and two others, five miles off, the latter being less than three miles apart. The field is an isosceles triangle. My extreme distances are not over nine miles the longest way. The roads are Minnesota's best, concrete and bithulitic pavement, tarvia and gravel, kept perfectly clear all winter by power plows. The farms and market gardens are so thick that the roads are like streets. A fine creamery here that can make half a ton of butter at a churning, and 1500 gallons of ice cream a day at the same time. Did it last summer. Between 300 and 400 families connected with my churches. It is hard in spots, discouraging sometimes, interesting mostly, and worth-while all the time. Have decided to go into the new Pension Plan, even if I have to pay the whole 10% myself."

ANDERSON—"My work in Savannah has developed beyond my expectations. The congregations have been growing, and the work developing along constructive lines. Just now we are planning to construct a new $25,000 mission building in the eastern section of the city, and have received the gift of some beautiful lots in the western section for a mission. We are supporting a number of missionaries in China and Korea. In China, we have completed the erection of ten churches and manses in Kashing Province, and our women have completed a memorial to one of our members who died in Chun-ju. I have been hoping to publish a volume of sermons and a volume of Services of Praise, interpreting the life of our Lord in song. Perhaps there have never been any services held in this city that have attracted more general attention and been more beneficial from an evangelical standpoint." Anderson has supplied the Park St. Church, Boston, the past three summers and preached this year the Baccalaureate at Davidson College.

BISHOP—Children all married, but one. Have second wife. Five children and five grandchildren. Last pastorate, Central Church, Portland, Oregon 1916-1918. Since then, engaged in evangelistic work. Expect to re-enter pastorate if the way be clear.

BRYANT—Wrote his letter from a hospital bed as follows: "Am dressed today for first time after illness from pneumonia. Expect to preach for Paterson on May 24 and June 14. For three and a half years, I have been an "honest-to-goodness" newspaper man. I am the official news-camera-man for the Pawtucket Daily Evening News. I also edit a Monday morning column each week, called "Echoes from the Pulpit." I cover for news one section of the city and an adjoining district. Am the Librarian of the paper, listing and filing cuts. The work is very interesting and I receive an excellent salary for it. I prefer a parish, and, if the way opens, will take one again. I now preach about half the time."

FENWICK FRASER—"They have made me Stated Clerk of Mahoning Presbytery. I have been in it for thirteen years. Came near getting into the necrological report last year (1922). Was driving my new Buick coupe, when I collided with a street car. Splinters cut my face, one a quarter of an inch from my eye. Damage to car, $300."

Commissioner this year to G. A. for fifth or sixth time. Preach in Geneva gown, made in Exeter, Eng., and have vested choir. Presided at Synod and introduced Campbell Morgan. Better health than for a long time. Gardening, my tonic. Troubled some with K. K. K., but hope the fever is going down.

GIBBONS—With pardonable pride, writes of his daughter Frances' trip around the world: "A year ago, she went to India to help her sister Eleanor who was breaking under the strain of being left alone in the station by death and furloughs. She has returned 30 lbs. heavier than ever. She came back via the Pacific, thus circling the globe. Since she has returned, she has been much in demand for missionary addresses. It has been a wonderful year for her, more valuable than a postgraduate course. She can never be provincial in her thinking and her sympathies again."

LYNN—Truly had a bitter disappointment. He has not been back since he graduated and, with Mrs. Lynn, was surely counting on this year's visit. "Alas! about six weeks ago, Mrs. Lynn scalded her limb very seriously and the Dr. says, it will take about ten weeks to heal. I retired from the pastorate a little over a year ago, and put in about one quarter of my time supplying. My first pastorate was in Pottsville, Pa., for four years; second, in Bergen, N. Y. for 13 years; and my last, in Baden, Canada, for 14 years. I am in my 76th year and have had only three weeks in that time when I was out of my pulpit. The Lord has been very gracious to us as a family. My daughter has been in charge of a City Mission in Oshawa and seems to enjoy the work."

MACBETH—From Vancouver, B. C., writes: "Things are in some confusion in the churches of Canada. I have had a certain degree of leadership in the struggle to continue our Presbyterian Church. We are winning in that regard, even though some leave us for the Modernistic merger. I stand for the Princeton theology and the Standards, at work, both at home and abroad."

From his letter-heading, we see that Macbeth has done a good deal of publishing, eight books being listed of which he is the author. He was with us only in Junior year.

McLEAN—Writes of Flordia: "We have a great State, and it is now the most prosperous State in the Union. People are crowding into it from all parts of the world. I have been very busy wih church work ever since coming into the State. I am a delegate to the G. A. meeting in Lexington, Ky. Hope all the Class are Fundamentalists."

MATTHEWS—With us one year—Dean of Cathedral, Farbault, Minn., 1913-1915; Professor Seabury Divinity School, 1913-1915;

Bishop of New Jersey, 1915. Settled for life in Princeton. Honors as follows: D. D. from Seabury, from Trinity College, Hardford, and from Princeton University, S. T. D. from General Theological Seminary.

MOORE—(Here is where the Redactor gets in his work. If it is poorly done, charge it up to his Princeton training. From four or five letters, personal and otherwise, we glean the following:)

First of all I want to thank you for the kindnesses, that you have shown me who tho in a different church and far separated from you most of the intervening years, seem to have been remembered by you in a very special and exceptional manner. I thank you very very much for your help in the education of the two boys named for two of the class, which was as much of a surprise to me as anything I have ever had I think. James Erskine is a Junior at Davidson College this year, and we hope will graduate there at 20 and get his M. A. the next year, and we are trying to hope that he will be willing to come out and teach in the Higher Commercial school here where his older bro. Wallace H. is expected to come this fall but this is a good way ahead. Mason Edwards is at the Green Briar Military school in West Va. (Lewisburg). I do not know when he will graduate there, but I suppose in the course of time. My hope is that both these boys may show their appreciation of your help thru life.

Once more it is my very pleasant duty to thank you for still another lift toward a Ford car. Entire honesty compels me to say that this was a complete surprise to me also. I sent to Everitt, some of the sheets of a sort of a circular letter that I was sending to some 70 or 80 churches selected by our Com. on Stewardship, and feeling that you might like some of your wealthy parishioners to help along the good work, since we are one church here in Japan, any way. But I did not for a moment suppose that you would make the effort to raise any large sum among yourselves. I have received and have deposited here the sum of one hundred and eighty eight Yen, and it is safe against the day when I can get the full amount and get the new Ford.

May I say that I propose to carry the Gospel to every soul in this our exclusive field. May I say that already I have carried the Gospel to practically every school! We have I think three small schools on one of the Islands of this field and some three or is it four where we have not been able to get, as it is right up among the Mts. and it would take an entire day in some cases to reach say sixty or seventy children. Of course we tell the old old story, and we give out simple tracts, and teach them the songs, that if properly understood, will lead to Salvation, and we have selected the most intelligible of all the songs we know.

Of Moderism, he writes: "I do wish that you could get ready for a real fight. For I believe that it is coming. I have felt it more than ever for the last four or five years. I think that Fosdick and his crowd will stop at nothing. We are all mixed up here, and while we have our Missions in separate organizations, there can not be the least doubt that the Liberals are strong enough now to show their hand, and it is not a question of "live and let live," but it has come to this, either get rid of these rats that are gnawing the bottom out of the ship, or we sink with them. There can be no middle ground. My own forecast is, that unless you at home stiffen up a bit, there will be nothing to show for your missionary efforts."

"As Dr. Patton said: 'we are not floating. We know where we are headed, and we are making for the port. We have not all the truth, but what we do have, is the truth, and further search is what we need, NOT a denial of what we have'!"

Of health: "except for the tremendous attack of neuralgia that Mrs. Moore had, we are as well now as we could wish to be, and tho the muscles tire a good deal quicker than they used to do, we are able to have four or five meetings a day, when we can get out."

Of results: "I have not had the super abounding number of results that every young missionary longs and works and prays for. There have been some, and we thank God and take courage. For there is a wide field, and many adversaries, and we find encouragement enough to keep as busy as can be."

"When I am tired, I like to sit and day-dream of how fine it will be to see you and yours in 1930. I honestly plan to spend more time with the classmates if they will allow me—to visit the churches for a few weeks before going South. In the fall of 1930, I plan to take Mason Edwards, named after Prinieton's great President, all the way from N. C. to Princeton to see the old college give Yale the biggest trouncing she ever had."

Note—Moore's letters are mighty interesting, and the Secretary will be glad to pass them on, upon request, as space here forbids more quotations. He plans to be with us in 1930.

MOOREHEAD—With us only in Junior year, writes from Banbridge, Co. Down, N. Ireland: "It is good to hear from you. What an attractive prospect, foregathering with my old Princeton classmates. But only a prospect, for distance and the calls of duty make attendance impossible. I shall be around the old Rabbi's house in thought and may catch heartening glimpses of the proceedings. Myself, a wife who takes good care of me, and a daughter who is lecturer in French at Queen's University, Belfast, make up the family circle. I have been in the ministry of the Irish Presbyterian Church all these years and have sought to the best of my ability to keep the old blue banner of Princeton unfurled. By paying special attention to the training of the young, I have the gratifying record of seeing all in the district over fourteen years of age enrolled in full communion and leading worthy lives. The roots of the faith were badly shaken before and after the war, but life is now practically normal again. I shall be delighted if any of the classmates who come to Wembley during the summer give me a call."

FRANK HYATT SMITH—"I came here for my wife's health in 1923. I am on a delightful place in a house 100 years old. We lived here before and I write and fill pulpits in the region about here. Am happy and contented and feel like Elijah when he dropped his mantle. I hope if you come this way, you will stop to see me. I don't get any younger but am spry at 66. Lost a brother who brought me up and my guide and counsellor and defender for fifty years. A big loss. But we are all moving on and Jerusalem looks good to me."

TROMPEN—"I had a sort of a vague hope that there might be a possibility of being at the Re-union this year, but know now that it will be impossible. My son, Nicholas, still lives in Brooklyn, N. Y., and is in the employ of the Brooklyn Edison Co. His son, Milton J. Trompen, was defeated in a wrestling match at Princeton not long ago. He is now a student at the Brooklyn Polytechnic. He may be the first grandson of the Class of '90. My second son, Harry, died five years ago. Twelve years, I was State Worker for the Congregational Churches of Colorado. Since the death of our son, I have been home. At prèsent, I am supplying a church twelve miles from Denver. We have a Dodge car, and in church work, make over 1000 miles every month. Added 44 members last year. We are hoping and planning to be at the next Re-union. So put our names down."

Thinking you would all be especially interested in Will Jessup, who died in Beirut, on Dec. 12, 1920, we quote from his two last letters, and add the Minute of the Board on his life and death.

From his letter of April 6, 1920, we read, "I was entitled to a year's furlough after nearly ten years of service in Syria. I had four and a half months in America, and have had five months here to rest after the hardest experiences of my life. Really I cannot describe to you these years. We were suspected of political propaganda by the Turks, who said our Relief Work was simply to win favor with the people of Syria to love America and to hate the Turks. We had no such designs, but the result of the work was as they described it.

When we had done all we could for the people with $50,000 per month and had given all our small income could possibly spare, we had to do as the Levite did, pass by in seeming indifference at times where the people were dying on the streets of hunger and typhus and exposure. Oh, it was dreadful, I hate to bring up these scenes. The nerve tension was too much to bear and keep strong.

Everything is kept hung in suspense here in Syria even now. France occupies this part of Syria and has her airplanes, tanks, armored cars, artillery and foot and horse here in an increasing strength. There is a great feeling of opposition to France."

His letter of July 15, 1920, was written from his summer home, called "The Heights" at Aaleih, Lebanon, Syria: "How I wish John Moore would return to Japan via Syria. Haw long before some classmate makes a trip to Palestine and makes me a visit! Here I am on a spur of Lebanon in a stone cottage belonging to me where I spend the summer. Beirut and the plain and seashore lie ten miles away and 2700 ft. below me. When the sun sets behind Cyprus, we can see it from our porch. There is a nice young growth of oak and ilex and pines on my lot and on the top of the hill I have a tennis court. My duties of Stated Clerk of the Mission have been returned to me and I have a good job to attend to once more. We are hoping for an advance in our work and are occupying new parts. We sadly need more ordained men. The political situation is going from bad to worse. How it will end is impossible to forecast."

Minute of the Board of Foreign Missions of the Presbyterian Church, in the U. S. A., December 20, 1921, as presented
by Dr. Stanley White

Dr. Jessup was ordained in May, 1890, by the Presbytery of New Brunswick, Dr, James McCosh giving him the charge. He continued to maintain his relationships with the American Presbyterian Church and at the time of his death was a member of the Lackawanna Presbytery. Dr. Jessup went to Syria as a regularly appointed missionary to represent the Board of Foreign Missions in November, 1890. In February of 1891 he was assigned to the station at Zahleh where he remained until 1915, devoting himself to the educational and evangelistic work of the station. In 1915 he was assigned to Beirut as professor in the theological seminary. Except for the purpose of his fhrloughs in 1899, 1908, 1913, and 1919, Dr. Jessup has spent the thirty years of his service in Syria.

His work in Zahleh was marked by efficiency and unselfishness, and even after he left there the influences which he started were potent in the upbuilding of the Syrian church. When visiting Zahleh in 1919 the writer found Dr. Jessup's name frequently mentioned by those whom he had served and who would never forget the kindnesses which he extended to those who were in need. In 1915 Dr. Jessup was transferred to the Beirut Station to take up the task of teaching in the theological seminary. His change of work, taking place as it did just as the world was being plunged into a turmoil of strife, the Mission found its theological work seriously interrupted. The men of Syria were taken into the army and gradually the student body was diminished until practically the seminary had to be closed and its buildings and esuipment turned over as the headquarters of the relief society. Ae the time of Dr. Jessup's death plans were being perfected for again opening the seminary and everyone was looking forward with eagerness to the new opportunity for training ministers for the advancing work of the Syria Mission. The Mission was relying upon Dr. Jessup to be the leader in this work particularly in preparing men fitted to deal effectively with the Mohammedan problems which have come as an outcome of the war. While Dr. Jessup was waiting for an opportunity to begin his theological work he became the Secretary of the Mission and his work there was marked with the same accuracy and thoroughness that always had been characteristic of him.

For some time Dr. Jessup's health has been threatened by bronchial trouble. It seemed to affect his heart. After his last visit to America in 1919 he returned with the consciousness that he must work under certain limitations, physically. However, his strong constitution and his inherited physical power warranted his returning, particularly as he was "going home" as he said. The particulars of his final sickness are not known as yet but intimations have come that the trouble which caused his death was a development of the sickness which attacked him when at home.

Such is the record of the details of his life. The record of his influence cannot be recorded. Born as he was in Syria and the son of cultured missionary parents whose lives were woven into the lives of the people, Dr. Jessup was peculiarly equipped for his task. By birth he was able to understand the Syrians' attitude and to see the problems from their point of view. The language was second nature to him. The customs were familiar to him and he had no thought except that Syria was his home. As he went from station to station he was received as a leader and as one whom the people turned to with confidence and trust.

REPORT OF TREASURER

Submitted May 11, 1925

RECEIPTS

May 1920....Balance on hand	$ 4.10
Dec. 1920....From McLean	1.00
Feb. 1923....From Whitaker	2.00
Dec. 1924....From Cummings and Paterson $1.00 each	2.00
Dec.-April 1925....Gibbons and Whitaker, $2.00 each..	4.00
Lynn and R. J. Campbell, $1.00 each	2.00
Thompson and McMillan, $2.00 each	4.00
Anderson $2.00, Levingood $3.00	5.00
Paton and Bannerman, $5.00 each	10.00
McLeod and Trompen, $5.00 each	10.00
Doughty $1.50, and W. H. P. Smith $1.00	2.50
Bryant	10.00
Total receipts ...$56.60	$56.60

EXPENDITURES

Printing bills (not including History) $18.50		
Postage and stationery 7.13	25.63	
Balance on hand ...$30.97		$56.60

John Moore Fund, of 1920

RECEIPTS

H. M. Campbell	$10.00
Adams $5.00; Polk $10.00	15.00
Wylie $15; McMillan $10	25.00
Cummings $2.00; Mr. and Mrs. Whitaker $10	12.00
Paterson $5.00; Gardner $5.00	10.00
McLeod $10; Warne $5.00	15.00
Paton $5.00; Gibbons $5.00	10.00
Mrs. Allen $10; Everitt $3.00	13.00
Bannerman $10; Hugh Miller $5.00	15.00
Thompson $10.00	10.00
Total ...$135.00	$135.00

EXPENDITURES

July 10, 1920 By N. Y. draft to him ...$110.00	
Aug. 10, 1920 By N. Y. draft to him 25.00	$135.00

John Moore Account, 1925
RECEIPTS

Cummings $5.00; R. J. Campbell $1.00	$ 6.00	
Dr. C. R. Erdman	30.00	
H. M. Campbell $5.00; Everitt $4.00	9.00	
Whitaker $10 and his church $20	30.00	
McMillan $20.00	20.00	
The Goodwill Presbyterian Church, per Thompson	80.00	
Total	$175.00	$175.00

EXPENDITURES

March 3, 1925 Sent him by N. Y. draft	75.00	
June 10, 1925 Sent him by N. Y. draft	100.00	$175.00

Note.—19 contributors this year out of 41. Where are the 22? This History is costing more than usual and will completely deplete the treasury unless more contributions are sent in. "S. O. S."

Report
Fortieth Anniversary
Monday, May 5th, 1930
Class of 1890
Princeton Seminary

CLASS MINUTE

The Class of 1890 held its fortieth Anniversary Re-union and Dinner at the Peacock Inn, 20 Bayard Lane, Princeton, on Monday evening, May 5, 1930.

Nineteen members of the Class were present, or one-half of those living, this, being the largest number at any Re-union since our graduation. These men were Adams, Bannerman, Henry Campbell, R. J. Campbell, Cummings, Everitt, Gardner, Gibbons, Levingood, McMillan, Hugh Miller, Moore, Parker, Paterson, Thompson, Voorhies, Warne, Whitaker, and Wylie. Of the One-Year men, Alexander was again present. Long distances were covered in reaching this Re-union, Moore and wife coming from Japan, Henry Campbell and wife from California, Adams and wife from Minnesota, and R. J. Campbell and wife from Canada, all except Moore, driving in by auto.

Our guests were the following wives of Class members, viz, Mrs. Adams, Mrs. Allen, Mrs. Bannerman, Mrs. Henry Campbell, Mrs. R. J. Campbell, Mrs. Cummings, Mrs. Everitt, Mrs. McMillan, Mrs. Moore, Mrs. Oates, Mrs. Parker, Mrs. Paterson, Mrs. Warne, Mrs. Whitaker, together with Miss McKinney, and the Rev. M. J. Hyndman, D. D., of Philadelphia, Mr. and Mrs. J. Clyde Foose, of Cranbury, Paul and Henry Bannerman, and Sidney Levingood, while as guests of honor, we again had Dr. and Mrs. Charles R. Erdman. 43 in all were present, with forty-one at the Dinner.

President Whitaker presided. A letter of regret was read from the Rev. J. H. Dulles, who was absent thro' illness. The roll was called, and each present answered as to any changes within the last five years. Dr. Erdman was heard, and then excused to attend other Seminary functions. Dr. Hyndman, Mrs. Allen, Mrs. Oates, and Mr. Foose were also briefly heard. Letters from absentee members were read by assignment to those present. The Secretary presented his report as Treasurer, showing a balance on hand of $11.30. He was instructed to print again a summary of the Class and its work during the last five years. Gardner, one of two lone bachelors surviving, gave the toast to the ladies. (Hugh Miller is the other.)

A pleasing innovation this year came in a surprise gift to the Class Secretary of a purse of $30.00, later increased to $54.50, in recognition of his forty years of service as Secretary. The presentation was made by R. J. Campbell, and warmly seconded by Henry Campbell, and Wylie. The Secretary responded in deepest feelings of appreciation, assuring the Class, it had been a real pleasure to serve so fine a body of men.

General discussion of our work followed for a season, after which Everitt closed with prayer.

The next Re-union will be held (D.V.) in 1935. We record grateful praise to the giver of all good for the fine spirit and fellowship of the gathering and the evidences of good health and continued vigor on every side.

Frank B. Everitt,
Secretary.

CLASS ROLL, 1930.

Name	Address	Occupation
Adams, Crofton Craig	Maple Plains, Minn.	Pastor
Anderson, Neal L.	25 W. Oglethorpe Ave., Savannah, Ga.	Pastor
Bannerman, William S.	Titusville, N. J.	Pastor
Bryant, Seelye	114 Trenton St., Pawtucket, R. I.	Rector
Bull, Kent M.	Kennett Square, Pa.	Farmer
Campbell, Henry M.	Stege, Cal.	Retired
Campbell, R. J.	Poplar Plains Crescent, Toronto, Can.	Retired
Carrington, Wilmot A.	Woonsocket, R. I.	Retired
Cummings, George M.	1628 T St, S. E. Washington, D. C.	Pastor, S.C
Doughty, James W.	819 15th St., Union City, N. J.	Pastor. (Ref)
Dunlap, Edward P.	Maryville, Mich.	Business
Eddy, George T.	Cape Vincent, N. Y.	Pastor
Everitt, Frank B.	Cranbury, N. J.	Pastor
Fraser, Fenwick W.	1600 Meadow Brook Ave. Youngstown, Ohio.	Retired, S. C.
Gardner, Murray H.	Brewster, N. Y.	Pastor
Gibbons, William F.	State College, Pa.	Teacher
Johnson, Andrew F.	316 N. Rowley St., Mitchell, S. D.	Gen Miss
Jungeblut, J. F.	407 Eden St., Lodi, Cal.	Pastor. (Ger. Ref)
Levingood, J. C.	Berwyn, Pa.	Pastor
Lynn, J. E.	Kitchener, Ontario, Can.	Retired
McLean, James T.	5112-31st. Ave, S. St. Petersburg, Fla.	Pastor
McLeod, Malcolm J.	1 West 48th. St. N. Y. City	Pastor. (Ref)
McMillan, John	239 Metropolitan Avenue, Atlantic City, N. J.	Pastor
Miller, Hugh	R. D. 2, Phillipsburg, N. J.	Retired
Moore, John	Takamatsu, Kagawa Ken, Japan	F. Miss.
Nelson, W. F. S.	1711 Grand Ave., Santa Barbara, Cal.	District Missionary
Parker, A. G.	Paw Paw, Ill.	Pastor
Paterson, A. McD.	Woodbury Heights, N. J.	Pastor
Paton, Lewis B.	359 Fern St. West Hartford, Conn.	Teacher
Remington, A. W.	R. D. 1. East Hampton, Conn.	Pastor
Smith, Frank Hyatt	31 Garrison Road, Williamsville, N.Y.	Retired
Smith, W. H. P.	R. D. 1. Wyoming, N. Y.	Farmer
Thompson, John H.	Montgomery, N. Y.	Pastor
Trompen, John N.	1095 Dallas St. Aurora, Col.	Pastor.(Cong.)
Voorhies, W. S.	Eddington, Pa.	Pastor
Warne, D. Ruby	730 Riverside Ave. Trenton, N. J.	Retired
Whitaker, Charles H.	8 E. Township Line, Jenkintown, Pa.	Retired
Wylie, S. Beattie	Franklin Apartm'ts, Wilmington, Del.	Retired

SUMMARY

Still in active pastorate (53%) 20
Retired, with occasional preaching 10
In Missionary work, home or foreign 3
In Teaching two; in Farming, two; in Business, one 5

                Total 38

Deaths since 1925 F. L. Fraser, MacGinness, and Carson 3
Total deceased of Class 19

AUXILIARY ROLL, 1930
(widows only, of members of Class.)

Name	Address	Occupation
Allen, Mrs. William	307 Kings Highway, East Haddonfield, N. J.	At home
Annin, Mrs. William A.	3715 McCausland Ave. St. Louis, Mo.	School Principal.
Baskerville, Mrs. H. C.	9260 California Ave. Seattle, Wash.	At home.
Erskine, Mrs. J. S. E.	Pine Bush, N. Y.	At home.
Fraser, Mrs. Frank L.	438 Magnolia Ave., Long Beach Cal., or Kennewick, Wash.	At home.
Heaney, Mrs. James	30 Highland Ave., Bala-Cynwyd, near Phila.	
Hedges, Mrs. Charles S.	Address unknown.	
Jessup, Mrs. William	Yonkers, N. Y. care of brother, Mr. Prime.	At home.
MacGinness, Mrs. C. E.	9 Madison Ave., Danbury, Conn.	Sanitarium.
Mason, Mrs. R. W.	1800 W. Bethune St. Detroit, Mich.	With son.
Oates, Mrs. Luther A.	Tarrytown, N. Y. care Castle School.	Matron.
Rankin, Mrs. Robert J.	60 Washington Ave, Berlin, N. J.	At home.
Williams, Mrs. James W.	Riverdale Country School, Riverdale-on-the-Hudson, N. Y.	Exec. Sec'y.

Mrs. Carson, Mrs. McCuish, Mrs. Phraner, Mrs. Polk, died as well as their husbands.

ROLL OF ONE AND TWO-YEAR MEMBERS, 1930

Name	Address	Year with us.	Occupation
Alexander, James A.	14 Emerson Ave. Crafton, Pittsburg, Pa.	Junior.	Miss. Supt., U. P.
Allison, Matthew G.	City Y. M. C. A. Madison Wis.	Jun. & Mid.	Univ. Pastor.
Barackman, Samuel P.	12 Tenth St. West New York, N. J.	Jun. & Mid.	Pastor (U. P.)
Bishop, Arthur F.	2240 N. Park Ave. Phila. Pa.	Junior	Evangelist.
Coffin, F. J.	112 Prince St., Charlottestown, P. E. I. Canada.	Jun. & Mid.	Retired
Gulick, Nelson J.	5025 Pulaski Ave Germantown, Phila.	Junior	Retired
Hays, Charles E.	Address unknown.	Junior.	
Heuver, Gerrit D.	Ipava, Ill.	Middle.	Pastor.
Hudnut, William H.	245 N. Heights, Youngstown, Ohio.	Jun. & Mid.	Pastor.
Latimer, Robert M.	Died March 2, 1918.	Junior	
Lippincott, Charles A.	Died March 14, 1929.	Junior.	
Macbeth, Roderick G.	335 11th West Avenue, Vancouver, B. C.	Junior.	Pastor.
Matthews, Paul C.	Princeton, N. J. Bayard Lane.	Junior	Epis. Bishop.
Moorhead, Joseph	Not located.	Junior	
Penrose, S. B. L.	515 Boyer Ave., Walla Walla, Wash.	Junior.	College Pres.
Phillips, David G.	Not located.	Jun. & Mid.	
Ricketts, Joseph B.	Died April 13, 1919	Junior	
Twinem, Leonard,	Wooster, Ohio.	Junior.	Retired

CHILDREN OF THE CLASS

The children of the Class are scattered far and near. It will interest all of the Class to know their home addresses and their work. So we give it in alphabetical order, with the hope that members of the Class will be interested enough in these children of '90, that if ever near them, they will give them a friendly call "for father's sake."

ADAMS
- (1) Rev. Arthur, pastor, Gibson City, Ill. No children.
- (2) Harold, electrician, 3830 Linden Ave., Seattle, Wash. Two boys.

ANDERSON
- (1) Margaret, wife of Legh R. Scott, pastor of First Presbyterian Church, Valdosta, Ga. Three children.
- (2) Ruth, wife of Alan S. O'Neal, Esq. Winston-Salem, N. C. Four children.

BANNERMAN
- (1) Harold, Engineer, Worcester, Mass., with American Steel and Iron Co., Aerial Tramway Dept. Has just been in Mexico, inspecting silver mines. In world war, army. One child, Edith.
- (2) Norman, head of Classified Advertising Dept., Morning Call, Allentown, Pa. In world war, army. One child, Virginia.
- (3) Paul, Trenton, N. J. Was with Murray Rubber Co., In world war, army. One child, Ethel.
- (4) Arthur, Studied law, now teaching in Asheville Farm School, N. C. In the world war, navy. Unmarried.
- (5) Henry, engineer, with the Bell Telephone Co., Trenton. At home, unmarried.

BRYANT
- (1) Lee, New Britain, Conn. Supervisor of teaching English in Junior High Schools.
- (2) Dorothy, Pawtucket, R. I., teaching English and Public Speaking.

BULL
- (1) Helen, Teacher, Westchester, Pa.
- (2) Anna, teacher at Teacher's College, Millersville, Pa.
- (3) Harriet, teacher, at Westchester, Pa.
- (4) Mary, teacher, at Kennett Square, Pa.
- (5) Edward C., student at Kennett Square, Pa.

CARRINGTON
- (1) Mrs. F. Earl Whitman, 219 Clarencedale Ave. Youngstown, Ohio, husband in employ of N. Y. Central, R. R.
- (2) Mrs. Oscar P. Lafere, Hinckley, N. Y., husband, a barber.
- (3) Elizabeth P., at home, employ of R. I. Hospital Trust Banking Corporation.

CUMMINGS
- (1) Florence, now Mrs. Fowler Dugger, Birmingham, Ala. Advertising agent for the Progressive Farmer, with a million circulation. Two sons.

- (2) Albert, Insurance, Des Moines, Iowa. One daughter, Barbara Jane.
- (3) Harold, Stock and Bond Salesman, Washington, D. C. Single, with parents.

DOUGHTY
- (1) Helena, wife of Reuben Peterson, Jr., 62 Chauncey St. Astoria, N. Y. City. Husband, newspaperman. Two girls.
- (2) John, 61 Chauncey St., Astoria, N. Y. City. Traffic Manager of New York Telephone Co.
- (3) Adaline, the blind daughter, living at home.
- (4) Richard, a defective, at Litchworth Village, Rockland Co., N. Y., in largest and finest home for defectives. A fine boy, but never will be over seven years of age.

EDDY
- (1) Alfred G. Port Washington, N. Y. Sales Representative.
- (2) Mrs. T. A. Sproull, N. Y. City. Sec. of N. Y. Academy of Medicine.

EVERITT
- (1) Kenneth, on staff of Farm School for Mountain Boys, near Asheville, N. C. Farm Supervisor. Married June 7, 1930, to Miss Carolyn Nelson, of teaching staff of Asheville Normal School for girls.
- (2) Helen, wife of J. Clyde Foose, now in Cranbury, N. J. Husband will enter Princeton Seminary in Fall. She is employed now in University Library, Princeton, N. J.
- (3) Donald, teacher of English, West Nottingham School for Boys, Colora, Md.

GIBBONS
- (1) Rebekah, Lincoln, Neb. Head of Division of Nutrition, School of Home Economics, University of Nebraska. Ph.D., from University of Chicago.
- (2) Eleanor, wife of Mason Olcott, Ph.D., Vellore, India. Supt. of Village Education, Dutch Reformed Church of America. One child.
- (3) Margaret, M. D., physician in Mary Lott Lyles Memorial Hospital, Madanapalle, India, North Arcot Mission, Ref. Dutch Church, U. S.
- (4) Frances, wife of M. A. Farrell, instructor in biology, in Lehigh University, Bethlehem, Pa.

JOHNSON
- (1) Julius Kenneth (Magaska), 304 Stratford Ave., Pittsburgh, Pa., Salesman for the Bessemer Cement Co.

JUNGEBLUT
- (1) Mrs. Henry F. Mettler, mother of seven sons and two daughters, living on a ranch, at Lodi, Cal.
- (2) Calvin, with two sons and three daughters, on ranch at Lodi, Cal.
- (3) Edna, wife of Dr. T. C. Rinder, three daughters, 315 Oak St., Lodi, Cal.
- (4) Laura M., at home.

LEVINGOOD
- (1) Sidney, Ph.D., Assistant Professor Dept. of Modern Languages, Princeton University.
- (2) Madeline, wife of John H. Stevens, Wayne, Pa. He is District Advertising Manager of Ladies Home Journal, Philadelphia, Pa.

LYNN
- (1) One daughter at home, active in church work.

McLEAN
- (1) Joseph T. at Annapolis, Md. In Aviation Service of U. S. Government.

McLEOD
- (1) Malcolm J. Jr., in School at Hackley.
- (2) Mrs. Jean McLeod Kennedy, wife of Robert E. Kennedy, One son, 425 East 51st., Street,New York City.

MOORE
- (1) John Watson, Principal High School, Winston-Salem, N. C. Two sons, two daughters
- (2) Wallace, teaching at Culver, Ind. One daughter.
- (3) James Erskine, teaching at Salisbury, N. C.
- (4) Eleanor, teaching at Kobe, Japan.
- (5) Boude Chambers, missionary at Kuru, Japan. Three sons, one daughter.
- (6) Lardner W., missionary at Gifu, Japan. Two sons.
- (7) Catherine Boude, living at Red Springs, N. C.
- (8) Bertha L., graduated from High School, Kobe, Japan, in June.

NELSON
- (1) William Franklin, the "Class boy" or first-born of the Class, Single, and at home, acting Secretary to father, active Legionnaire.

PARKER
- (1) John, teacher, Memphis, Tenn.
- (2) Rev. Albert G. Jr., Ph.D. President of Hanover College, Hanover, Ind. One boy, two girls.
- (3) Rev. Edwin G., missionary, A. P. Mission, Fatehgarh U. P. India. Has adopted son.
- (4) Malcolm, teacher, Memphis, Tenn. Two sons, one daughter.
- (5) Rev. Kenneth, missionary, A. P. Mission, Fatehgarh U. P. India. One son.
- (6) Donald, teacher, in Philippines, under Foreign Board. One daughter.
- (7) Elliott, teacher at Coffeyville, Kas. also medical student at Kansas University.
- (8) Norman, 852 Chalmers Place, Chicago, Ill., with the Continental Illinois Bank and Trust Co.
- (9) Beulah, graduated from Presbyterian College of Christian Education, Chicago, and now Director of Christian Education in Second Pres. church, Newark, Ohio.

PATERSON
- (1) Ruth, wife of John Mahon, New Bedford Mass. Florist.
- (2(Josephine, teacher in High School, Flint, Mich.

- (3) Jean, Assistant Superintendant Palmerton Hospital, Palmerton, Mass.
- (4) Elise, wife of Wm. Burd, Essex, Ontario, Can. Farmer.
- (5) Allan, with the W. T. Grant Co, Davenport, Iowa.

PATON
- (1) Only child, Suvia Lanice, wife of Arthur E. Whittemore, of the law firm of Nutter, McClennan and Fish, of Boston, Mass. Two children.

TROMPEN
- (1) Nicholas, 456-79th St., Brooklyn, N. Y. Supervisor of Brooklyn Edison. Has summer home at Morris Plains, New Jersey.

VOORHIES
- (1) Paul, Youngstown, Ohio. Agent for A. and P. Stores.
- (2) W. Sinclair, physician, Mendham, N. J.
- (3) Robert R. Auto insurance, Hartford, Conn.

WARNE
- (1) Helen, kindergarten teacher in her own home, Zanesville, Ohio.
- (2) Margaret, teacher of physical culture in schools of Johnsonburg, Pa.

WYLIE
- (1) Hugh, Providence, R. I.
- (2) Jeannette, married in Surrey, England.

CHILDREN OF DECEASED MEMBERS OF THE CLASS

ALLEN
- (1) William, 3rd. One girl. Westmont, N. J. At present out of work because of ill health.
- (2) Louis, Two children, boy and girl. Broker, with Munda & Winslow, N. Y. City. Winter home Plainfield, N. J. Summer home, Bay Head, N. J.

ANNIN
- (1) Pauline, wife of Manuel S. Galvarro, Bolivian Counsel in Chicago. Took A. M. degree from Columbia University, N. Y., and taught a few years before marrying. Has one son.
- (2) John, with the Real Estate Mortgage Trust Co., St. Louis, Mo. Married in 1926, and has two children.

BASKERVILLE
- (1) Julia, wife of Prof. Hensel, in Jamestown College, Jamestown, N. D.
- (2) Rev. Wm. E. 9260 California Ave. Seattle, Washington. In Metaphysical Library.
- (3) Rev. Robert, pastor Fauntleroy Congregational Church, Seattle. Lives at 9260 California Ave.
- (4) Rev. Arthur, 214 Summit Ave., Seattle, Wash. Five ministers in this family, two deceased, one a missionary to Persia, and Charles, by drowning.

CARSON
- (1) Donald, lives at 251-75th, St., Brooklyn, N. Y. married.

F. L. FRASER
- (1) Sibyl, married, living in Oregon.
- (2) James, in business in Alaska.

HEANEY
- (1) Only child, Spencer, was a mining engineer, in which he was very successful, but is now Assistant to the Vice President of the American Store Co. in Philadelphia, in the buying dept. Is married, has three children, and his mother lives with him. Address 30 Highland Place, Bala-Cynwyd, Philadelphia, Pa.

JESSUP
- (1) Theodosia, wife of Rev. Edward Thompson, now in Oxford, England. He was Chaplain to forces under Allenby, in Palestine, was a professor in India, and this year was exchange professor at Vassar College, where he lectured on the Indian Situation. Has two boys.
- (2) Elizabeth, wife of Kingsley Blank, X-Ray specialist at Watertown, N. Y., Hospital. Has two boys.
- (3) Helen, unmarried, living for awile at Poughkeepsie, to be near her sister, while visiting in this country.
- (4) Faith, wife of George Karhl, now finishing his studies at Graduate School, Princeton. Has been living in Princeton, opposite the Inn.
- (5) Marie, is finishing her course at Dobbs Ferry, N. Y.

MASON
- (1) Robert, Jr. is a physician, graduating from Rush Medical College, in Chicago, and now at the Henry Ford Hospital, in Detroit. Is married, and has his mother with him.

McCUISH
- (1) Helen, wife of Dr. Theodore V. Oltman, of Las Vegas, Cal, preparing to go as medical missionaries. She is a trained nurse, and has one daughter.
- (2) John B. Jr., is in Newton, Kas., on the staff of the Kansan Republican, a daily evening paper.
- (3) Anna Margaret is a Senior at Park College, lives at Newton, Kas. Their guardian is Miss Katherine McCuish, sister to our classmate, who lives in Newton, Kas.

OATES
- (1) Robert Luther, engineer, has been working on a water tunnel near Worcester, Mass. While working in California, found his wife.

PHRANER
- (1) Stanley, 615 E. 21st St. Brooklyn, N. Y. Four children. Until recently, Managing Editor of Wall Street News Bureau. Now in Europe.
- (2) Wilson, lives at 702 E. 19th St. Brooklyn, N. Y., is an active elder in the Central Presbyterian Church, member of Board of National Missions, Secretary-Treasurer, Baker & Williams Storage Warehouse, N. Y. City.

POLK
- (1) Rebeka, wife of Paul Dietz, lives at 5543 Minerva Ave. St. Louis, Mo.
- (2) James, married, living at Atlanta, Georgia.

RANKIN
- (1) Robert, after ten years in the consular service, has resigned. Not engaged in other work as yet.
- (2) Ella May, Company Secretary of Peacock Dahlia Farm. Dahlialand, N. J.
- (3) Helen E., teacher of English, at High School of Commerce, Springfield, Mass.

Brothers Henry Campbell, R. J. Campbell, F. W. Fraser, John McMillan, A. W. Remington, F. H. Smith, W. H. P. Smith, J. H. Thompson, and Charles H. Whitaker have not the joy of children of their own. Remington educated one boy, and Thompson, two, one of whom is now a lawyer.

BARACKMAN
- (1) Rev. Paul F. Barackman, 330 West Englewood Ave. West Englewood, N. J. Professor in the Biblical Seminary, in New York.

GULICK
- (1) Prof. Lee Nelson Gulick, Towne Scientific School, University of Pennsylvania, Philadelphia, Pa.

HEUVER
- (1) Eleanor M. teacher of history in Blackburn College, Carlinville, Ill.
- (2) Rev. Gerald Austin, pastor, Hanover, Ill.

HUDNUT
- (1) Dorothy, unmarried, at home.
- (2) Marjorie, wife of Jasper Coghlan, 540 Parker Street Newark, N. J.
- (3) Rev. Herbert Beecher, pastor Windermere Presbyterian Church, East Cleveland, Ohio. Three children.
- (4) Katherine, wife of Henry Bischoff, 18 Holmcrest Court, Oceanside, N. Y. One child, a son.
- (5) William Herbert, Jr., Student in Union Seminary, N. Y. Class 1930. Licensed by Presbytery of Mahoning, January, 1930.

PENROSE
- (1) Mary, wife of Paul Copeland, The Loleta, 916 University, Seattle, Washington.
- (2) Frances, Woman's University Club, Seattle, Washington. Training Director, Frederick and Nelson's
- (3) Clement, 338 W. Milford, Glendale, Cal. With Equitable Life Assurance Society, Los Angeles, Cal.
- (4) Nathaniel, The Normandie, Seattle, Washington. With National Bank of Commerce.
- (5) Virginia, 515 Boyer Ave., Walla Walla, Washington. Assistant to father.
- (6) Stephen, Jr. The American University, Beirut, Syria. Instructor in Physics.

SUMMARY

Of these children of the Class, 29 boys have married and 25 girls. Twelve boys are still unmarried and 22 girls, while of sixteen, the Secretary is uncertain. As these are all boys and no statement was given as to their families, they are presumably unmarried.

64 grandchildren are reported, as follows: 23 grandsons, 17 granddaughters and 24 unclassified (sex not given.) Jungeblut leads the Class with seventeen grandchildren; Moore, next with eleven.

The Class has sent nine into the ministry, Baskerville furnishing five, Parker three and Adams, one. Of these, seven are living. Of the one-and-two-year men, Hudnut has given two to the ministry, Barackman, one, and Heuver, one. Three girls have become wives of ministers or missionaries.

On the foreign mission field are eight representatives, three each from Moore's and Parker's family, and two from Gibbons.'. Two are on the Home field, and, in the same school, viz.: Arthur Bannermann and Kenneth Everitt, at Farm School, N. C. Stephen Penrose is at Beirut, Syria, teaching. Wilson Phraner is a member of our Board of National Missions. The former Helen McCuish is soon to go as a medical missionary with her husband.

Teaching is the favorite profession, no less than 24, being so engaged. Bull leads, with four girls teaching. One has reached the dignity of a College President, viz. Rev. Albert G. Parker, Jr., President of Hanover College, Ind. Rebekah Gibbons, Sidney Levingood, John W. Moore have reached enviable positions in that profession.

Only two boys and one girl have become physicians. Each boy is a namesake of his father, viz. Robert Mason, Jr., and W. S. Voorhies, Jr. The girl is Margaret Gibbons, in India.

Only one has taken up with' the latest profession of aviation, viz. Joseph McLean.

To one, and all, we extend our heartiest good wishes and assure them of an undying interest in their future welfare. Fellows, pass this on to your children.

RE-UNIONS.

1895—May 6, Nine present, viz, Whitaker, Trompen, Wylie, Parker, Levingood, Warne, Oates, Paton and Everitt. Mrs. Trompen also.

1900—May 7, 13 men back. Wives also. List was Adams, Mr. and Mrs. Everitt Mr. and Mrs. Gibbons, H. Miller, Oates, Mr. and Mrs. Parker, Mr. and Mrs. Polk, Remington, Thompson, Mr. and Mrs. Trompen, Warne, Whitaker and Williams. Also Kenneth Everitt and Donald Parker. Met at Mrs. Leigh's.

1905—Record Lost, if any meeting held. Does any one know?

1910—At Princeton Inn. Twelve men present, including Bannerman, Erskine, Everitt, Levingood, McMillan, H. Miller, Parker, Paton, Thompson, Warne, Whitaker and Williams As guests, we had Drs. Erdman and Davis, Dr. Phraner and his grandson, Wilson Phraner, Mrs. Erskine, and Beulah Parker. Everitt spoke for Class at Alumni Dinner.

1915—At Princeton Inn, May 3. Nine present, H. M. Campbell, Mr. and Mrs. Everitt, Gibbons, Levingood, Mr. and Mrs. Polk, Thompson, Warne, Mr. and Mrs. Whitaker, and Williams. Also, Sidney Levingood and Robert Baskerville, Thompson spoke for Class at Alumni Dinner. Mr. and Mrs. Bannerman and Wylie present next day.

1920—At Orange Inn, May 3, 17 men there, 25 in all. Mr. and Mrs. Whitaker, Mr. and Mrs. H. M. Campbell, Mr. and Mrs. Adams, Mr. and Mrs. Polk, Mr. and Mrs. Bannerman, Mr. and Mrs. Moore, Mr. and Mrs. Everitt, Mrs. Allen, Warne, Carson, Thompson, Gardner, Eddy, Frank H. Smith, Carrington, Parker, Wylie and Levingood. Next day, also Mr. and Mrs. Fenwick Fraser.

1925—Orange Inn, May 11. 12 men there, total 22. Mr. and Mrs. Whitaker, Mr. and Mrs. Everitt, Mr. and Mrs. McMillan, Mr. and Mrs. R. J. Campbell, Mr. and Mrs. Bannerman, J. A. Alexander, Parker, Mr. and Mrs. Thompson, Wylie, Gardner, Levingood, Mrs. Allen and Paton. Also Dr. and Mrs. Erdman, Dr. and Mrs. Davis, and Prof. Smith, Also Donald Everitt, Miss Hetzel and Miss Clingan, of Lewisburg, Pa.

GLEANINGS FROM THE QUESTIONNAIRE

The average age of the Class is now 68, and yet 23, or 60%, report their health, as good, some as fine, "never better", etc. Nine can only say, "fair", while but three are actually in poor health. Four failed to reply as to their physical condition. Heuver has had two very serious operations in last four years. Lynn has recovered from a foot disease. Mrs. Mason had accident which left her lame.

Ten have retired, or soon will. Seven are still under retiring age (65), and may be hailed as the "kids" of the Class. These are Adams, Bryant, R. J. Campbell, Carrington, Everitt, McMillan, and Moore. Twelve report themselves, as pensioned. More should be, if they take advantage of their newly-given rights.

The following changes have taken place in the last five years: six have retired, viz, Henry Campbell, Carrington, F. W. Fraser, Lynn, Warne, and Whitaker. Five have moved to new fields, viz: Eddy to

Cape Vincent, N. Y., Everitt to Cranbury, N. J., the home of his wife in early girlhood, and only five miles from his own boyhood home; Parker to Paw Paw, Ill., to be nearer his children; Paterson to Woodbury Heights, N. J., suburb of Philadelphia; and Remington to East Hampton, Conn. One (Bryant) has gone into the Episcopal Church, from the Congregational, and is a full-fledged Rector. However, the roving days of the Class seem to be over, as 27 are still on the same job in the same place.

Lynn is our "Patriarchus Maximus", reaching the golden eighties on Nov. 23, of this year. Mark the date, boys, and write him a line. Eight have passed the 70 line, but none are near Lynn.

Twenty-seven enjoy the luxury of a radio, Frank W. Fraser, having a Radiola 16, given him by the men of his church. Seven do not refresh their souls with such modern means. How they can stand, missing "Amos and Andy", deponent saith not.

Honors have not hurt the Class any in the past decade. Perhaps, we are all getting too old for that now. But Anderson was made Moderator of the Synod of Georgia, as well as of the Presbytery of Savannah, and was sent, as Commissioner, to his General Assembly this year. Cummings taught one-term course in the School of Religion at Howard University. George still reads his New Testament in Greek every morning, and is headed for a Greek professorship * * * somewhere. Hudnut received an L. L. D. in 1929, and MacBeth was similarly honored by the University of Manitoba. McLeod gave the Annual Alumni Dinner Address in 1929 and was President last year of the Alumni Association.

Publications are none too numerous by the Class. Gibbons has some "in prospect". You recall, his first book, "Black Diamond Men", was a great success. McLeod has issued, "Challenge of the Changing". Paton tops the list, with his prolific mind, and has published "Early Hebrew Ethics", "Ethics of the Hebrew Prophets", "The Evolution of Ethics" (edited by E. H. Sneath, Yale University Press, 1927). He also has given out the "Summaries of Archaeological News" in the American Journal of Archaeology, numerous articles in journals, as also articles in the New Standard Bible Dictionary, of 1926, and was lecturer at Summer School of Union Theological Seminary, in 1926. Penrose has issued a pageant, entitled "How the West was Won". MacBeth is a prolific writer, his latest book, being "The Print of the Nails", or "The Outside Challenge to the Church". Alexander issued a pamphlet for his Mission Board entitled, "Home Missions, the Beginning of the Enterprise". It was sent to all ministers and elders of the U. P. Church.

RECENT FAMILY CHANGES.

There are reported four new sons-in law, and four new daughters-in law, thirteen new grandsons, ten new granddaughters.

Marriages have been as follows; Paton was married, for the second time, on July 14, 1925, to Katherine Hazeltine, B.D., graduate of the Hartford Seminary, and Professor of Biblical Literature in Vassar College, Poughkeepsie, N. Y. Warne did likewise, on July 31, 1926, taking to wife Miss Nellie M. Wallace, of Trenton, N. J., where they are living most happily; while Jungeblut married on April 12, 1929, Mrs. Louisa Schinkenburger, of Lodi, Cal. Of the children of the

Class, Jeannette Wylie was married in January, 1926, to W. F. Field, of Leatherhead, Surrey, England, where they now reside; John Annin was married in June, 1926, to Miss Alice Henderson, while his sister, Pauline, was married the same year in September, to Manuel S. Gabarro, Bolivian Consul in Chicago; Kenneth Lawrence Parker was married on Dec. 22, 1926; Robert Mason on Aug. 23, 1927, to Anna Katherine Winne, of Denver, Col.; Helen Gladys Everitt on June 25, 1927, to James Clyde Foose, of Altoona, Pa; Donald Dean Parker, on Feb. 8, 1928; and Robert Luther Oates, on May 13, 1928, to Patricia Louise Careness, of Oakland, Cal. Faith Jessup married in June, 1929, George Kahrl, of Princeton; and Kenneth Everitt married on June 7, 1930, Miss Carolyn Nelson, of Asheville, N. C.

Others married during last five years but no dates given were: Alfred and Catherine Eddy, Frances Gibbons, Jean McLeod and Wallace Moore. Penrose had three children married in same time, and added three grandchildren. A good start. Macbeth had two daughters married. Parker had six grandchildren born and Moore had eight.

Deaths saddened the home as well, Levingood losing his beloved wife soon after our last reunion in 1925, with a granddaughter as well. Mrs. Alexander died on April 10, 1926, Warne's oldest daughter, Helen Insley, died. While in Japan, John Moore received the tragic news of the sudden death of his boy, Mason, named after our classmate, Bob Mason. He was studying in North Carolina, and died in an auto accident, when driving alone. Mrs. Barackman has also recently died.

THE CLASS AND PRESENT-DAY QUESTIONS

Opportunity was given the Class, if it chose, to express itself on some of the pressing questions of the day. Two of the questions bore on present conditions, and four referred to the future. The replies may be summarized briefly as follows:

ON PRESENT CONDITIONS.

1.—What is your candid opinion as to the ordination of women?

To this, seven gave unqualified assent, while fourteen opposed it, five were doubtful, one neutral, and rest non-committal.

Some oppose it as unscriptural; others, as displacing men; more, as unsought by the women themselves. Some are sure, it is coming, but see little practical good in it, unless it be in small rural churches.

Here are some of the comments: "Most of the women who qualify are likely to be more embarrassment than real help." "No serious danger, but no great success." "Not natural for men to look to women for leadership." "When men are Spirit-filled, women will not be needed in the ministry, but will be in demand, as mothers in Israel, in producing preachers and preparing men of merit for the ministry."

The optimist is heard in this: "One sees a great opportunity for women in the ministry in rural parishes." And this: "More able women will enter the ministry, because fewer professions are open to them, just as Y. W. C. A. leaders are conspicuously more able than Y. M. C. A. leaders." "Women rule the church, and ought to be in the pulpit. When she is, the pink teas will disappear, and Armageddon will come."

On the other hand, the pessimist is also heard, as follows: "The church is sufficiently feminized now." "A sign of the apostasy of the modern church." "A blunder, if not worse, from every point of view." "She is running the risk of losing much and gaining nothing."

Of our one-and-two-year men, most seem to favor the proposal. One would "leave it to the next generation," and one would "give them all to which they aspire."

II—What is the weak spot in religion today?

Some think this question is misleading, as there is NO weak spot in religion, it is all in the application of religion.

Seven declare that the weakness can be traced back to lack of faith; six point to a failure to apply the principles of religion to the daily life; "profession without possession." Five seem to think that the weak spot is in our mental attitudes, in a failure "to get hold of the real thing;" or in "too much thinking," or "piece-meal thinking;" or in "flabby training, craze for philosophy, psycho-analysis, etc,." while one frankly says: "the church is out of touch with modern thought and life," and so fails.

Several lay the blame on the leaders of the church, "the wabble of would-be noisy leaders;" "leaders who know not the Spirit of God." "Modernism in the pulpit."

Others declare it is the secondary place now assigned to religion; "not a major concern, only one of many interests;" and "insistence on the irrelevant and immaterial things." One says quite pointedly; "super-re-organization, and super-programs to the neglect of her Commission." Another laments its failure in Christian fellowship and love.

Other striking replies are: "the church is not converted;" "the weakness is in lack of parental control of children in the home." while another points to the lack of the vision of God, and a failure to realize the power of prayer." "Division of Protestantism, and eagerness of so many ministers for big salaries." "Too many fearful souls in and out of the ministry." "Too many pastors convictionless, passionless, fruitless." "Lack of sacrificial spirit." All of which reasons should move us to new searchings of heart.

THE CLASS AND QUESTIONS AS TO THE FUTURE

I—The future of Prohibition.

The general tone of the replies is hopeful, even enthusiastically so. Only one declares himself opposed to the Eighteenth Amendment —"always has been." One looks for some revision—perhaps "a happy medium." A warning is heard from the South in "direct action by the church as such, in the interest of sumptuary legislation retards rather than helps such great social movements." One expresses some fear of failure, but, outside of these, the replies are unanimous for the continuance of Prohibition, and are full of confidence of ultimate victory. Evidently the Digest poll did not reach our Class—nor men like us. One says: "it must succeed or our high-powered civilization will be wrecked." Another adds: "Retreat means a fifty-year setback." Another: "It is an American necessity under present conditions."

R. J. Campbell declares, the Canadian liquor-control system, a failure. Paton hopefully says, "it is bound to win ultimately, like the abolition of slavery, but it may take many years and there may be temporary setbacks." Remington saw only one drunk in a long trans-continental trip, and Adams, only one possibly tipsy driver in his auto trip east to the Re-union. He sees success, if we can return to temperance education and emphasis on law observance.

Two laconic and characteristic replies are worth noting: Gardner says, "good enough, if the decent are not irritated by the press into a 'kick-me-out-and-have-done-with-it' state of mind." Frank Hyatt Smith says: "sure to come, opposed by intelligentsia, modernists, and such. Preachers, too many, fear the ridicule of others, ought to put on the sword of Gideon, give up the use of cosmetics, and marshmallow apologies."

Let us all be stirred to new endeavor in this great cause by the knowledge of such solid support, as this Class gives.

II—The future of Princeton.

Upon the future of our beloved Seminary, it may surprise some to find almost universal optimism. Only two or three seem to be otherwise. Four might be classified as somewhat doubtful, yet "hopefully waiting." Perhaps the worst pessimist of all wrote in this vein: "I see no hope, unless they can get free from entangling endowments that prevent all teaching of modern thought," while another warning of a similar nature comes in "perils of reactionism are as deadly as the perils of radicalism."

Several base their hope on the new regime, and openly say so. A few citations may be of interest: "full of promise;" "Princeton has advanced steadily through all the years, and will continue to do so;" "It shall remain, as at present, our first denominational Seminary, orthodox, evangelical, aggressive." "As glorious as its past. It is sound, sane and successful." "All right, and will be better than ever." "Its rootage going back to 1746, and its steady growth through the long decades are prophetic of its splendid future."

A few other comments may be recommended to the new regime for consideration, viz: "not hopeless, if brains are imported and temperament excluded;" "Princeton will be O. K., when Presbyterians, who are 'born again' are the teachers." Will depend on the trend of religious thought, which has already affected Princeton, but I look for no further change;" "My sympathies are with the Fundamentalists, and if it prove true, that the new order of things in Princeton leans toward Modernism, I shall not hesitate to stand with the Fundamentalists;" "I know Erdman and his parents before him, and as long as men like him are there, Princeton will send out men who know how to preach the real gospel of Jesus Christ."

III—The future of Religion, in view of Radicalism.

The attitude of most of the men is, as one expresses it, "I am not worrying about it; "the gates of hell shall not prevail against it." Several affirm a well-known truth, viz, there has always been Radicalism, and Religion has survived. One says: "Radicalism is not the real trouble. It is money, prosperity, vastly increased pleasure." Another: "a church filled with the Spirit of God is the antidote." One quotes Matt. 15;3. "Faith will suffer much, but it will come thro the fire-testing purified."

Some of the more serious replies are: "the peril today is in the church' masking its attack under the guise of a gospel which is no gospel at all. If the popularly called Naturalism be true, there is nothing in Religion that makes it worthy of a future."

"Radicalism will not overthrow Religion until God is dethroned, and the thirst for God is rooted out of the human soul."

"The very Radicalism of the Radical will ultimately react toward true Religion." "The pendulum will swing back."

A worth-while saying comes from the West: "As a pre-millenarian, I do not look for the church to conquer the world, or save society. That is not her job. She is to bear witness to Jesus Christ. And this will be done."

The following may need a little exegesis from the writers: "The future is mighty promising, if Karl Barth will get an apologist of his own calibre for a partner." And "Calvin's cruiser rides serene among the confectioner's creations of Behaviourism, Hegelianism, and Mary Eddy's shallop."

One of the most suggestive replies is: "Denominationalism seems to me to be dying, but I have no fear for the future of religion. Out of the present scientific movement, I expect a re-birth of Christianity far more significant than the Protestant Reformation." Another, in like strain: "I think the tendency will be to base religion on the supreme doctrine of love to God and man, and the elimination of much dogmatic theology." (shades of Warfield!) Another: "religion will be more liberal."

IV— The Future of the Church.

The general feeling is hopeful and assuring. How could it be otherwise, in view of the promises of God? "Built on a Rock." What a refuge we have in Matt. 16:18! One exultingly shouts: "bright, brighter, brightest."

Nevertheless, an undertone of serious heart-searching is manifest." "The church represents Jesus indifferently." "Its future depends on itself." "The church today is having a hard time to convince the world, it is a church of the living God. That is not surprising when pulpit and pew confound the church with organizations, buildings, machinery of church work, in which the Lord is not interested."

That changes are coming, most foresee, "surprising changes." "But still there will be the church, as it is God-ordained, Christ-headed, and founded upon a Rock." "The church must be loyal to fundamental truth, yet learn how to adjust itself and teaching to modern conditions." "In the near future, the church will be more wealthy, more worldly, but in the distant future, glorious."

Among the changes that will come are: "stress will be laid on likeness to Christ, rather than creedal conformity." Several emphasize the trend toward church unity: "The church moves toward vital unity, and the trend toward organic union will increase the expression of unity and demonstrate to the world the larger values of the church. It is still the whitest thing on earth." "Denominations must unite, especially Presbyterian and Reformed." "An English prelate recently said: 'In one hundred years, there will be no Protestantism'. I think he has named too long a time."

A solid Princetonian says: "The Presbyterian Church has the best body of truth of all the churches, and when we preach what Christ and our fathers have given us, our church will always be victorious."

Perhaps the most penetrating and concisive answer comes from one who thinks, and thinks deeply: "I expect the rise of a new church, that will meet the needs and voice the worship of the new age more adequately than any of the antiquated existing sects."

And so we compass all sides of the question, from conservative to liberal. Enough to make us all think—and pray.

V—Optimism, or Pessimism, as to the future.

Of course, optimism by 18 to 1, and more! Only one seems fully persuaded of dire evils to come, and writes: "How can one be optimistic, when the family altar has broken down, the Bible is becoming an unknown book, and people are declining more and more to take responsibility."

One or two style themselves, "meliorists." One says: "an optimist of the type of Isaiah. (see Is. 28;16) Another would refer us to Luke 12;32. One calls himself, "rationally optimistic." Another says: "I was born an optimist, but I hope, not a fool optimist." Some seem to hang around No Man's Land, and are neither. "I am neither, as both are extremists. As to the immediate future, we are joy-riding in both church and state, with a telephone pole ahead. He who runs may read." "The near view makes me pessimistic, but the distant view, optimistic."

While it is refreshing to read, "I am optimistic, except on Mondays when I am tired." How very natural! So say we all of us.

IN MEMORIAM.

Record must be made of the death of three members of the Class since our last metting in 1925.

Frank L. Fraser.

This good brother of the far West passed to his reward just before our last Re-union, on April 30, 1925, at the age of fifty-nine years. Word was not received of it in time for that meeting, or for the printing of that history.

Fraser was one of ten Canadians in our Class, being next to the youngest, Johnson, who was born six months later. He was a graduate of Manitoba College in 1886. He served numerous fields in Canada, Minnesota, and California, until he finally settled in Kennewick, Washington. There, with his preaching, he also engaged in fruit ranching, and in educational matters.

Fraser was well beloved by all, his genial qualities showing themselves in good sportsmanship on the athletic field, while in the Seminary. He left a widow and two children. Mrs. Fraser divides her time between a sister in Long Beach, Cal., and her fruit ranch in Kennewick. The daughter is married, and lives in Oregon, and the son is in business in Alaska.

Charles E. McGinniss, Ph.D.

McGinniss died in Hoosic Falls, N. Y., on March 30, 1927, at the age of 62 years and six months. He had had some heart trouble for several years, diagnosed as enlargement of the heart, and the end came suddenly.

McGinniss was born in Joy, Ill., and graduated from Princeton University in 1887. He was ordained by the Presbytery of Troy on April 22, 1890. His first work was as Assistant Pastor in the Lansingburgh Church of Troy, of which he later became pastor in September, 1891. From 1899 to 1913, he served as pastor at Whitehall, N. Y., and from 1914 until his death, he was pastor at Hoosic Falls. His entire ministry, therefore, was spent in the one Presbytery of Troy.

Many years ago, after the death of his daughter, his wife lost her mind, and his care of her was most devoted and tender. She is now in the Sanitarium at Danbury, Conn., well provided for by his will, with such luxuries as a radio, and a good automobile, which she enjoys very much. The Manufacturers National Bank of Hoosic Falls is in charge of her estate, while her sister-in-law, Mrs. Helen B. Judson, looks after her personal needs and comforts. No children survive.

McGinness received the degree of Ph.D., from the University of New York in 1892. He lies buried in Woodlawn Cemetery, of Troy.

Robert H. Carson.

Carson was one of our youngest members, of winsome personality and brilliant mind. The Stated Clerk of his Presbytery, the Brooklyn-Nassau, says, he was the "best loved man in the presbytery."

His going was a great shock to all. His health had not been good for some time, due to prostate trouble, but in June, 1928, he was able to visit his brothers and sisters in Ireland. On his arrival there, he had to go to a hospital, but recovered sufficiently to make an early return home. In October of that year, he was operated upon, which operation seemed completely successful and he resumed his work. This was probably a wrong step, as he had not sufficiently recovered. For he soon had to go to the hospital again. His strength there seemed to gradually ebb away, influenza and pleurisy set in and on July 25, 1929, he died.

His wife had died March 17, 1929. One son, Donald Newlin, survives. He is now 27 years old, lives in Brooklyn, and was married on June 14, of this year, to Marie Elizabeth Cornwall.

Our sympathy goes out to all these sorrowing circles, and we pray God's richest and abiding comfort to be with them all in this hour of their deepest need.

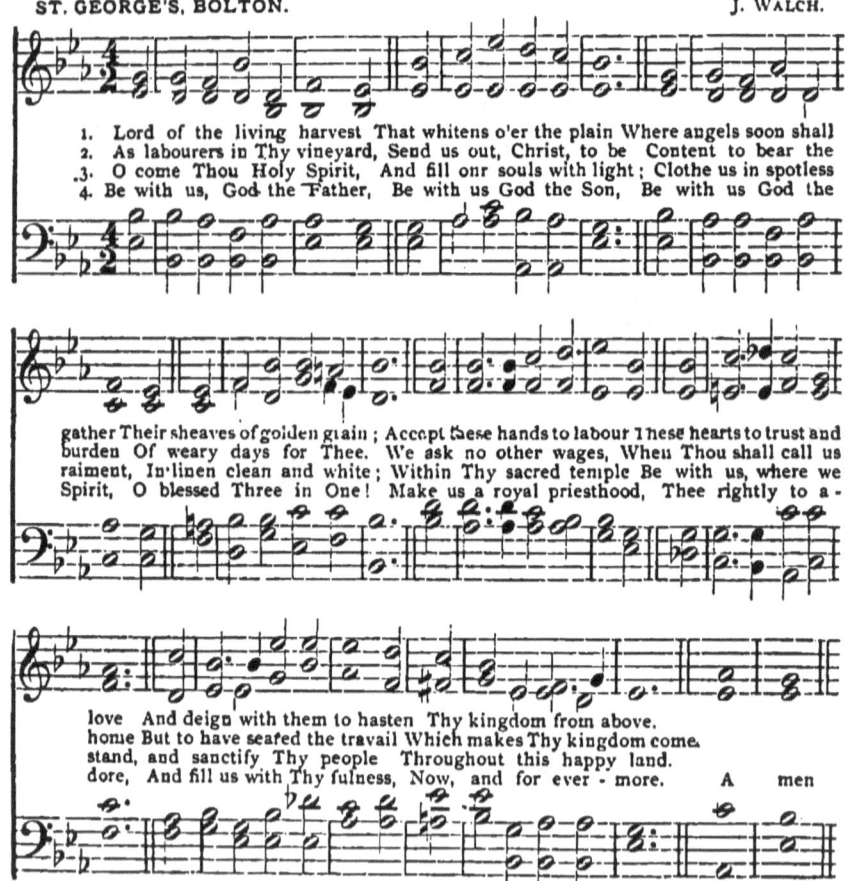

MESSAGES TO THE CLASS.

In this, the Secretary will depart from his custom hitherto, and give the name. He thought that the other answers would be of greater advantage if separated from any questions or suspicions of unorthodoxy. All the replies are kept on file, and will be available for any that may have a personal interest in them.

But these final messages of the Questionnaire are very personal, and we are glad to attach the sender's name to each.

ANDERSON—Come South, young man.

BULL—Greetings to all. I rejoice with rejoicing and weep with weeping. I Timothy 6;20.

R. J. CAMPBELL—Thy work is His. He'll reward to the end. Work with might and main. He will do the same.

CUMMINGS—I hope the closing days of life of each one may be the best.

DOUGHTY—A long life and continued prosperity, and the love of God and peace and contentment in life for every member of the old Class is my hearty wish.

EDDY—2 Thessalonians 3;16.

F. W. FRASER—Toil on, faint not!

GARDNER—Goodwill and good wishes.

JOHNSON—I am most grateful for the noble personnel of '90 and their good judgment in electing their Class Secretary. It is the genuineness of the fellowship that will characterize the Re-union dinner that I will so much miss.

LYNN—Please convey to the Class the love and respect of a warm heart, and one that never regrets his sojourn in dear, old Princeton. May God's blessings and smiles rest upon her while humanity lasts. May the Lord's richest favors be the portion of her sons and servants everywhere.

MACLEAN—Best wishes to all of the Class that is left.

McMILLAN—Wish we could all meet at this re-union. May we all meet in the great church above, saved by the grace of Jesus Christ, our Lord.

NELSON—Tell the boys I am still working in the oil fields, have ten points where I preach, and ten Sunday Schools. Hope to hold on until the great Class Re-union. Tell the fellows I will be with them in spirit and only wish I could be there in person. I think of them all as the best fellows I ever knew, and am proud of their lives and records. May God bless and keep them all and may we all serve Him for many years yet.

PARKER—Always interested in the activities of classmates, and send greetings, hoping that their service for the Kingdom will long continue to bear a rich fruitage.

PATERSON—Nothing more than that the present calls for men of clear heads, pure hearts, and courageous souls. We need men who will go to the stake for Jesus Christ, if necessary.

REMINGTON—The heartiest greetings and best wishes. Wish I could be at the Re-union, but adversity smiles upon me, and I grin back and hope for better things some other time.

FRANK HYATT SMITH—Best class since Reformation. When I have a church again, I will hang a ribbon of orange and black at the lecturn, and put the purple in the waste basket. Keep away from Episcopalians, and Baptists, and Unitarians. Pound out Patton's theology in a new dress, and let the galled jades wince. Keep away from all seducers and penny fathers. Beecher could have coughed up more ability than resides in 33 presbyteries.

W. H. P. SMITH—Remember we are not responsible for what happens, but for what we preach and what we teach and how we live.

TROMPEN—My prayer and best wishes to all.

VOORHIES—Best wishes.

WARNE—Mizpeh, and "God be with you till we meet again."

MACBETH—I have most kindly memories of the Class. My message would be, the text of Dr. Patton's on the 100th anniversary (which I attended,) viz, "Earnestly contend for the faith, once delivered to the saints." That is the worth-while work.

HEUVER—I am trying to reproduce in my life the spirit of Jesus, and am working hard to get people to follow Him. I have the dearest wife and children.

Other messages were given in person at the Re-union, and some failed to send any.

TOURING WITH THE CLASS OF '90.

What car? Well, make your own choice. The reliable Ford is the Class Favorite, with five using it, viz, Heuver, Moore, W. H. P. Smith, Voorhies, and Whitaker. But the Oldsmobile with three, viz, Everitt, Levingood, and Warne; the Dodge with three, viz, Gardner, Nelson, and Trompen; the Chevrolet, with three, viz, Adams, Bryant, and Johnson; and the Buick, with three, viz, H. M. Campbell, R. J. Campbell, and F. W. Fraser, are pressing it close. Thompson and Remington are almost in a class by themselves, as they swear by the Franklin, as will also McMillan and Penrose, by the Packard. But other cars are heard from in Anderson for the Essex, McLeod for the Chrysler, Wylie for the Nash, Hudnut for the Hudson (a new Brougham). What more can we offer you? We may be conservative in our Theology, but we are very liberal in our offer of a choice of machine. Some fellows are wise * * * and have none. Frank Hyatt Smith says: "remember Elijah."

Now, why not hit the trail for an "over-night" with the fellows? Why not R. J. Campbell, in Toronto (who drives a new car every time he comes to Princeton, because he has to have something new in that town), pick up our gracious Lynn in Ontario, and together leave the King's dominions for the time, and ramble thro the States. Of course, they will start in New England as all good pilgrims did, and do, touching on the way, however, Eddy, at Cape Vincent, N. Y. up near their Canadian border. They will find Bryant, with latch-string out, in Pawtucket, R. I., and perhaps Carrington nearby at Woodsocket, if he has not moved by that time to his new home in the south. Over in the Nutmeg State (Conn.) is Lew Paton at Hartford, and Remington at East Hampton, while Mrs. MacGinness is at Danbury.

The busy metropolis has little time for tourists, yet has many, and you may get McLeod's ear for a moment by phone, or call at 1 West 48th St; or run out into the suburbs, up into Westchester Co., or beyond, to Gardner's bachelor domicile, or to Thompson's hospitable country home in Orange Co., where your machine * * * mental, of course * * * will most likely break down with his logic; or still further, on to our farmer-preacher, W. H. P. Smith, at Wyoming, N. Y. Nor must we forget Mrs. Jessup at Yonkers, Mrs. Oates at Tarrytown, and Mrs. Williams at Riverdale. The beautiful shores of the Hudson will soon be the haven of all our good women, and they could not choose better. Mrs. Erskine is near Thompson at Pine Bush.

In the "wettest State in the Union", you will find here and there an arid spot * * so we hope. Doughty, in Union City, N. J., Barackman at West New York, N. J., are near enough to New York to be "moist", but we trust not. If they are, come on over to your Secretary's home, and big verandah, at Cranbury, just half-way between New York and Philadelphia, and only nine miles from Princeton itself; or to Warne's at Trenton, and Bannerman's at Titusville, only ten miles above. A detour north would reach Hugh Miller, near Phillipsburg. Paul Matthews is the only one who had nerve enough to settle in Princeton itself where he keeps close to Henry VanDyke next door, and directs the work of the great Episcopal Church, as its Bishop for the State. Just over the line from Trenton is Voorhies at Eddington, Pa. Below him you can cross the Delaware by bridge, and head for South Jersey, where you will find Paterson at Woodbury Heights, Mrs. Allen at Haddonfield, and Mrs. Rankin at Berlin, while on the sunny strands of Atlantic City, you will find the most genial host and hostess of all, John McMillan and his good wife.

The City of Brotherly Love (ask the Philadelphia Presbytery!) cannot but be inviting, with Whitaker and Levingood, and Bishop and Gulick, all within its limits. If the "blue laws" are not broken down by that time, it might be well to spend a Sabbath there. Bull, at Kennett Square, not far away, would later carry you over "Blue Monday" with fresh milk from his dairy.

From Philadelphia, two routes call you; one to the southland, in which case, you can enjoy Wylie's Irish humor at Wilmington, sup with George Cummings in the Capital City of Washington, and then "step on the gas" for a long run over fine roads to "reminisce" with Anderson, in Savannah, and see his wonderful church plant, and then finish up with McLean in the balmy sun of Florida at St. Petersburg.

Or from Philadelphia, take the western trail, not forgetting Gibbons at State College, Pa., nor Alexander, at Pittsburgh. The Buckeye State of Ohio holds for you F. W. Fraser and Hudnut in Youngstown, from which a short detour north to the vicinity of Buffalo will bring you to Frank Hyatt Smith and his witticisms, at Williamsville. Thence, you skirt the shores of Lake Erie to visit Mrs. Mason in Detroit, living with her son, and hunt up "Dunnie" at Maryville, Michigan, and hear again his thrilling "ladder story."

Taking up again the trail westward, you come upon Parker at Paw Paw, Ill. and Heuver, at Ipava, Ill. You can pass by Chicago, the "payless" city, in detouring north to call on Allison, at Madison, Wis., and Adams among the beautiful lakes of Minnesota at Maple Plains. Still further is Johnson, our Indian missionary, at Mitchell, S. D. Retracing, we find Mrs. Annin in St. Louis. Amid the towering

Rockies, we have one lone representative, Trompen, at Aurora, Col., who holds the record for automobile endurance in having run his Dodge car, 156,920 miles. Think of it, you poor fellows, with your 10,000, etc!

Facing the glories of the setting sun, in the mellow atmosphere and sunshine of lower California, we find Nelson at Santa Barbara. Stege, across the bay from 'Frisco, will welcome you to Henry Campbell's comfortable home. Jungeblut is at Lodi, in the same State. Mrs. Baskerville is at Seattle, Mrs. Frank Fraser at Kennewick, Penrose at Walla Walla College, all in the State of Washington. A few miles further on, we come to the end of the trail with MacBeth, in Vancouver, B. C. Thence, our Canadian pilots can find their way back to their Eastern Canadian homes as best they can. But they must first stop long enough to kowtow to Moore, via cable, and tell him, that they have either missed the boat to Japan, or their money has run out.

So endeth the story. But what these * * or any other fellows * * found out from their classmates en route wouldn't go in any book yet written. Who will be the first to try it out? Carrington is soon to travel across the continent. Maybe this will help him. Look up all addresses in the rolls elsewhere in this history. Henry Campbell drove over from California to the Class Re-union, as did also Adams from Minnesota, and R. J. Campbell from Toronto. All enjoyed it. Moore, without auto, visited many of the fellows on his journey east, and is very grateful for their hospitality and advises more fellowship of this character among the Class. Why not be increasingly sociable to the end? Drive up, open up, speak up, and all will feel better for it.

TREASURER'S REPORT

CLASS OF 1890.

In account with Frank B. Everitt, Secretary-Treasurer.

RECEIPTS

To balance on hand	$8.82	
From Cummings	1.00	
From W. H. P. Smith	1.00	
From Nelson	1.00	
From Bannerman	3.00	
From Whitaker	5.00	
From Alexander	5.00	
From Eddy	3.00	
Total	$27.82	$27.82

EXPENDITURES

Printing Christmas postals	$4.00	
Printing Questionnaire	6.00	
Printing postal notices	2.50	
Postage and Telephone	4.02	
Balance on hand	11.30	
Total	$27.82	$27.82

CLASS HISTORY ACCOUNT

From Johnson	$2.00
From Trompen	2.00

CLASS NOTICES

Copies of preceding histories of the Class can be secured of, the Secretary, upon request, free of charge, especially the silver anniversary number of 1915.

Th Secretary has reserved not a little data, sent him by members of the Class, as to their children. This will be kept on file for future use, if the way opens.

As the roll of widows increases, it is becomingly increasingly difficult to locate these, and the Secretary would greatly appreciate notices of removal, death, etc. We have been unable to locate Mrs. Hedges who married again after her husband's death.

Note this especially! Will the members of the families of the men, now living, promptly notify the Secretary of the death of any member of the Class, and the time of the funeral. He will then, in turn, notify members of the Class, especially those near at hand, so that, if at all possible, the Class may be represented at the funeral. This can only be done however, when there is full co-operation by the family of the deceased. He would also appreciate a letter from some one of the family giving some particulars about the last illness and death, all of which would be filed for the next issue of the Class History.

☞ The cost of this publication is met by voluntary contribution. ☜
It is the wish of the officers that every widow of the Class should have a copy. The cost of this issue of sixty copies is $122.20. A balance is on hand now of $10.20, leaving $112.00 to be raised to cover all bills, with no money in the treasury for postage &c., up until 1935. Figure out for yourselves what each of 38 members should give to ease the mind of the Secretary-Treasurer, and let your checks come promptly. For he, wants his credit good with the printer. The three cuts have added not a little to the cost, but your Secretary thought they should be preserved, Extra copies of the Class Hymn have been printed on separate sheets for future Re-unions, or will be mailed on application.

Now, please, fellows before you forget it, mail a check of not less than two dollars—and as much more as you can—to your Secretary to pay ALL bills. No more appeals until 1935.

If Class funds warrant, and data is sufficient, the Secretary would like to issue each year in April, a brief summary of Class news, together with the Commencement program of that year. He hopes to meet many of you each year at Commencement, and also in his home. Make Cranbury, your headquarters.

The Class officers wish to thank all for their hearty co-operation, and for the fine spirit all have manifested in the work and life of the Class.

CHARLES H. WHITAKER, President,
Jenkintown, Pa.

FRANK B. EVERITT, Secretary,
        Cranbury, N. J.

OUR FACULTY 1887-1890

THE PRESS
CRANBURY, N. J.

HISTORY

CLASS OF 1890

PRINCETON SEMINARY

FORTY-FIFTH ANNIVERSARY

—o—

MAY 1935

CLASS MINUTE

The Class of 1890 held its 45th Re-union Dinner at the Peacock Inn, Bayard Lane, Princeton, on Monday, May 13, 1935.

Those present were Adams, Mrs. Wm. Allen, Henry Campbell, Mr. and Mrs. R. J. Campbell, Mrs. Eddy, Mr. and Mrs. Everitt, Mrs. J. C. Foose (daughter of Everitt), Levingood, McLeod, Mr. and Mrs. McMillan, Mr. and Mrs. Paterson, Thompson, and Mr. and Mrs. Warne —eighteen in all.

The Secretary announced the death of our beloved Class President, Charles Whitaker, on January 2, 1934. The Class expressed its deep sorrow and instructed the Secretary to convey to Mrs. Whitaker its sympathy.

McLeod was elected Chairman of the meeting.

The Secretary read his report, which was received, and ordered printed, with such additional data as may be of interest to the Class. It was decided, until further notice, to meet every two years, instead of five, with the same dinner arrangements as we have enjoyed at reunions. The following Class Officers were then elected: President, M. J. McLeod; Vice-President, Henry M. Campbell; Secretary and Treasurer, F. B. Everitt. The Class again expressed its appreciation of the work of the Secretary in a substantial gift, which was gratefully acknowledged by him. He reported a balance in the treasury of $12.98.

The members then spoke of their present work and it was a real pleasure to hear from Mrs. Allen and Mrs. Eddy, widows of our deceased brothers.

The meeting closed with prayer by Henry Campbell.

FRANK B. EVERITT,
Secretary.

CLASS ROLL, 1935

ADAMS, CROFTON CRAIG..........Maple Plains, Minn...........Pastor
BRYANT, SEELYE.......114 Trenton St., Pawtucket, R. I........Rector
BULL, KENT M...........Kennett Square, Pa...........Dairy Farmer
CAMPBELL, HENRY M.......330 S. 16th St., San Jose, Cal.......Retired
CAMPBELL, R. J.....74 Poplar Plains Crescent, Toronto, Can.....Retired
CARRINGTON, WILMOT A....420 Magnolia Ave., Orlando, Fla....Retired
CUMMINGS, GEO. M., 1628 T St., S. E., Washington, D. C., Supply, S. C.
DOUGHTY, JAMES W.......819 15th St., Union City, N. J.......Pastor
DUNLAP, EDWARD P.............East Jordan, Mich............Business
EVERITT, FRANK B.............Cranbury, N. J.............Pastor
FRASER, FENWICK W., 1665 Meadowbrook Ave., Youngstown, O.
Retired, and S. C.
GARDNER, MURRAY H..............Brewster, N. Y..............Pastor
GIBBONS, WM. F..............State College, Pa..............Professor

JOHNSON, ANDREW F....316 N. Rowley St., Mitchell, S. D....Miss. Supt.
LEVINGOOD, J. C..................Berwyn, Pa..................Pastor
MCLEAN, JAMES T.....5112-31st Ave.,S., St. Petersburg, Fla.....Pastor
MCLEOD, MALCOLM J...Cedar Knolls, Bronxville, N. Y...Retired, P. Em.
MCMILLAN, JOHN..239 Metropolitan Ave., Atlantic City, N. J...Pastor
MILLER, HUGH...........Phillipsburg, N. J., R. D. 2..........Retired
MOORE, JOHN.......Takamatsu, Kagawa Ken, Japan.......For. Miss'y
NELSON, W. F. S.....1711 Grand Ave., Santa Barbara, Cal.....Miss'y
PARKER, A. G....1010 Third Ave. and 10th St., Mendota, Ill...Retired
REMINGTON, A. W...........Portland, Conn., R. D. 1..........Pastor
SMITH, W. H. P................Wyoming, N. Y.................Farmer
THOMPSON, JOHN H..........Montgomery, N. Y., R. D..........Pastor
TROMPEN, JOHN N.........1095 Dallas St., Aurora, Col........Pastor
WARNE, D. RUBY......730 Riverside Ave., Trenton, N. J......Retired
WYLIE, S. BEATTIE......280 Slater Ave., Providence, R. I......Retired

SUMMARY

Number in Class at graduation 57
Deceased members 29
Living members 28
    As follows:
    In active service: Pastors, 11; Missionaries, 3; Supply 1....15
    Retired from active service 9
    Other vocations: farming, 2; teaching, 1; business, 1....... 4
                                                   — 28

AUXILIARY ROLL, 1935
(widows only, of members of Class)

ALLEN, MRS. WILLIAM..307 Kings Highway, Haddonfield, N. J. Home
ANNIN, MRS. WILLIAM, 375 McCausland Ave., St. Louis, Mo., Sch. Prin.
ANDERSON, MRS. NEAL L., 1622 W. First St., Winston-Salem, N. C.
                                                                                 With daughter
BANNERMAN, MRS. WM. S............Titusville, N. J...........Home
BASKERVILLE, MRS. HENRY C., 3804 Edmunds St., Apt. G., Seattle, Wash.
                                                                                             Home
EDDY, MRS. GEORGE A. T...Merriam Home, Newton, N. J...Pres. Home
FRASER, MRS. FRANK L., 605 Catherine St., Walla Walla, Wash.
                                                                                  With daughter
HEANEY, MRS. JAMES, 30 Highland Ave., Bala-Cynwyd, Pa., With son
JESSUP, MRS. WILLIAM.....50 A. Locust Hill, Yonkers, N. Y......Home
JUNGEBLUT, MRS. J. F......407 Eden St., Lodi, Cal......With daughter
LYNN, MRS. JOHN E., 256 Frederick St., Kitchener, Ontario, Can., Home
MCGINNESS, MRS. CHAS. E., Care of Manufacturers Bank, Troy, N. Y.
                                                                                                Traveling

OATES, MRS. LUTHER A., Kent Place School for Girls, Summit, N. J.
House-mother
PATERSON, MRS. A. M...672 Rockdale Ave., New Bedford, Mass...Home
PATON, MRS. L. B......359 Fern St., West Hartford, Conn......Home
RANKIN, MRS. R. J................Berlin, N. J................Home
SMITH, MRS. FRANK HYATT, 217 E. Delavan Ave., Buffalo, N. Y.
Luth. Home
WHITAKER, MRS. CHAS. H...514 Cheltena Ave., Jenkintown, Pa...Home
WILLIAMS, MRS. JAMES W., 3615 Greystone Ave. Riverdale, N. Y., Home
VOORHIES, MRS. WM. S............Mendham, N. J............With son

ROLL OF ONE AND TWO-YEAR MEMBERS

ALEXANDER, JAMES A., 14 Emerson Ave., Crafton, Pittsburgh, Pa.
Miss. Supt. U. P.
ALLISON, MATTHEW G.............Madison, Wis.............Retired
BARACKMAN, SAMUEL P., 12 Tenth St., West New York, N. J.
Pastor (U. P.)
ERDMAN, CHARLES R.........Princeton, N. J.........Prof. Seminary
HEUVER, GERRIT D...............Rockford, Ill...............Retired
HUDNUT, WILLIAM H......245 N. Heights, Youngstown, O......Pastor
MATTHEWS, PAUL.....Bayard Lane, Princeton, N. J......P. E. Bishop
MONTGOMERY, THEO. E.....Mercer House, Ambler, Pa.....Pres. Home
PENROSE, S. B. L....Whitman College, Walla Walla, Wash...Professor
No word has come from BISHOP, COFFIN, or GULICK.

CHANGES NOTED IN QUESTIONNAIRE

CLASS MEMBERS

PARKER, A. G., to Mendota, Ill.
CAMPBELL, R. J., to 74 Poplar Plains Crescent, Toronto, Can.
CARRINGTON, W. A., to 420 Magnolia Ave., Orlando, Fla.
HEUVER, G. D., to Rockford, Ill.

CLASS CHILDREN

ADAMS, HAROLD C., electrician, to 7021 16th Ave., N. E., Seattle, Wash.
ALLEN, WILLIAM, JR., to Haddonfield, N. J.
ANNIN, Pauline, or Mrs. Galvarro, husband died Dec. 20, 1933, now teaching in the National College of Education, Evanston, Ill.
John, in St. Louis, with the St. Louis Investment Co.
BANNERMAN, Harold, in Mexico.
Arthur and Henry, married, latter in Titusville, N. J.
BASKERVILLE—Julia—widow of Prof. Hensel, now dean of women and teacher in Jamestown College, N. D. One daughter.

William E.—pastor of Pres. Church, Groton, S. D. Two children.

Robert (Rev.), studying for Ph.D. in the University of Washington in Seattle. Two sons.

Arthur an Analytical Psychologist, practising at 1514 Bellevue Avenue, Seattle.

BULL, Harriet, married James W. McFarland, teacher, in Downington, Pa., on July 5, 1930. William, born May 15, 1931.

CARRINGTON, Mrs. F. Earl Whitman, 205 E. Phila. St., Whittier, Cal. Husband in real estate.

Ruth H., and Elizabeth P., at home, in beauty parlor work.

CUMMINGS, Mrs. Fowler Dugger, now at 30 Sherwood Avenue, Pelham Manor, N. Y.

Harold G., married July 3, 1932, to Anna Pauline Adams. Harold George, Jr., born July 14, 1934. In Farm Credit Administration Work.

EVERITT, Kenneth, with Graham School (orphanage), Hastings-on-the-Hudson, N. Y.

Helen, wife of Rev. J. C. Foose, in pastorate at Pottsgrove, and Mooresburg, Pa., near her old home in Lewisburg.

Donald, married, teaching Senior English in High School, Woodbury, N. J.

FRASER, Sibyl, daughter of Frank L., married and living in Walla Walla, Wash. Barbara, born 1930, Donald, 1932, and Kathryn, 1934.

GIBBONS, Margaret, a doctor at the Christaluka Ashram, Tirupattur, India. All workers serve without pay, live as one family and dress in native costume. No fees charged, and clinics always crowded. In one day, when in charge, she had cases of leprosy, cholera, and bubonic plague. Very happy in her work and very successful.

Eleanor at Vellore, India, wife of Rev. Mason Olcutt, in a hard climate.

Frances, wife of Prof. A. M. Farrell, bacteriologist in State College, Pa., at home with her father, has three children.

HEDGES, only son, Charles L., lives at 119 Henderson St., Marietta, Ga.

JESSUP, Theodosia, wife of Edward Thompson, Oxford, Eng. Two boys.

Elizabeth, wife of Kingsley Blake, X-ray specialist, 155 Webster Ave., Scarsdale, N. Y. Two boys and a girl.

Helen, in Hartford, Conn.

Faith, wife of George Kahrl, temporarily in Waltham, Mass.

Marie, after studying for two years dramatics in London, is at home with her mother, in Yonkers, N. Y.

JUNGEBLUT, Mrs. Erna Mettler, on ranch, near Lodi, Cal. A new son, making a family of eight sons and three daughters.
LEVINGOOD, Madeline, wife of J. H. Stevens, now at Ithan, Pa. A son, Martin H., was born on June 21, 1931.
MCCUISH, Helen, wife of Dr. Theodore V. Ottman, a medical missionary in Amoy, China.
> Anna Margaret, dietician in N. Y. Hospital, and Cornell Medical College.
> John B., Jr., manager of the Harvey Co. News, Newton, Kans. Their aunt, who was appointed guardian, died last year.

MASON, Robert, Jr., a specialist in children's diseases, lives at 5140 Second Ave., Detroit, Mich.
MCLEOD, Malcolm, Jr., in school at Phillips Exeter, Mass.
> Mrs. Jean Kennedy, in New Canaan, Conn. Two boys and a girl.

MOORE, John Watson, Jr., Supt. of Education, Winston-Salem, N. C. Baby boy died soon after birth.
> Wallace, at Palo Alto, Cal., in post-graduate work. Two daughters, second born Oct. 1934, named Margaret Anne.
> Eleanor, Assistant to Principal, Canadian Academy, Kobe, Japan. Returns next year.
> James Erskine, pastor of Mt. Washington Presbyterian Church, Baltimore.
> Catherine, teaching mathematics in Salisbury, N. C. H. S.
> Lardner, missionary at Toyohashi, Japan. Three sons, one born March, 1934.
> Bertha, in Nurses College, Johns Hopkins, Baltimore, Md., training for medical missions.

OATES, Robert Luther, working as an engineer in Washington, D. C., in construction work, electric tunnels, building excavations, etc. Married.
PARKER, Donald, after six years in Philippines, now home on furlough.
> Norman, in the University of Chicago.
> Beulah, wife of Mrs. James W. McMillan, Hamilton, Ill. One son.

PATERSON, Jean, now Instructor of Nurses in Elliot Hospital, Manchester, N. J.
> Allan, Manager Grant Stores, Norwalk, Ohio.

PATON, Suvia, wife of Arthur E. Whittemore, has a new son, named after her father, Lewis Bayles, born Jan. 24, 1932.
RANKIN, Ella May, back at teaching, near her home in Berlin, N. J.
> Robert left consular service, has taken his M.A. at University of Penn. At present at home.

WARNE, Helen, teaching at Westfield, N. J.
    Margaret, teaching physical culture, at Easton, Pa.
WYLIE, Hugh, in oil business, 280 Slater Ave., Providence, R. I. Three children, Nancy, 15;. Barbara, 13; and Herbert, 11.
    Jeannette, wife of W. F. Field, St. Mary's Road, Leatherhead, Surrey, England. Two children, Hugh, 8, Jean, 6.

CHILDREN OF ONE-YEAR MEN

ERDMAN, Calvin Pardee, Pasadena, Cal. One son, two daughters.
    Mrs. Henry Lewis, Ann Arbor, Mich. Three daughters.
    Charles R. Erdman, Jr., Princeton, N. J. Five sons.
    Mrs. Francis Grover Cleveland, Boston, Mass. One daughter.
BARACKMAN, Rev. Paul F., pastor Central Pres. Church, Brooklyn, N. Y.
HUDNUT, Dorothy, single, at home.
    Marjorie, wife Jasper Coghlin, 540 Parker St., Newark, N. J.
    Herbert Beecher, 150 S. Euclid Ave., Bellevue Station, Pittsburgh, Pa. Pastor of Bellevue Church, 1446 members. Four children.
    Katherine, wife of Henry Bischoff, 18 Holmcrest Court, Oceanside, N. Y.
    William H., Jr., married Elizabeth Kilborne, Nov. 21, 1931. Pastor of Glendale Pres. Church, Glendale, Ohio. Three sons, the oldest, William Herbert Hudnut, III.
PENROSE, Mary, wife of Paul Copeland, 4730-19th Ave., N. E. Seattle, Wash.
    Frances, wife Henry Owen, 406 Conover Ct., Seattle, Wash.
    Clement, 3807 Boyce Ave., Los Angeles, Cal. With Equitable Life Insurance Co.
    Nathaniel, 3858 Cascadia Ave., Seattle Wash. With People's Bank and Trust Co.
    Virginia, 7 College Ave., Walla Walla, Wash. Teacher and Dean of Girls at Prosser, Wash.
    Stephen, Jr., 7 College Ave., Walla Walla, Wash. Assistant Professor of Philosophy in Whitman College.

The above is NOT a complete record of the families of the Class, but only some corrections in addresses, etc. For complete list, see History of 1930. No word has come from the children of Polk, Carson, and Phraner, although repeated letters were sent. That, to James Polk, at Atlanta, was returned.

THE SECRETARY'S REPORT

In the good Providence of God, we are permitted to meet once more in a Class Re-union, the ninth since graduation. We cannot but be grateful that the Lord has spared us and given us the rich measure of health that we seem to enjoy. We congratulate Bro. Warne on his fine return to health, since our last Re-union. Shuffleboard and Florida sunshine have surely done wonders for him. Gardner had to try the same remedy last winter. With McLean living there, if many more head for "St. Pete", we will start a boarding-house down there for the men of '90.

Naturally, a Secretary runs almost to seed in statistics. So here are some idle ramblings of this Secretary's mind.

I—AGE. The average age of the 29 men of the Class who have passed on, is 57 years, 5 months, and 14 days. You recall that three of our men died before they were thirty-five; MURCHIE, the first to go, after only four years and two weeks of active service, at the age of 33; RANKIN, with a record of only two weeks longer in service, had just passed his 28th birthday; while PHRANER, with a service record of only four years and seven months, was but 34 years and 7 months old, at death.

Three of the Class passed away in the first decade of 1890-1900, four in the first decade of the new century, viz, Hedges, Mason, Oates, and Heaney; five between 1910-1920, Allen, Baskerville, Erskine, McCuish, and Williams; seven in the decade, 1920-1930, viz, Carson, Annin, Frank Fraser, Jessup, McGinness, Ed Miller and Polk; while no less than ten have left us in the past five years.

The break in this pentad began in 1931, when Anderson was called home while on a visit to his former charge in Montgomery, Ala. Lynn, our patriarch, after reaching his eighty-first year, died on September 2, of that same year, and on December 19, of that year, Jungeblut, in far-off California, fell asleep—three in one year. That same year also brought heavy sorrow to Levingood in the death of his second wife, whom he had married but a year before.

1932 found our beloved Paton at death's door, his going, being on January 24th. The next year, Eddy was laid to rest in Newton, N. J., on December 5th.

The last year has been especially heavy in its toll. Our genial President, Charlie Whitaker, was called home on January 2nd. Soon after, on March 12th, Voorhees fell under a sudden apoplectic stroke. In August, three of us laid to rest our beloved Bannerman, the man with the stalwart missionary spirit. On November 8th, Frank Hyatt Smith yielded up his life here at the age of 77 years. That same year brought the crushing blow to Henry Campbell in the death of Mrs. Campbell on January 10th. Likewise, were Wylie and Remington called into the same shadow, the latter's wife dying on October 27th. Since our Re-union in May, Paterson suddenly died on September 9, 1935.

To all our sorrowing circle, we extend our deepest sympathy, and pray God's richest comfort on them all. Verily, "He giveth His Beloved, Sleep".

II—THE LIVING MEMBERS. Twenty-eight still remain in the Class, and it is a real source of satisfaction that each has been heard from. Only eleven of these can be said to be in actual pastoral service. Two or three more àre on the point of retiring.

The average age of the living members is now 70 years, 5 months, and 15 days. Rate yourself accordingly. (Ages can be compared in a later schedule.)

III—MINISTERS AND TEACHERS. Our Class can be proud of eight grandsons in the ministry; Adams, one; Moore, one; Parker and Baskerville, three each. The Parker, Moore, and Gibbons families are the missionary families, as far as furnishing workers for the mission field goes. Parker has three in that field, two in India, and one in the Philippines. Moore has two in Japan. Gibbons has two in India. McCuish has one in China.

As sons in the ministry, not missionaries, Baskerville has two, Moore has one, Parker has one, Hudnut has two.

Two are practising medicine, Robert Mason and W. Sinclair Voorhees. Teaching probably claims the next largest number some attaining high distinction therein, as Albert G. Parker, Jr., now President of Hanover College, Indiana. Rebekah Gibbons is at the head of the Division of Nutrition, in the School of Home Economics, in the University of Nebraska, and has been freely used by the State in much of its work. Ruth Anderson is at the head of the Moravian Woman's College Y. W. C. A. in Winston-Salem, N. C., and teaches two classes in Bible there. Sydney Levingood is an Assistant Professor in the Department of Modern Languages, Princeton University. John W. Moore heads the Educational work of Winston-Salem, N. C., as its Superintendent. Penrose has a son, assisting him in teaching Philosophy in Whitman College.

IV—THE QUESTIONNAIRE. The replies to the questions asked, furnishes much food for thought. On the question of retirement, Adams, McMillan and Trompen seem too healthy or too busy to think of it. And it does not look very promising for your Secretary—those restful days in seclusion—when he doubles up in his work by the merging of the two Presbyterian churches in his town, each of them large and prosperous. It gives him now a combined membership of over 700, and all rural, probably 350 families. One of the largest rural churches anywhere in the Synod. Cummings, Henry Campbell and Nelson, find it very hard to keep "unemployed", the latter even serving without pay, and at considerable physical difficulty, as not very well. McLeod has retired—BUT is to preach once a month, or the like. Has a very nice pension from his church. He expects to write and travel. Levingood says, he will retire soon, but no date as yet set.

On the question of National Recovery, the almost unanimous reply is negative. Doughty expresses himself as in entire sympathy with the efforts of our President, but is doubtful. Levingood is "hopeful, but very doubtful". Hugh Miller says, he is doing the best he can, with which Nelson agrees, saying: "he is at least trying". Warne is, like Wilson, "watching and waiting". I believe, we all want to be sympathetic and patient, but there are so many serious questions aroused by any extreme measures, that it seems the part of wisdom to withhold conclusions for the time being. There is still too much political propaganda and scheming to warrant final decisions. There is unquestionably much that is good in the New Deal, and, at the same time, much that is without question in error.

As to the action of the General Assembly on the Independent Board, there is, as was to be expected, a wide range of varying opinion. And that, not on any theological ground, but rather a question of expediency and constitutionality. Both extremes are found in the replies, from "absolutely necessary", to "unwise, autocratic, and unconstitutional". While it might be enlightening to give more in detail, and a good argument might be enjoyed—as was the famous Revision Debate in our student days,—yet the Secretary sees no gain in printed discussion and prefers to give no names. It seems a matter of purely individual judgment.

As to the condition of the church, it is, in every case but one or two, regarded as critical and discouraging. Nelson thinks, he sees improvement. So does Trompen. But most cry for a real revival. Cummings thinks, the religious conditions are simply the reaction from the political. As a whole, the nation is in a deplorable condition spiritually —and what is worse, it does not seem to sense it.

As to the future, it is "as bright as the promises of God". There seems to be a "waiting for the blessed hope", with keener expectancy, for that Return.

The times call for stalwart men, and the men of '90 have now had that experience that should make them that type of men. With renewed consecration and with invincible spirit, let us continue the task, that the Lord has so graciously given to us. May the end find us with our grip firmer than ever upon the "things that are spiritual and eternal".

FRANK B. EVERITT,
Secretary.

THE ITINERANT SECRETARY

Of the twenty-eight men remaining, it has been the privilege of the Secretary to visit personally fifteen of them in their own homes. He would bear witness to their kindly hospitality and their happy estate. Sickness and sorrow have visited some, but faith and courage remain.

None welcomed the Secretary and his wife more cordially than Seelye BRYANT in the summer of 1934 in his home in Pawtucket, R. I. While greying in locks, Seelye has not lost the keen sparkle in his eyes, and his genuine interest in the old Seminary days and associations. How the midnight hours looked down on two old chums, poring over those old Seminary photographs that Seelye treasures so dearly! Some of you athletes of those days would smile at yourselves in your old "togs". Thompy is but a shadow. Seelye is now an Episcopalian rector, although "always a Congregationalist at heart". And why not? After three generations of Congregational preachers behind him! His Bishop lives near him, and he is very happy in his relations with his Episcopal brethren. His daughter lives with him, Mrs. Bryant being in poor health. Seelye has had some close grips with rheumatism, which really kept him from our last Re-union.

BULL is weathering the years fairly well on his dairy farm near Kennett Square, Pa. His 74 years has put a few more kinks in his joints, and he is doing more work than he should be doing. His wife, long an invalid, is no better.

Our visit this summer, with the McMillan's, to the home of "the late" R. J. CAMPBELL in Toronto was both a revelation and an inspiration. For Richard has a hillside of beauty in his rock garden in the rear of his home—mostly planned by himself—and a whole firmament of sunshine and loveliness in his amiable little wife. It is no wonder, that his life is bound on all sides by the wonderland of joy and happiness, and he says, he expects to live to be a hundred years old. But, my boy, if you do, put on the brakes, and don't lose your nerve with the police. For Richard is some driver! and every time, he wants to break in a new car, he somehow manages to get one to bring him down to class re-unions at Princeton.

George CUMMINGS still holds forth in Washington, busy as a regular supply at Bethesda, Maryland, his Greek New Testament, being his chosen companion,—pardon me, Mrs. Cummings. Both he and his wife enjoy splendid health, and George continues to be the guardian of ecclesiastical procedure as Stated Clerk of Synod, and Permanent Clerk of Presbytery.

DOUGHTY has been visited twice lately, the last time, in company with Thompson and Henry Campbell, when we secured, not fingerprints, but a good photo of him. So, if he does not show up next time at our

Re-union, we will expose him—through his picture. For over fourteen years, he has been laboring in his field in a Reformed Church in Union City, N. J. Family well, but a blind daughter at home.

Murray GARDNER writes enticing letters from Brewster, N. Y., up among the suburban hills of Dutchess County, just above New York. That is as near as he dared to get to the metropolis, lest the city be too much disturbed. Murray is a believer in community service, and heads up various enterprises, such as the town library—and the local "aviary". For don't miss his birds, when you call. He spent last winter in Florida and yearns for another flight—solo? of course. What other kind could he take, wifeless as he is. Murray follows the injunction, "'he that is single, let him be singular still".

GIBBONS surprises us all. Though our Nestor in age, he hammers away in State College, Pa., on the fine points of Journalism, to a deeply interested group of young literary hopefuls. Health fine, so he says, and still happily at work. And why not? for he has as fine a family of real achieving merit as any man in the Class, two of them in India. Six grandchildren, three in India, three at home, and "as proud of them as any grandaddy can be". Why shouldn't he keep young?

McLEAN is hidden away under "his own vine and figtree" on the shores of the Gulf of Mexico, at Gulfport. All Class visitors to St. Petersburg, look him up. He is trying to keep going in a new church, with good equipment, but poor financially. He has suffered a heavy blow in the death of his only son, an adopted boy, who went through the World War, and finally died last year.

John McMILLAN is our perpetual wonder. He steps on the gas so fast in his church work, that it makes us dizzy. When John gets down to figures of weekly attendance at his services, all slams at Atlantic City as a worldly city are "called off" at once. With the biggest Sunday School in Atlantic City, and a church program that never lags, he is in a whirl of excitement all the time. With two exceptions—and both of these churches having over a thousand members—John led all his Presbytery last year in additions on confession of faith—forty-four in all. With that S. S. of over 800, what a field for soul-winning, and John knows that work to perfection. But such a pace is only in keeping with that new Packard, which we had the pleasure of handling this summer on a 3000-mile trip to Canada and the midwest. Some car and some royal good time, as we visited the famous foot clinic of Dr. Locke at Williamsburg, and the Dionne Quintuplets, Canada's greatest wonder. John is a real traveller, his visit last year to the old country, and his stay on the king's estate at Balmoral, a never-to-be-forgotten memory. He has a student helper in the winter from Princeton.

Hugh MILLER, we visited this Fall. Found him, living alone (never married) on a back road near his first charge at Harmony, N. J. He is getting very deaf and, because of that, seldom goes anywhere. Yet he has still his gleaming eye, that tells of a keen mind and interest in things. Hugh was very cordial and would certainly appreciate a letter now and then from some classmate. Address him at Phillipsburg, N. J., R. D. 2.

In the summer of 1934, Mrs. Everitt and I looked up REMINGTON, on the eastern shore of the Connecticut River, where he ministers to a small rural Congregational Church. Our camera came in good here, too. Mrs. Remington was not very well, and has since died but was then able to be around. Since her death, we learn that he has toured to California, stopping a month at El Paso, Texas. He has a fine summer home on the top of the New Hampshire hills. He expects to retire soon.

The Goodwill manse, near Montgomery, N. Y., has always breathed a wholesome atmosphere of quiet contentment and genial cordiality as more than one member of the Class can testify. For forty-five years in the same place cannot but do something just like that. If you want a real pleasure, spend a Sunday as we did with Mr. and Mrs. THOMPSON there. We saw about everything—except, Dunnie, the Yost. Saw his fine congregation who love them dearly, even though he asks them every Sunday from the pulpit the Catechism. That was a new one to us, using the Catechism in public worship. But they want it, he says. We even had the pleasure of showing the Thompsons the beautiful Lake Minnetonka, not so far away from him, but which they had never seen. A fine recognition of their 45th wedding anniversary was given them by their people recently, when a purse of $125 was placed in their hands. Here's, to their fiftieth!

WARNE still suns himself—when he is not playing shuffleboard with his neighbors on his concrete run in his basement—on the quiet banks of the Delaware, in Trenton, and yet not in it. For his outlook is quite rural. Ruby surely is a Florida booster, and hies away every winter to try his hand at excelling in shuffleboard—just as he used to do in tennis. Ask Seelye. Mrs. Warne suffers much from arthritis, and needs the warmer climate.

This about complete the itineration, as far as your secretary goes. We, in Cranbury, have kept open house for the Class, especially at all times of Princeton gatherings, and our memories recall happily many hours spent with the boys, who have honored us with their presence. Last May, I had the pleasure of four classmates in the pulpit with me, McLeod to preach, R. J. Campbell to read the Scriptures, McMillan to pray, and Henry Campbell to say a few words in introducing McLeod. Warne was also in the audience, unknown to us, or he would also have had a part. It was a delightful pre-Re-union fellowship.

We still live in the hope of seeing the others in their homes, especially those near at hand, as McLEOD in his comfortable home in the Bronx, near New York, or even in his summer home at Eldon, Prince Edward Island, Canada. And LEVINGOOD at Berwyn, suburb of Philadelphia, if he does not retire and depart to realms unknown before we get a chance. He holds his own very well, although much alone, since his wife's death, but feels the end of active work is nearing.

WYLIE can only be visited in winter, as he spends his summers with his daughter in Leatherhead, England. He winters with his son, Hugh, in Providence, R. I., where, we are glad, he has met Bryant and enjoyed renewed fellowship. One time, in Minneapolis, at the General Assembly, we saw Wylie get a whole suite, when others were going begging; and it seems, he can still pull the trick, for he now travels in a special suite on board the steamer through the courtesy of the Captain. Pardon me, he and R. J. had better team together. Or does it take an Irishman to "get there"?

We hope before many moons to again hie away to Florida. In fact, it is our fondest dream to always spend our winters there, when we retire. Our summer home at Rehoboth Beach, Del., looks good to us for one-half the year, and then, Florida for us! When we go, of course, we will look in on CARRINGTON in his new home in Orlando, where he is entertaining tourists, and enjoying the social and religious life of a truly wonderful city with its many lakes and churches. Look him up at 420 Magnolia Avenue. Two daughters are at home, one soon to be married. A few years ago, with the McMillans, we called on him in his former home in the same city, on McLEAN, and also on DUNLAP, then wintering in Delray. Dunnie can still regale you with wit and humor, and it was a delightful time we had, while dining with him. He surprised us this year with a good, long letter sent by special delivery from Daytona Beach, Fla., in time to be read at our gathering in May. Both he and his wife are well, and enjoy Florida winters, with a summer home in northern Michigan, which we came near visiting this summer.

We were also not so far away from FENWICK FRASER and HUDNUT in Youngstown, Ohio, but our time was limited. FRASER writes that he has been re-elected Stated Clerk of Mahoning Presbytery for a term of three years—this being the fifth or sixth time. His wife's new play, "The Woman Who Turned Back" is in its second edition of 5,000 copies, while her first play, "Two Masters", first published twenty years ago, is now in its 13th edition, over 35,000 copies having been sold. She is a fine missionary leader, being President of the Ohio Synodical, and has shown her spiritual and intellectual qualities in these plays.

JOHNSON and his wife had a beautiful tribute shown them recently, when an Indian woman presented them with a handsome picture, "The Rock of Ages", suggestive of the faith which they have so long and so faithfully tried to impart to the Indian folk. Johnson put over a wonderful pageant of Indian missions before their Indian Conference last year. It involved tremendous effort but was well worth it all. He is most beloved by all those Dakota Indians, now one of the most Christianized tribes of our Indian life.

PARKER, too, will come in for a visit some of these days. He has now moved to Mendota, Ill., and is enjoying now the luxury of a son home on furlough from the mission field. HEUVER also clings to the Prairie State, and may be found also in his new home at Rockford, Ill.

The way that ADAMS returns to Re-unions with cleanly shaved face and unwrinkled brow, making him look younger than ever, is a reminder to all of us wrinkled fellows to "go and do likewise". What keeps Adams so young must be his outdoor life. For he lives the life of a circuit-rider of old with his three rural churches. But, my! how they do respond. One of his three churches the past winter increased 50% in attendance. Its midweek meeting runs from 40-100. The C. E. Society has forty members with an average attendance of fifty. It maintains a cottage-prayer meeting in addition to its regular C. E. meeting. A dozen young people are studying for full-time Christian service. A student assistant has been secured so that four services a Sabbath can be held. We are glad that the Minneapolis Presbytery recognized the work of this dear brother, and made him recently their moderator, an experience which Craig describes as "pleasant, but hectic". We were sorry to hear at Re-union that Mrs. Adams was not well, and could not be with us, as she has been at so many of our gatherings. Craig enjoys an oil-burner for heat, and says, he had the laugh on all of us easterners last winter. For they had a mild winter, and we nearly froze.

The rest of you fellows will have to wait on that long-hoped for trip to the coast. Mac and I may yet try it. Mrs. Trompen and Henry Campbell keep hurling at us all kinds of luring bait. What a joy it would be to look in on the TROMPEN'S. For we know, from experience in a visit they made to us, that it will be a real spiritual reviving when we meet again. For no lovelier people abide this side of heaven. Their beautiful Christian spirit is a benediction to any home. They labor on, rejoicing as ever in the "marvellous work of God" in saving men. Both keep unusually well. They journey east quite often to visit their son in Brooklyn. We hope to see them soon again.

And California! the land superb, in spite of EPIC, etc., Henry CAMPBELL, the genial soul, never relaxes in his cordial invitation to come out. He is as fine a correspondent as he is a lovable character.

The Secretary just cannot help, putting in an extra bit of emphasis into the word, brother, when he speaks of Henry. For we went west together, straight from the old halls in Princeton. He followed me in Kansas City, and our love for each other has never wavered. Never mind, Henry, we are coming. Don't close up those two houses of yours in San Jose, and do not take that trip to Siam yet. His former parishioners in Phoenix, Dr. and Mrs. George MacFarland, are pressing him to visit them in Bangkok. Maybe, the Clipper will soon be heading straight for that city, and then, go, my boy.

NELSON is now living at Santa Maria, to be near his oil men, with whom he continues to work even without pay, as they are too poor to pay anything. He has had a slight stroke lately, and somewhat incapacitated for work, but he says, "the Class of '90 never quits". His boy is with him, his wife, having died a few years ago.

This completes the round of our living members, except John MOORE in Japan, our lone representative on the foreign field. John is still going strong in that Island Empire, but looks with some misgiving ahead to May 18, 1936, when he reaches retirement age of seventy, and he cannot, or will not, be re-commissioned as an active worker there. His allowance from his Board is enough to live on, but he will be left without native help and other accessories, as we understand it. He does not yet think of returning home for good. Has two children now over there. His youngest girl, Bertha, wants to go out as medical missionary to Thibet, and John is anxious about financing her preparation, as she is only beginning her special training. She is at present in the Johns Hopkins College for Nurses in Baltimore, and if there is any possible way to get into the medical college, she wishes to do so. How we all wish we were millionaires to help her! If you have any contacts, or know of any scholarships along that line, John would appreciate any suggestion from any one. His daughter, Eleanor, is leaving Japan next summer for America. She has been secretary to the Principal of the Canadian Academy in Japan.

John is much concerned over the status of belief on the foreign field, and is disappointed in Kagawa, as he is too socialistic in his views, and seems to preach a mixed gospel. One thing we are sure of, viz., that there will be no compromising of the truth, when John Moore preaches. For he is Fundamentalist to the core, and we all can sympathize with his concern over present day conditions in the church. But, John, let me pass on one sentence I heard last night from a prominent pastor: "When there are no problems in the church, then the Lord is getting ready to call his servant home".

Under date of Nov. 5th, 1935, I have just received a three-page letter from John whose letters are most deeply appreciated. For he is a very busy man. I shall be glad to share this letter with any classmate, upon request, and am only sorry that I cannot give more of it in this brief account of our classmates.

Our Auxiliary Roll

One of the most gratifying things to the Secretary has been the ready response of the widows and children of our deceased members to our questionnaire. We now have twenty widows living—two, Mrs. Erskine and Mrs. Mason—having died recently. Mrs. Carson, Mrs. McCuish, Mrs. Hedges, Mrs. Phraner and Mrs. Polk had already passed on with their husbands. Of these twenty living, all have been heard from—a wonderful record of loyalty!

The replies of these sisters would make an interesting thing in itself. No man can put into words what has gone into the silent, lonely struggle of those bereft of long-time companions, especially of those who have no children to comfort them with their presence. Among such are the following: Mrs. MacGINNESS, who writes: "My occupation seems to be, enjoying myself. I am very well, indeed." She has enjoyed a trip to California, and last winter, to Florida, where she met, in Georgia, her first auto accident. A cow disputed her right of way—ergo, a broken collar-bone. She was kind enough to call on me while passing through one of her trips, and showed a deep interest in all members of the Class.

Mrs. FRANK HYATT SMITH is another cheerful soul, in spite of her lone vigils. For she keeps herself still interested and busy in church and community affairs, as did her husband. She resides in the Lutheran Home in Buffalo, where her husband died, and where, he said just before death, "it has been, in some respects, the most contented year of my life". She serves still, with her fine intellectual ability, on numerous committees in service. R. J. Campbell and wife recently called on her, and found her most genial and cordial.

Mrs. WHITAKER has felt very keenly her loss, and finds it harder to be reconciled. But she, too, is seeking some kind of Christian, or other, service that will occupy her mind and strength. She has rented her home, while taking a temporary apartment in Jenkintown, Pa.

Mrs. WILLIAMS answered very fully and interestingly our letter. She resigned her executive position in the Riverdale Country School two years ago, and is now doing special work there, but only in the busiest seasons. She lives in Riverdale-on-the-Hudson, where she is happily and actively interested in the work of the Riverdale Presbyterian Church.

Of the sisters near at hand, we have met in person lately the following: Mrs. ALLEN, who has never missed a Re-union, even after her husband's death, is lying helpless with a broken hip, suffered in a fall last July in her home. Little hope is held out for recovery, although at this time, she is showing commendable improvement and more comfort. But it has affected her mind as well as her body.

Mrs. BANNERMAN is in her new home on the banks of the Delaware in Titusville, where he served so long, and where his body lies. She is still most active in church and missionary work, and finds congenial fellowship in her new pastor, and his wife, returned missionaries from Persia.

Mrs. EDDY was present, for the first time, at our last Re-union in May. She lives in the beautiful Merriam Home for Presbyterian Ministers and their wives, in Newton, N. J., where her husband is buried. She has her own car, and drives herself, even to Florida. The Class truly rejoiced in her presence with us, and in her good health and enjoyment of life.

Mrs. LYNN and daughter, Lida, opened their doors to us itinerants last summer and served us with such a delicious dinner, and good fellowship, that their lovely home in the heart of Kitchener, Ontario, will always be a blessed memory. We found Mrs. Lynn unusually well for a woman in the eighties, with mind keen, and heart contented. The daughter, in a real way, is carrying on the work of her father, being an ordained evangelist, and going a good deal of special revival work. She is also an active W. C. T. U. worker. Lynn went into the United Church movement in Canada, and was pastor of one of their churches.

Mrs. OATES has always been a most worthy exponent of that charming American quality, known as Southern Hospitality. Two visits to her have proved that beyond all question. In the old town of Princess Anne, Md., in the Makemie country, she holds property and calls it, home, although she really lives in Summit, N. J., where she has been house-mother and librarian in the Kent Place School for Girls. But her old ancestral home on the banks of the Pocomoke to which she took us one pleasant Sunday, and the old Rehoboth Church, the oldest Presbyterian Church in the country, we are told—these, with that wonderful box-wood garden, and the old Eastern Shore traditions, keep her heart still in the Southland. Of course, she is wrapped up in that boy, Robert Luther, who is doing engineering construction work in Washington, D. C.

Mrs. PATERSON had just moved into comfortable apartments in New Bedford, Mass., to be near her daughter, and where her husband expected to find some supply work and congenial fellowship with friends of former days, when his end suddenly came. They were both at our Re-union in May. She will still reside in New Bedford.

Others near at hand—on whom we may call some of these days—are Mrs. HEANEY living in Bala, near Philadelphia, with her son. She writes most appreciatively of our writing her, and our keeping in touch with her.

Mrs. JESSUP still resides in Yonkers, her home before marriage. She reports three new grandchildren, seven in all, which is a good tonic for age. The newcomers are Stanley Jadwin Karhl, Thomas Allen Karhl, and Ida Jadwin Blake. Two daughters are unmarried, the fifth daughter, being the wife of an Englishman, and living in Oxford, Eng.

Mrs. RANKIN remains still at Berlin, N. J., her home also before marriage. She has been through a severe strain in the illness of a sister, brother-in-law, and a daughter. Ella May is back at teaching, commuting every day. Helen has been for twelve years teaching English in Springfield, Mass. Robert is now out of work, although with an A. M. in physics and mathematics.

Mrs. VOORHEES replies that she is now living with her son, a practicing physician in Mendham, N. J. Is housekeeping in a small way. Three sons live to comfort her.

Mrs. PATON has most interesting understudies in her three grandchildren, two of whom—ages ten and six—have developed a "strong interest in the Egyptian exhibits in the Boston Museum, which would delight their grandfather Paton". She herself is still pursuing studies in Biblical Literature in Bryn Mawr for her Ph.D., which she hopes to get in a year or so. She is a real collegian, with interests also in Wellesley and Hartford. Her association with her husband in his researches has opened a whole new world to her, that gives her great pleasure.

Still further away is Mrs. ANDERSON, whose interesting letters entitle her to a Belles Lettres degree—"or something". She, too, is a most happy grandmother, with seven grandchildren to entertain, which she does when in Winston-Salem, while her daughter attends to her school duties in the Moravian School for Girls. So, she says, "Ruth is carrying on her father's work" referring to her Bible teaching in that school. Mrs. Anderson has passed through a serious and painful illness, as the result of her strain after her husband's death, but she cheerfully writes: "working every waking moment, forgetting self, and memories, and doing for others is the only way you can endure the changed life (in widowhood)." She spends her time between her two daughters, one a minister's wife in Valdosta, Ga., and the other a lawyer's wife, in Winston-Salem.

Mrs. ANNIN writes from St. Louis, where she has a position in the Lindenwood School about her family, the account of which is given elsewhere. She takes deep interest in all Class news and history.

Mrs. FRANK FRASER is now a resident of Walla Walla, where her daughter, Sibyl, lives with three children. In the summer, she goes back to her apple ranch in the Yakima Valley, where his last pastorate was.

Mrs. BASKERVILLE was not heard from directly, but through her son, we learn that she is well and is enjoying life in a nice apartment in Seattle, Washington.

The same is true of Mrs. JUNGEBLUT, who reached us through her daughter, Laura, with whom she lives in Lodi, Cal. Will Parker and Moore take notice, that her oldest daughter, Mrs. Mettler, has eight sons and three daughters? Jungeblut showed his staunch orthodoxy by naming one son, Calvin, who is blessed with two sons and three daughters. Both of these are ranchers. A third daughter, Mrs. Rinder, has three daughters—so nineteen grandchildren in all, and all live nearby in Lodi. We wonder what is the "batting average" of that family, and what there is in the air of Lodi, that is so opposed to race suicide. Hats off, to the Class of '90 contingent in Lodi!

The full address of these beloved sisters can be found on another page, as also more about their families. We thank again, one and all, for their splendid responses, and especially for the oft repeated expression of their interest in the Class and its history. We hope to see more of them at our next Re-union in May, 1937.

And the Grandchildren!

Your Secretary has been heartened not a little by the interest that even the next generation is taking in the Class History. For years, we have been out of touch with the family of our colored brother, HEDGES. Now, after much earnest searching, comes a letter from his only son, Charles Lyman, living in Marietta, Ga. He sends full data of his father's life as follows: taught in Paine College, Augusta, 1891-2; pastor of Ebenezer Church, Rome, Ga., 1893-1901; married May 14, 1894, Gwendolyn Lyman, who died July 28, 1895; health failed (through tuberculosis) and he went to Texas in 1902; married again in 1903, to Elizabeth McCall, of Houston, Texas. He died in that city on May 23, 1906, his second wife, dying soon thereafter. The son does not say much about himself, but does write a fine letter. He adds: "I have all my father's papers and cherish more than all his picture of the Class of '90."

The family of McCUISH is again heard from through his son, John B., Jr., and their record can be found on another page.

Bob MASON—Dr. Bob, as his mother called him—wrote us fully of the death of his mother on August 4th of this year—a most loyal daughter of the Class. She had not been at all well for the past four or five years, being a hard sufferer from asthma and bronchitis. In '33-'34, she spent most of her time in bed or in the hospital; went out to California, seeking relief through a change of climate. This failed, although she spent a considerable time on the top of Mt. Baldy with a nurse, "fighting for breath". Came home in March, suddenly developed pneumonia, and died on June 11th. Cremated, as was her wish, her ashes are placed at the head of the grave of her beloved "Bob" in Spring Grove Cemetery, Cincinnati. Friends, who would have given flowers, by request, gave to a Memorial Fund at her church. Robert Judson is an active church worker, being Superintendent of the Junior Department in the Sunday School.

Arthur BASKERVILLE has also written fully about their family. To all these new correspondents, we wish to extend our heartiest thanks.

The One-Year and Two-Year Men

Following the Seminary Biographical Catalogue, we call the roll, as far as we have any information.

ALEXANDER, faithful supporter in every way of our Class, is in active service, and carrying a "heavier load than ever". He is not only Superintendent of the Pittsburgh U. P. Synod, covering 165 churches, but also the Chairman of the Department of Comity of the Pennsylvania Council of Churches, and the President of the Pittsburgh Council of Churches. His CMO movement (Christ, Myself, Others) among young people has met with remarkable success. He had a very prominent part in the recent historical celebration of his denomination and wrote out its program or pageant.

ALLISON (so Fenwick Fraser writes) had a stroke last year, then a gland operation, now back in Madison, Wis., but with no use of his right hand, and little use of one leg.

BARACKMAN, visited by Henry Campbell, Thompson and myself last May, was happy to see us in his home, overlooking the Hudson at West New York, N. J. He is still hard at work over the First U. P. Church there, with prospects very poor, for retiring. His son, Paul F., is pastor of Dr. Carson's old church in Brooklyn, with over a thousand members.

ERDMAN in Princeton, is retired as a pastor, still teaches in the Seminary, but looks forward to retirement from that in another year. He gives much time to writing his New Testament Commentaries, and to his work, as President of the Foreign Board. He rejoices in twelve grandchildren.

HEUVER has retired from service at Ipava, Ill., and moved to Rockford. He was recently honored by his Presbytery, who came in a body to hear his farewell address on "Forty-five Years in the Ministry".

He writes: "I am growing old gracefully—enough to live on comfortably. Began at fourteen years of age to look out for myself, and have never been a day without work—sixty years in all." At 68, he was invited to two different fields, and at 69, more overtures were held out to him.

HUDNUT keeps going strong, in Youngstown, Ohio, over a church of 1441 members. Has two sons in the ministry, Herbert in Pittsburgh, and William H., at Glendale, Ohio. Keeps company with Erdman on the Board of Foreign Missions. Mrs. Hudnut recently died, the two sons, conducting a most impressive Memorial Service for her. Our sympathy is extended. Hudnut underwent, last June, a serious operation in Presbyterian Hospital, N. Y.

MATTHEWS is living in Princeton on Bayard Lane, and rules as Bishop over the Diocese of New Jersey. He has been with us for a brief while at some of our Re-unions, and we enjoy much his company. He is a lovable Bishop, whose visits we know to be helpful; not like the boy's idea, who replied to Bishop Colton's question, in Bombay, what a Bishop's visitation was; the boy replied: "an affliction sent of God". The good Bishop has intimated retirement in another year.

MONTGOMERY—he with the long name, Theophilus—and a long body—lives in the lovely Minister's Home in Ambler, Pa. Meanders down to Princeton now and then to see if everything is all orthodox.

PENROSE retired lately as President of Whitman College, in Washington State, but is still teaching philosophy, with a son, as assistant. He has written one book, entitled "Whitman, an Unfinished Story".

The death of two in this group is noted. We have had no direct word, but we understand that MacBETH, out in Vancouver, has passed on, which the Class will regret to hear. For he was a strong man with power behind every sermon he preached or word he spoke or wrote. He was a vigorous opponent of the United Movement in Canada, and had been Moderator of his Assembly.

Leonard TWINEM died on September 19, 1935, at Akron, Ohio, at the age of 75 years. He had served numerous churches in West Virginia and Ohio, and had retired from active work in 1920. He was a writer of note of poems and hymns. He is survived by his widow and three children.

AT HOME WITH THE LORD

The following brief records of men who have passed away in the last five years is given in the order of their deaths. We wish that there was space for more extended accounts, as each deserves such recognition.

NEAL L. ANDERSON

Born in Yorkville, S. C., on July 15, 1865. Graduated from Davidson College in 1885, took M.A. there in '87, and received his D.D. there in 1904. Pastor at Marion, Ala., '90-'91; s. s., Central Church, Montgomery, Ala., 1891-1907; pastor, Winston-Salem, N. C., '08-'16; President, Austin Theological Seminary, Austin, Texas, '16-'17; pastor, Independent Presbyterian Church, Savannah, Ga., '17-'30; Evangelist, '30-'31. Died in Montgomery, Ala., May 19, 1931, at the age of 66. He had gone thither with his wife to visit some old friends, had passed a wonderfully happy day, when at nightfall, he was suddenly stricken, and passed away before morning. He lies buried in that city, his grave, being lovingly cared for by the Session of that church. Anderson was a man of versatile gifts, and led in many denominational and national movements in the South. He was one of the Southland's ablest leaders and preachers.

JOHN E. LYNN

Born in Kilsyth, Ont., Nov. 23, 1850. Educated at McGill University. Professor of Latin and French in Lebanon Valley College, '84-'87. Upon graduation, he became pastor of the Second Church of Pottsville, Pa., and remained there from '90-'94; s. s. Bergen, N. Y., '94-1907; pastor, Berlin, Ont., '10-'16; pastor, Kitchener, Ont., '17-'25, and pastor of United Church, Kitchener, '26-'28. Died in the latter city on September 2, 1931, after suffering for some time from hardening of the arteries, at the ripe age of eighty-one, the only one in the Class as yet to reach the fourscore mark. He is buried in Woodlawn Cemetery, Kitchener. Lynn impressed all with his mature judgment and earnest purpose. While in the Seminary, his home in Princeton was open to many students who will recall its genial hospitality.

J. F. JUNGEBLUT

Born in Germany, November 9, 1859. Graduated from Dubuque Seminary in '87, and from Princeton in '90. Was a Home Missionary in Milwaukee, '90-'91; then s. s. over the First German Church in Milwaukee, '91-'95; at Alexandria, Neb., '95-1900; at Arcadia, Iowa, '00-'01; at Alexandria again, '01-03; at Eureka, S. D., '03-'04; at Lodi, Cal., from 1905 until his death on December 19, 1931. Jungeblut will be remembered as the accommodating mail-carrier at the Seminary, and many the days, when his visits were longingly awaited. He was a deep student, and well liked by all his fellows.

LEWIS B. PATON

Born in New York City, June 27, 1864. Graduated from New York University, from which he received his D.D. in 1906. Took his Hebrew Fellowship in Berlin, and received his Ph.D. from the University of

Marburg. He began his teaching work in Hartford Theological Seminary in 1892, was made Associate Professor of O. T. Exegesis, and Criticism in 1893, full Professor of same in 1900, and continued in same position until 1932. He was made Director of the American School of Oriental Study and Research in Jerusalem, and labored there in that holy city in 1903. He had been in poor health since 1931, when he had pneumonia and pleurisy. In July, a serious throat condition somewhat alarmed him. It eventually developed into cancer. Radium treatments failed, and it reached the pleura. Strength waned, and he quietly passed away on January 24, 1932. He had been teaching in that Seminary for 39 years, and the Seminary held a beautiful Memorial Service in his honor. His last message to his Class was: "I now recognize that my malady is incurable, but I am not in despair. I realize Jesus' confidence in the unfailing love of God, His unfailing love for God and His divine love for men, and, therefore, I still take hope." He believed, in his dying, he was entering upon the greatest of all adventures, and his courage, patience and triumphant faith inspired all. By his extensive and valuable literary labors, he won his place in America's "Who's Who".

GEORGE T. EDDY

Born in Belvedere, Ill., Nov. 22, 1863. Graduated from Princeton University in '86, where he distinguished himself in oratory and in classics, carrying off a Fellowship. In the Seminary, he again captured a Fellowship, the one in New Testament, falling into his hands. He remained to study a year. In 1891, he became pastor at Beverly, N. J., staying until '95. He was Assistant-Pastor at the Washington and Compton Avenue Presbyterian Church, St. Louis, '95-'97; s. s. at Boonville, Mo., '97-1901; pastor, First Church, Huntington, L. I., '01-'09; pastor at Wyoming, N. J., '10-'23; University Pastor at Columbia University, N. Y., '23-'28; pastor at Cape Vincent, N. Y., '28-'31. Eddy, in later years, struggled with some mental difficulty, passing away on December 2, 1933, with burial in Newton, N. J. A warm-hearted soul, gentle beyond measure, and true to the old Gospel.

CHARLES H. WHITAKER

Born in Philadelphia, Dec. 7, 1862. Graduated from Princeton University in '87. His first charge was Avondale and West Grove, Pa., '90-'93; then Lower Walpack, Pa., '94-1900; in Union Seminary, N. Y., for B.D., '97-'99; pastor, Bordentown, N. J., '00-'11; assistant pastor, West Hope Church Philadelphia, '11-'18; s. s. Green Hill Church, Philadelphia, '18-'22; and same at Elkins Park, Pa., '22-'29. Died in Jenkintown, Pa., where he had bought a home, on Jan. 2, 1934, after a gradual decline, at the age of 71. The secretary assisted his pastor, Dr. Muyskens, in the final service, Paterson also being present. Charlie had been our genial President through all the years, never missing a Re-union and presiding at each with dignity and with grace. He was a true follower of the Lord, and will be sorely missed at all our gatherings.

WILLIAM S. VOORHIES

Born in Jersey City, N. J., Jan. 26, 1862. Graduated from Lafayette, 1887. Pastor at Elmer, N. J., '90-'92; at Second Church, Trenton, '92-1902; s. s. at Yardville, N. J., '02-'04; pastor at Milford, N. J., '04-'09; and at Thompsonville, Conn., '09-'16; s. s. at Lyndhurst, N. J., '18-'20; pastor at Garfield, N. J., '21-'23; and at Edington, Pa., '23, until his death suddenly from apoplexy on March 12, 1934. Ill and unconscious for a day and a half from the first stroke. Your secretary also assisted in the final service. He received his D.D. from the University of Chicago in 1895. A man, beloved for his work's sake.

WILLIAM S. BANNERMAN

Born in Chatsworth, Ont., Feb. 2, 1856. Teacher and Principal, Normal School and Teacher's College, Toronto, '74-'77; and at St. Catherine's Collegiate Institute, '77-'79; in the University of Toronto, '80-'81; then teaching until '87, when he entered the Seminary. Missionary at Gaboon, West Africa, '90-'91, at Ogove River station, '92-'93, and again at Gaboon, '94-'97. On his return from that torrid clime, he tried the very opposite, and became a home missionary in Juneau, Alaska, '99-1900, then Sitka, '00-'07. Retiring from active missionary work, he found a most congenial pastorate at Titusville, N. J., where, from 1909, until his death on August 13, 1934, he labored most earnestly and successfully. He died from hardening of the arteries at the age of 78. So loyal was this beloved brother to his Class, that he requested that his classmates have charge of his last services. This they did, Warne presiding, Everitt speaking, and Paterson, offering the prayer. They also laid him to rest beside the beautiful river he loved. He will long be remembered for his quiet ways and his lovable spirit.

FRANK HYATT SMITH

Born in Auburn, N. Y., July 22, 1857. Graduated from Princeton University, 1887. After two years in Union Seminary, N. Y., he came to Princeton. His first charge was over the North Avenue Congregational Church, Cambridge, Mass., from '91-'95; then s. s. over Park Presbyterian Church, Buffalo, '96-1910; lecturer on Literature, in University of Buffalo, '05-'07, and again '10-'12; pastor at Kenmore, near Buffalo, '13-'23. Died in the Lutheran Home in that city on Nov. 8, 1934, where he said to his wife shortly before he died: "in some respects this year in the Home has been the most contented in all my life". Frank will always be remembered for his brilliant mind, his sparkling wit and humor, his letters never failing to be eagerly read. He was a master in aphorisms, and startling phrases of speech. He attained very high rank as an astrologist, and his fees for such work were said to be very high. He also ranked as an authority on Shakespeare, possibly none higher in this land. His loyalty to the Masonic order could never be questioned. He lies at rest in Woodlawn Cemetery, Buffalo.

ALLEN McDONALD PATERSON

Born in Glasgow, Scotland, April 3, 1858. Graduated from Knox College, Toronto, in 1886. Home Missionary in Ontario, '86-'87; pastor at Mechanicsville, N. Y., '91-1908; pastor, First Congregational Church, Shelburne, Mass, '08-'09; pastor, Old South Presbyterian Church, Newburyport, Mass., (where, under the pulpit, George Whitefield lies buried), '09-'26; pastor, Woodbury Heights, N. J., '26-'35. He retired from active work last June, and had just settled in a nice home in New Bedford, Mass., when an old heart trouble returned, and death suddenly took him on Sept. 9, 1935. Burial at Mechanicsville, N. Y.

Since coming back to New Jersey, Paterson never lost a chance to meet with his classmates at every Princeton function. He had successful pastorates, and his work was done. He will be remembered for his steadfastness to the truth and his warm friendliness.

Other deaths since 1930 have been Mrs. J. C. LEVINGOOD, the second wife of our brother, who, after only a short married life of a year, passed away on Feb. 14, 1932, after a lingering illness from cancer. Mrs. ERSKINE died in 1933, but no direct word has come about the details. Mrs. Henry CAMPBELL, beloved on the whole Pacific Coast, for her good deeds and her missionary leadership as the President of her Synodical Society, went home on Jan. 10, 1934, leaving a very lonely Henry behind. Mrs. WYLIE joined the goodly company on the other side on Jan. 31, 1934, at the home of her daughter in Leatherhead, England. Burial in Belfast. Mrs. REMINGTON died in Middlesex Hospital, in Middletown, Conn., on Oct. 27, 1934, of cancer, but with little suffering. Burial was in Milford, Conn. Mrs. HUDNUT also passed on during the past year.

McLEAN lost his only son, an adopted boy, Joseph. He went overseas in the World War, in 1917, and served to the end. Spent a year in Germany in garrison duty. Came through without a wound, and with six bars for fine service. Entered the aviation department of the Navy, became an officer in Air Service, but died of malignant cancer in the naval hospital at Mare Island, Cal. It is thought that it was induced by being gassed on the other side. And comes as a crushing blow to the loved ones in St. Petersburg, as they had put their hope in him for their advancing years.

BIRTHDAY DATA

(Thanks to Seminary Biographical Catalogue)

BORN IN

1859—Nov. 12—James T. McLean
Nov. 18—Hugh Miller
Dec. 31—Wm. F. Gibbons
1860—July 15—W. H. P. Smith
1861—Jan. 20—D. Ruby Warne
April 19—Kent M. Bull
May 6—Henry M. Campbell
1862—April 28—J. H. Thompson
July 26—Geo. M. Cummings
Aug. 28—M. H. Gardner
1863—Jan. 13—E. P. Dunlap
March 4—J. W. Doughty
April 23—J. N. Trompen
April 30—A. G. Parker
July 17—W. F. S. Nelson
Dec. 13—A. W. Remington
1864—Aug. 17—C. C. Adams
1865—May 24—M. J. McLeod
June 22—S. B. Wylie
July 11—W. A. Carrington
Aug. 6—F. W. Fraser
Oct. 5—John McMillan
Nov. 22—R. J. Campbell
1866—Jan. 9—J. C. Levingood
March 8—F. B. Everitt
May 18—John Moore
Aug. 6—A. F. Johnson
Dec. 11—Seelye Bryant

The honors go to McLean, as the Patriarch, and to Bryant, as the "kid".

BIRTHDAYS AGAIN

By months, for convenient reference for greetings.
Born in January—Levingood, Dunlap and Warne.
in March—Doughty and Everitt.
in April—Bull, Thompson, Trompen and Parker.
in May—Henry Campbell, McLeod and Moore.
in June—Wylie.
in July—Smith, Cummings, Nelson, and Carrington.
in August—Gardner, Adams, Fraser and Johnson.
in October—McMillan.
in November—McLean, Miller, and R. J. Campbell.
in December—Gibbons, Remington and Bryant.

Every month represented except February and September. For exact date, see schedule above. Why not a birthday greeting for each one, when the time for each birthday rolls around? You fellows on "retired" list need something to do.

RE-UNION DATA

Our Fifth in 1895—Nine present, including eight men of the Class and one woman.
Our Tenth in 1900—Twenty present, including thirteen men, five women, and two children.
Our Fifteenth in 1905—No record.

Our Twentieth in 1910—Eighteen present, including twelve men, one woman, and five guests.

Our Twenty-fifth in 1915—Fourteen present, including nine men, three women, and two guests.

Our Thirtieth in 1920—Twenty-five present, including seventeen men, eight women. Two others present the next day.

Our Thirty-fifth in 1925—Twenty-seven present, including twelve men, seven women and eight guests.

Our Fortieth in 1930—Forty-three present, including twenty men, fourteen women and nine guests. This was our banner year for attendance.

Our Forty-fifth in 1935—Eighteen present, including ten men, seven women, and one guest.

Summary

In all, thirty-one members of the Class have been back to some Re-union, leaving twenty-six, who have never been fortunate enough to be back in Princeton on Re-union years. Whether or not, they have ever been back since leaving in 1890, we know not.

Everitt is the only one to have bene at all Re-unions, with Whitaker present at every one during his life-time. Parker, Levingood, Warne and Thompson have attended six of the seven; Wylie, Bannerman, and Henry Campbell, four; others, three or less. Moore has come twice from Japan, Henry Campbell four times from the Pacific Coast or farwest; Adams, three times from far-away Minnesota, and usually with his wife with him; while R. J. Campbell rambles down every year from Toronto. To these, go the crown of loyalty, as tested by distance. Some near at hand have never been back.

Our Class has the unique distinction in Seminary Re-unions of always having invited the good wives, and even children, of the Class to attend. This innovation has added untold joy and distinction to every gathering.

PRINCETONIANA

Gardner—no increase in family! mirabilis dictu.

McLeod lives the primitive life in the summer on his ancestral estate in Prince Edward Island with oil lamps, etc.

Johnson can still boast the most unique name for an heir—Magaska.

Jessup had a unique experience, when on the birth of a son, he cabled to his brother in New York these words: "King Jessup, New York: son and heir born." The brother's law firm was King and Jessup. But when the Syrian censor got hold of that wire, all Beirut was in an uproar, and couriers went flying hither and yon, as in Jerusalem of old.

For it was interpreted that a rival to the Syrian throne had been born. Only after Jessup had made a complete explanation, was the coffee passed and good fellowship restored.

Alexander sends a good definition of an optimist. "An optimist is one who goes out on a dark night when clouds are black and scans the horizon when there is no light and *sees a light*. The pessimist goes out the same night, when clouds are black and mists are thick and scans the horizon and *tries to blow that light out*."

Wylie states that he has preached in 103 churches on the other side of the sea, thirty-eight of them, being in Belfast; and in 87 churches on this side, forty of them in the Presbytery of Newcastle. He enjoyed meeting many old friends at the General Assembly of the Irish Church last June.

"John" Kelley of the Class of '89 is in the Minister's Home at Ballston Spa, near Saratoga, N. Y. He is losing his sight and very much alone since the death of his sister, with whom he had lived for many years. He is Secretary of his Class, and we enjoy exchange of letters and data. John would surely appreciate a letter, for he just hungers for a bit of sunshine from old friends. He sends a reminder for us old fellows, who persist in "holding on". It used to be a saying among his farmer friends, "There's a worn-out preacher. He wants still to plod. Knock him in the head and put him 'neath the sod." Well, boys, really how long should a sane man keep his job from the hands of a younger man? Who will answer?

The Seminary enrollment is now 191. The selective policy of the Seminary has considerably reduced the number of entering students, each year a goodly number being turned down. This has resulted in a better student body as a whole. Wheaton College still leads in students enrolled. Twenty-eight states and nine countries are represented, there being one each from Alaska, Ireland and South America; two each from Germany and Hungary; three from Canada; four from Korea; five from China; and six from South Africa. New additions to the faculty include Dr. Edward Kase, from Grove City College, and Dr. Sherman Gapp, both teaching Greek.

The total subscription of our Class to the Current Expense Drive of last year was $63, given by eight subscribers. The amount needed was raised, but the Seminary faces a similar deficit this year of about $15,000, and subscriptions will be gladly received. Make checks payable to Princeton Theological Seminary.

If you wish to know the life-history, or present location, if living, of your Seminary chums, of whatever Class, send to Rev. E. H. Roberts, Registrar, for the Biographical Catalogue, published in 1932, price, one dollar.

The Secretary plans to bind together all the printed copies of our Class History and present them to the Seminary Library. He can send, free on request, copies of former printed reports, especially the Silver Anniversary number.

A Patton anecdote. Apropos of Dr. Patton's recent death in Bermuda at the age of ninety, his Seminary students are recalling many amusing incidents of the classroom, in which the good Dr. figured. One is going the rounds as follows: some students, shelling peanuts in the classroom, got on his nerves. So he remarked, as only he could: "I realize that these lectures, to which you are compelled to listen put a great strain upon you, and I have no desire to interfere with your natural right to seek that refreshment, which will enable you to bear up under that strain. But I am a somewhat nervous man, and I must admit that the constant popping of peanuts is somewhat disturbing to me. I wish, in the future, that you would be willing to substitute some *less audible* means of refreshment—say, sponge cake."

And now we would—if we only could—like to let Dunnie, Thompy, and Oates fill out the page with more rambling stories of the classroom.

TREASURER'S REPORT

(Five Years)

Receipts

Balance on hand	$ 8.82	
McMillan	8.00	
Thompson and Paterson, each $6.00	12.00	
McLeod and Wylie, each $5.00	10.00	
Alexander, Bannerman and Johnson, each $4.00	12.00	
Bryant, Gibbons and H. M. Campbell, each $3.00	9.00	
F. W. Fraser, R. J. Campbell, Gardner, Warne and Cummings, each $2.00	10.00	
Levingood, Erdman and Trompen, each $1.00	3.00	
	$72.82	$72.82

Expenditures

For printing and mimeographing	$33.02	
For postage and incidentals	22.19	
For funeral expenses, flowers, etc.	5.93	
	$61.14	$61.14
Balance on hand		$11.68

CLASS MINUTE

On Tuesday, May 18, 1937 the following members of the Class of 1890 assembled at noon at the Prince of Orange Inn, in Princeton, for their 47th Class Reunion: R. J. Campbell, Doughty, Everitt, Levingood, McMillan and Warne. As guests, were Mrs. R. J. Campbell, Mrs. Doughty, Mrs. Everitt, Mrs. McMillan, Mrs. Warne, Mrs. John A. Hartpence, and Prof. S. M. Zwemer.

A telegram of regret at absence through illness, was read from our President, Dr. McLeod and Levingood was asked to preside in his absence. Other letters were read. The Secretary read his report which was ordered printed. He presented to the Class the complete bound copies of all our printed Class Histories, one volume of which is kept in the Seminary Library and the other copy in the hands of the Secretary. This is an innovation, we are told, in preserving Class records, no other Class having taken such action.

The Secretary, as also Treasurer, presented the financial report that showed receipts from four men, totaling $15.00, leaving a balance of $5.10; also, subscriptions to the History Fund from 21 subscribers, totaling $52, leaving a balance in this Fund of $6.00. Since making this report, a gift of $5.00 has been received from Mrs. Charles E. McGinness, making the total balance on hand of $16.10.

Dr. Zwemer, now retired from Faculty through age limit, but still to live in Princeton, being a member of the Class of 1890 of Rutgers Seminary, New Brunswick, N. J., was made an Honorary Member of the Class, to be included in all future invitations of the Class. It was decided to continue our former action to meet every two years, meeting again in 1939.

The Secretary presented to the Class the Academic hood of Frank Hyatt Smith, for use by the Class as needed, the gift of Mrs. Smith.

The members present were then heard in turn and a most enjoyable afternoon was spent in fellowship. The meeting closed with prayer by Brother Doughty.

FRANK B. EVERITT, Secretary.

REPORT OF SECRETARY

Since our last meeting, two years ago, six Class members have passed on: Fenwick W. Fraser, at Youngstown, Ohio, on Feb. 12, 1936, age 71; Kent M. Bull, at Kennett Square, Pa., on April 23, 1936, age 75; William F. Gibbons, at State College, Pa., on Aug. 21, 1936, age 77; James T. McLean, at St. Petersburg, Fla., on Nov. 7, 1936, age 77; Hugh Miller, at Easton, Pa., on Feb. 2, 1937, age 77; and Albert G. Parker, at Madison, Ind., on April 2, 1937, age 74.

The average age of these six at death was 75.

FRASER had been ill for some time with a heart affection. On the day of his death, he was out for a short walk, and was stricken on the street near his home and died soon thereafter. He was Stated Clerk of Mahoning Presbytery, and was five times sent to the General Assembly as a commissioner. He studied for a year at Yale and then had a Fellowship year at Harvard. A Nova Scotian by birth, he leaves a widow to mourn his going.

BULL'S death was unusually pathetic. He had long had an invalid wife. From nursing his wife, who was very ill, he contracted double pneumonia, and died in the hospital a few days after her death, whose passing he never knew. He had for many years operated a dairy farm. The family requested your secretary to make the funeral address, which he did.

GIBBONS was for his years one of the most active of the Class. He was teaching Journalism in Penn State, was to be retired last year. Stricken with prostate trouble, several visits to the surgeon failed to heal and he died in the hospital at Altoona, Pa. Your Secretary called upon him only a few weeks before his death, while he lay very weak at his home. We enjoyed prayer together.

McLEAN had been ailing for some time, but continued as best he could with his work in St. Petersburg. He, too, died in the hospital. While in Florida last winter, we called on Mrs. McLean, who took us out to his grave, where we again lifted a prayer for all. She is carrying on his work in Gulfport, a suburb of St. Petersburg.

HUGH MILLER never married and lived alone with his books on a by-road near his first charge at Harmony, N. J. I called on him a few years ago and found him with his usual happy smile and cordial greeting. His death came from broncho-pneumonia, after a week in the hospital at Easton, Pa. His niece from Ardmore, Pa., arranged the last services, a Methodist pastor having charge. He was laid to rest in the beautiful West Laurel Hill Cemetery, in Philadelphia, on the banks of the Schuylkill.

PARKER'S death was very sudden. He had been visiting a son in Memphis, Tenn., and then his son, the President of Hanover College, Ind. While there, he developed bladder trouble, that necessitated a cystcstomy operation at once. He was taken to the hospital at Madison, Ind., and seemed to be recovering, when a relapse came and after three days in coma, he passed away. He was planning to attend the fiftieth reunion of his college class this June in Princeton when he was to receive the Class's loving cup for the largest number of grandchildren in the Class.

ALL of these men were beloved and loyal members of the Class. They filled out their years with faithful service and we gladly and heartily pay them the tribute of our love and honor. They will be remembered for their untiring devotion to all that is best in life and for their fine spirit of brotherly love and mutual helpfulness. To the families bereaved, we extend our truest and deepest sympathy and love.

This leaves the Class Roster as follows: living, 22, deceased, 35. The average age of us who remain, is 73. W. H. P. Smith now becomes the Patriarchus Maximus, a quiet orchardist in New York State, up near Buffalo, enjoying life at the ripe age of 77. Warne and Henry Campbell are at his heels in age, the former swinging back and forth between Trenton and Florida, while Henry has been bold enough to invite your Secretary and his wife to be his guests this summer at Lake Tahoe, Cal., and we have accepted. He is suffering from cataracts which forbid much reading. His operation for this may come this Fall.

Only eight are still in active service, viz., Gardner, Johnson, Levingood, McMillan, Moore, Remington, Thompson and Trompen. John McMillan still keeps a church at high pressure, over 500 being in a recent picture of his S.S. Trompen thinks nothing of driving twenty miles each way every Sabbath in zero weather to his field. Your Secretary hopes to visit him this June. The retirements of late have been, ADAMS, who suffered a severe nervous breakdown last year due to the severe climate of northern Minnesota, and so retired to become permanent guest, with his wife, in the Penney Memorial Homes, at Penney Farms, Fla., near Jacksonville. There, they have found most congenial friends, and better health and are very happy and contented. We spent very pleasant days with them this winter.

CUMMINGS retires this July 1 to live on in Washington, and to keep his clerkships in Synod and Presbytery. George has completed a colossal task of annotating every Greek word in the New Testament and has ready for publication some 27 volumes, the work of seven hard years of study. As yet, the publisher has not been found to print it, but he is hot on some trails.

JOHNSON, through that fatal age limit of our church as to its missionaries and secretaries, was forced to retire last year from his great work with the Indians in Dakota, to which he had given his whole life, and has taken up work over a small church at Pompey, N. Y., near Syracuse. NELSON has, after 27 years of hard and constant service with the oil men on the Pacific Coast (where he is lovingly known as "Bill" Nelson) retired to live with his son, near Orcutt, Cal.

Your SECRETARY by mutual agreement, when the Cranbury merger was effected, has been released from that work, involving over 700 members in 350 families. His church was most generous in their thought and kind in their actions. He retires to live in the summer at Rehoboth Beach, Del., where he has been entertaining diplomats and college professors in his cottage at "so much per." With his wife, he is foolish enough to dabble in seashore real estate, and will be glad to inform all interested as to where the "best beach in the whole country" is. Incidentally, it would be great to have a little colony of old Seminary "cronies" camp nearby. The winters may find him contesting with such experts, as Warne, on the shuffleboard courts of Florida. Address us always at Rehoboth Beach, Del.

JOHN MOORE is also up against the age rule and must retire from active work next year. At present, he inclines then to live near Baltimore, where he has a son preaching.

REMINGTON also enjoyed a flying trip to Florida last winter and our paths crossed at Adams's. R. J. CAMPBELL and wife honored us with a recent visit at Rehoboth Beach. JOHN McMILLAN and wife expect to tour the Northwest and Alaska this summer, joining us for a week at Lake Tahoe, Cal. BEATTY travels back and forth summering with his daughter in England, and wintering with his son in Rhode Island. ALEXANDER says, he cannot retire, and it surely looks so. For he is at present the very active President of the Presbyterian Social Union at Pittsburgh and has just staged a dinner with 450 guests present. He leaves in early July to attend the second meeting of the Universal Council on Life and Work, to be held at Oxford, England; and then goes to the Ecumenical Conference on Faith and Order in Edinburgh, as the representative of the U.P. Church. HEUVER, although retired, keeps busy with weekly classes in religious education and in miscellaneous addresses. He reads a lot and enjoys good health in Rockford, Ill.

From the Auxiliary Roll, letters were received from Mrs. Eddy, Mrs. McGinness, Mrs. Paterson, Mrs. F. H. Smith and Mrs. Parker. A call lately on Mrs. Allen found her in fairly good health.

As no questionnaire was sent out this year, full replies were not sought and were not received. We are grateful for those letters that did come. We look for more from time to time. Let us keep our contacts with ALL our Class families intact, never failing to send to the Class Secretary any family item of real interest. Notice of deaths of Class members should be promptly sent him that he may, in turn, notify the rest of the Class. Funds are provided for this. It would also be true to the spirit of the Class if birthday greetings could be exchanged between the living members of the Class. For dates of same, see last printed report, page 29.

We greet you, one and all, in the name of our one Lord and Master.

FRANK B. EVERITT, Secretary.

www.ingramcontent.com/pod-product-compliance
Lightning Source LLC
Chambersburg PA
CBHW031830230426
43669CB00009B/1288